Human Development in Business

*Humanism in Business Series*

The Humanistic Management Network is an international, interdisciplinary, and independent network that promotes the development of an economic system with respect for human dignity and well-being.

The Humanistic Management Network defends human dignity in face of its vulnerability. The dignity of the human being lies in its capacity to define autonomously the purpose of its existence. Since human autonomy realizes itself through social cooperation, economic relations and business activities can either foster or obstruct human life and well-being. Against the widespread objectification of human subjects into human resources, against the common instrumentalization of human beings into human capital and a mere means for profit, we uphold humanity as the ultimate end and principle of all economic activity.

In business as well as in society, respect for human dignity demands respect for human freedom. Collective decision-making, in corporations just as in governments, should hence be based on free and equal deliberation, participation or representation of all affected parties. Concerns of legitimacy must, in economics like in politics, precede questions of expediency.

We believe that market economies hold substantial potential for human development in general. To promote life-conducive market activities, we want to complement the quantitative metrics which hitherto define managerial and economic success with qualitative evaluation criteria that focus on the human dignity of every woman and every man.

As researchers, we work towards a humanistic paradigm for business and economics, trying to identify and facilitate corporate and governmental efforts for the common good.

As a think-tank, we set out to spread intellectual tools for culturally and ecologically sustainable business practices that have the human being as their focal point.

As teachers, we strive to educate, emancipate and enable students to contribute actively to a life-conducive economy in which human dignity is universally respected.

As practitioners, we act towards the implementation of a humanistic economy on an individual, corporate, and governmental level.

As citizens, we engage our communities in discourse about the benefits of a human-centred economy.

*Titles include:*

BUSINESS SCHOOLS UNDER FIRE
BANKING WITH INTEGRITY
HUMANISTIC MANAGEMENT IN PRACTICE
HUMANISTIC ETHICS IN THE AGE OF GLOBALITY
HUMAN DEVELOPMENT IN BUSINESS

---

**Humanism in Business Series**
**Series Standing Order ISBN 978–0–230–24633–1**

You can receive future title in this series as they are published by placing a standing order. Please contact your bookseller or, in case of difficulty, write to us at the address below with your name and address, the title of the series and the ISBN quoted above.

Customer Services Department, Macmillan Distribution Ltd, Houndmills, Basingstoke, Hampshire RG21 6XS, England.

---

# Human Development in Business

## Values and Humanistic Management in the Encyclical *Caritas in Veritate*

Edited by

Domènec Melé
*Professor and Holder of the Chair of Business Ethics,*
*IESE Business School, University of Navarra, Spain*

and

Claus Dierksmeier
*Distinguished Professor of Globalization Ethics,*
*Department of Philosophy, Stonehill College, USA*

palgrave
macmillan

First published 2012 by
PALGRAVE MACMILLAN

Palgrave Macmillan in the UK is an imprint of Macmillan Publishers Limited, registered in England, company number 785998, of Houndmills, Basingstoke, Hampshire RG21 6XS.

Palgrave Macmillan in the US is a division of St Martin's Press LLC, 175 Fifth Avenue, New York, NY 10010.

Palgrave Macmillan is the global academic imprint of the above companies and has companies and representatives throughout the world.

Palgrave® and Macmillan® are registered trademarks in the United States, the United Kingdom, Europe and other countries

ISBN: 978–0–230–29682–4

This book is printed on paper suitable for recycling and made from fully managed and sustained forest sources. Logging, pulping and manufacturing processes are expected to conform to the environmental regulations of the country of origin.

A catalogue record for this book is available from the British Library.

A catalog record for this book is available from the Library of Congress.

10 9 8 7 6 5 4 3 2 1
21 20 19 18 17 16 15 14 13 12

Printed and bound in the United States of America

# Contents

## Part II Management and Human Development

# Abbreviations

| | |
|---|---|
| BE | Business Ethics |
| CDO | collateral debt obligation |
| CDS | credit default swap |
| CSR | corporate social responsibility |
| CST | Catholic Social Teaching |
| GNP | Gross National Product |
| ISO | International Standards Organization |
| O&D | originate and distribute |
| OECD | Organisation for Economic Co-operation and Development |
| S Th | Thomas Aquinas, *Summa Theologiae* (1273) |

# Pontifical Document Abbreviations with Sources

For ease of use the following abbreviations are used throughout the text. Where these occur they are not listed in the individual references section of each chapter. Numbers following abbreviations correspond with the official numeration of the document.

CA — John Paul II. Encyclical letter *Centesimus annus*, 1991. Available at: www.vatican.va/edocs/ENG0214/_INDEX.HTM (accessed January 31, 2012).

CCC — *Catechism of the Catholic Church*. Available at: www.vatican.va/archive/ENG0015/_INDEX.HTM (accessed February 3, 2012).

*Compendium* — Pontifical Council for Justice and Peace. *Compendium of the Social Doctrine of the Church*, 2004. Available at: www.vatican.va/roman_curia/pontifical_councils/justpeace/documents/rc_pc_justpeace_doc_20060526_compendio-dott-soc_en.html (accessed January 31, 2012).

CV — Benedict XVI. Encyclical letter *Caritas in veritate*, 2009. Available at: www.vatican.va/holy_father/benedict_xvi/encyclicals/documents/hf_ben-xvi_enc_20090629_caritas-in-veritate_en.html (accessed January 31, 2012).

FR — John Paul II, Encyclical letter *Fides et ratio*, 1998. Available at: www.vatican.va/holy_father/john_paul_ii/encyclicals/documents/hf_jp-ii_enc_15101998_fides-et-ratio_en.html (accessed February 3, 2012).

GS — Second Vatican Council, Pastoral constitution *Gaudium et spes*, 1965. Available at: www.vatican.va/archive/hist_councils/ii_vatican_council/documents/vat-ii_cons_19651207_gaudium-et-spes_en.html (accessed January 31, 2012).

LE — John Paul II. Encyclical letter *Laborem excersens*, 1981. Available at: www.vatican.va/holy_father/john_paul_ii/encyclicals/documents/hf_jp-ii_enc_14091981_laborem-exercens_en.html (accessed January 31, 2012).

MD — John Paul II. Apostolic Letter *Mulieris dignitatem*, 1988. Available at: www.vatican.va/holy_father/john_paul_ii/

apost_letters/documents/hf_jp-ii_apl_15081988_mulieris-dignitatem_en.html (accessed February 1, 2012).

MM John XXIII, Encyclical letter *Mater et magistra*, 1961. Available at: www.vatican.va/holy_father/john_xxiii/encyclicals/documents/hf_j-xxiii_enc_15051961_mater_en.html (accessed February 3, 2012).

PP Paul VI. Encyclical letter *Populorum progressio*, 1967. Available at: www.vatican.va/holy_father/paul_vi/encyclicals/documents/hf_p-vi_enc_26031967_populorum_en.html (accessed January 31, 2012).

QA Pius XI. Encyclical letter *Quadragesimo Anno* 1931. Available at: www.vatican.va/holy_father/pius_xi/encyclicals/documents/hf_p-xi_enc_19310515_quadragesimo-anno_it.html (accessed January 26, 2012).

RN Leo XIII. Encyclical letter *Rerum novarum*. 1891 Available at: www.vatican.va/holy_father/leo_xiii/encyclicals/documents/hf_l-xiii_enc_15051891_rerum-novarum_en.html (accessed February 1, 2012).

SRS John Paul II. Encyclical letter *Sollicitudo rei socialis*, 1987. Available at: www.vatican.va/holy_father/john_paul_ii/encyclicals/documents/hf_jp-ii_enc_30121987_sollicitudo-rei-socialis_en.html (accessed January 31, 2012).

# Acknowledgments

Most of articles included in this volume were originally presented at the 17th International Symposium on Ethics, Business and Society held by IESE Business School, University of Navarra. The editors show appreciation to the organizers of this conference for facilitating them the publication of these papers.

Gratitude to Libreria Editrice Vaticana for allowing the use of the official translation on the Encyclical *Caritas in veritate* in this book.

Many thanks to the board of The *Humanistic Management Network* who encouraged us to publish this book, and to Palgrave Macmillan for acting it within its collection of Humanism in Business Series.

# Editors and Contributors

## Editors

**Domènec Melé** is Professor and holder of the Chair of Business Ethics at IESE Business School, University of Navarra, Spain. He holds a doctorate in Industrial Engineering (Polytechnic University of Catalonia, Spain) and another in Theology (University of Navarra, Spain). He is the author or editor of several books on business ethics, Christian social thought and related topics, in addition to numerous articles and contributions to books and encyclopedias. He serves as section editor on the *Journal of Business Ethics*. His most recent books are *Business Ethics in Action: Seeking Human Excellence in Organizations* (2009) and Management Ethics. Placing Ethics at the Core of Good Management (2012).

**Claus Dierksmeier** is Professor of Globalization Ethics and Research Director of SUMMIT (Sustainable Management and Measurement Institute) at Stonehill College. His academic work focuses on the idea of freedom, political and economic philosophy, business ethics, and corporate social responsibility. Dierksmeier has completed research in Europe, the United States, and Latin America (Uruguay, Argentina). He has worked as a strategy consultant in politics and business (e.g. for the Strategy Institute of the Boston Consulting Group). He serves on the board of The Humanistic Management Network.

## Contributors

**Antonio Argandoña** is Professor of Economics and holds the "La Caixa" Chair of Corporate Social Responsibility and Corporate Governance at IESE Business School, University of Navarra. A member of the Royal Academy of Economics and Finance, he has been the Honorary Treasurer of the European Business Ethics Network (EBEN), and founder and Secretary General of EBEN-Spain. He is the author and editor of many books and articles on economics and business ethics, corporate social responsibility, and corporate governance.

**Michael Stefan Aßländer** is Professor of Business Ethics at the International Graduate School in Zittau, Germany. Between 2005 and 2010 he held the Plansecur Endowed Chair for Business Ethics at the

University of Kassel. He has studied management, philosophy, sociology, psychology, political economy and Russian language in Bamberg, Vienna, Bochum and Moscow and holds a Master's in Business Administration (1988) and Philosophy (1990), and a Ph.D. in Philosophy (1998) and Social Sciences (2005).

**Gregory R. Beabout** is Associate Professor of Philosophy at Saint Louis University, USA. With interests in the history of philosophy, his teaching and research areas include virtue ethics, Catholic social thought, and issues at the intersection of ethics and the economic sector. His books, as author, co-author, and editor, include *Freedom and Its Misuses, Beyond Self-Interest, A Celebration of the Thought of John Paul II*, and *Applied Professional Ethics*. He is working on a book tentatively titled *The Character of the Manager: From Office Executive to Wise Steward*.

**Paul H. Dembinski** is an economist and political scientist by training. He was educated in Poland, Switzerland, Cameroon and the United Kingdom (St Anthony's College, Oxford). He is Professor at the University of Fribourg, Switzerland, where he teaches International Competition and Strategy. He is the initiator and Executive Director of Foundation of the Observatoire de la Finance (1996) (www.obsfin.ch), the mission of which is to promote awareness of ethical concerns in financial activities and the financial sector. Dembinski is also the editor of the French/English scientific journal *Finance & the Common Good/Bien Commun* (1998). His most recent books include *Enron and the World of Finance: A Case Study in Ethics* (co-editor, 2005); *Finance: Servant or Deceiver?* (in French, 2008; in English, 2009); *Pratiques financiers – regards chrétiens* (edited by Desclée de Brouwer, 2009).

**André Habisch** is Professor of Christian Social Ethics in Business and Society at the Ingolstadt School of Management of the Catholic University of Eichstaett-Ingolstadt, Germany and Director of the Center for Corporate Citizenship (Ingolstadt-Germany). He holds a Ph.D. in Theology from Tubingen University and a professional degree in Economics from the Free University of Berlin. Habisch has published on CSR, social capital and Catholic Social Thought in German, English, and Italian. Among his multiple practical engagements he consults for the Catholic Entrepreneurial Union, UNIAPAC and serves on the German Parliament's commission on Civil Society and Civic Engagement. He is also research director of the European Academy of Business in Society (EABIS). His most recent books include *Responsibility and Social Capital* (co-editor 2004); *Corporate Social Responsibility Across Europe* (co-editor, 2005); *Handbuch Corporate Citizenship: Corporate Social Responsibility für Manager* (co-editor 2008).

**Robert Kennedy** is Full Professor in the Department of Catholic Studies at the University of St Thomas (St Paul, MN) and Co-director of the University's Terence J. Murphy Institute for Catholic Thought, Law, and Public Policy. He also holds a joint appointment (as a professor in the Department of Ethics and Business Law) in the College of Business, where he served as Chair of the Faculty in 2004–05. He holds a Ph.D. in Philosophy and an MBA. His research interests focus on topics in professional ethics and the application of the Catholic social tradition to problems in contemporary society. He has written articles on corporate social responsibility, professionalism, ethical investment, and just war theory, as well as a variety of issues related to culture and public life. His books include *The Good That Business Does* (2006).

**Cristian R. Loza Adaui** is a doctoral researcher at the Ingolstadt School of Management of the Catholic University of Eichstaett-Ingolstadt, Germany, and researcher of the Center for Corporate Citizenship (Ingolstadt-Germany). He holds a Master's in Catholic Social Thought from the Pontifical Lateran University (Rome-Italy) and a Master's in Management and Corporate Social Responsibility from the Pontifical University of St. Thomas Aquinas (Rome-Italy). He was director of the Center for Catholic Social Thought of St. Paul Catholic University (Arequipa-Peru), where he also researched and taught corporate social responsibility, business ethics and philosophy in undergraduate and executive programs. He is co-author of the book *Verso il metaprofit: gratuità e profitto nella gestione d'impresa* (2011).

**Jennifer E. Miller** is a researcher for the Markets, Culture, and Ethics Project at the Pontifical University of the Holy Cross, Rome. She is currently finishing a doctorate in Moral Theology that addresses poverty and the family in the works of Amartya Sen, investigating the capabilities approach in the light of integral human development, solidarity, and subsidiarity. Previously, she pursued postgraduate studies at the Pontifical John Paul II Institute of Studies on Marriage and Family in Rome.

**Cristian Palazzi** is Executive Secretary of the Càtedra Ethos at Ramon Llull University, Barcelona, where he is also the editor-in-chief of the *Ramon Llull Journal of Business Ethics*. He holds an Advanced Studies Diploma from the Faculty of Philosophy of Ramon Llull University, where he is working on a doctoral thesis about Hans-Georg Gadamer. He teaches courses on social philosophy in the Faculty of Tourism at ESADE Business School.

**Álvaro Pezoa** holds the *Fernando Larraín Vial* Chair of Business Ethics and Corporate Responsibility. He is also Director of the CGE Group Center for Business and Humanism, ESE – Business School, Universidad de los Andes, Chile. He acquired a degree in Business Administration at the Universidad Técnica Federico Santa María, Chile. In addition, he has a Master's in Political Science and Liberal Arts (Philosophy), and a Ph.D. in Philosophy and Arts. Pezoa has been a visiting scholar in the Graduate School of Business, Stanford University, and in the Markkula Center for Applied Ethics, Santa Clara University.

**Francesc Torralba** is Professor at Ramon Llull University, Barcelona. He studied Philosophy at the University of Barcelona, and Theology in the Faculty of Theology of Catalonia. He extended his studies at the University of Copenhagen, where his thesis was on the thinker Søren Kierkegaard. He gives courses and seminars in universities in Spain and South America.

**Stefano Zamagni** is Professor of Economics at the University of Bologna and Adjunct Professor of International Political Economy at the Bologna Center of Johns Hopkins University. He is also President of the Italian Agency for the Third Sector. His recent books include *Markets, Money and History* (2008, with R. Scazzieri and A. Sen), *Civil Economy* (2007, with L. Bruni), *The Cooperative Enterprise* (2010) and *Avarice* (2009).

# Introduction

# Values and Humanistic Management in the Encyclical *Caritas in Veritate*

*Domènec Melé and Claus Dierksmeier*

In the past decade, various scholars (Gioia 2002, Mitroff 2004, Mintzberg 2004, Adler 2002, Ghoshal 2005, Bennis and O'Toole 2005, Pfeffer 2005, among others), increasingly denounced the dominant role of neoclassical economics in the theory and practice of management. At the center of this critique was the crucial influence of the reductionist view of the human being as a *homo economicus* – beholden to nothing but the rational pursuit of self-interest. This *economism* was held responsible for "bad management theories" (Goshal 2005), whose negative repercussion was brought to everyone's attention in the recent financial crisis. In search of countervailing orientations for management, ever more scholars (Melé 2003, Rosanas 2008, Spitzeck et al. 2009, Pirson and Lawrence 2010, Kimakowitz et al. 2010, Dierksmeier 2011a, among others) have investigated the possibilities of a *humanistic* understanding of business and business ethics. Indeed, humanistic management might be an answer to many of the problems that plague the current economic system. Based on a more comprehensive and thus more realistic view of the human being, theories of humanistic management operate from a holistic perspective on business that offers interesting conceptual possibilities for the reconciliation of economic and ethical aspects in managerial and organizational theorems.

A significant voice in encouraging the theoretical development and practical implementation of humanistic management is Pope Benedict XVI. His encyclical letter *Caritas in Veritate* (Love in Truth; CV)[1] published on June 29, 2009 proposed "a *new humanistic synthesis*" (CV 21, italics in the original) in order to realign the economy with its social purpose. Instead of criticizing the practical shortcomings of the current economic system, the Papal letter investigates their methodological reasons. An "excessive segmentation" of economic knowledge and an excess of reductionism in economic methodology have, argues Benedict XVI, moved the human foundations and the humane goals of business activity out of focus. Oblivious to its qualitative and normative ends, present-day economics has shrunk to a mere quantitative analysis of the efficient use of ends whose ultimate purpose (material growth and gain) was allowed to reign supreme over all other societal projects. Against this trend, the encyclical recommends a reverse in the direction of, and a change in, the economic course to a generally more considerate and particularly more ethically responsible direction. The challenge so posed is undoubtedly great, and its realization will require a long journey.

*Caritas in Veritate* has attracted significant attention from the media and politicians,[2] business and financial leaders,[3] and the academic world.[4] The warm reception for this encyclical beyond Catholic communities[5] is indicative of its intention to speak not only to Catholics but to "all people of good will" (CV, introductory subtitle). The encyclical is an expression of the long-standing tradition of Catholic Social Teaching (CST) as moral theology (SRS 41), based on both faith and reason. Since the days of Thomas Aquinas, Catholic theology has advanced its moral postulates on two different but complementary roads: the path of Revelation and the path of the "lumen natural," the natural light of reason. "Faith and reason," wrote John Paul II, "are like two wings on which the human spirit rises to the contemplation of truth" (FR, Initial blessing). Reason tries to make faith understandable and provides complementary arguments. Due to their reasonable nature, CST arguments often find approval from people of all confessions and convictions. This extends to all social papal encyclicals and thus assures their relevance beyond the confines of the Christian faith, making their message accessible to people of all creeds.

Apart from this dual methodological approach, CST has some features – shared by *Caritas in Veritate* – which are worth noting. Its aim is not to design or propose technical solutions, nor to present action programs, but to provide moral guidelines for social life through principles, judgments, and criteria with a logical internal consistency. As CST is in constant dialogue with the various fields of knowledge concerned with the human being, it has a notable interdisciplinary character. This problem-based approach "allows faith, theology, metaphysics and science to come together in a collaborative effort in the service of humanity" (CV 31). The overall purpose of this transdisciplinary endeavor is to arrive at overarching insights about human life and its destination so as to provide society with moral guidance and orientation.

Presently, CST pays close attention to "the *explosion of worldwide interdependence*, commonly known as globalization" (CV 33; italics in original). The manifold processes (economic and cultural, political, and technological) of globalization have, in their conjoined effects, created a world which is very different from that inhabited by past generations. In many regards, we have already achieved a state of *globality* both practically, through the *de facto* approximation of our life-worlds, and theoretically, through the growth of a global consciousness and the increasingly cosmopolitan ways of our intellectual self-reflection. Neither theoretically nor practically can we wholly retreat from this state of globality (Dierksmeier et al. 2011b). We cannot shield ourselves from the practical assault of certain global problems, nor can we ignore the moral demands they make on us. *Caritas in Veritate* offers a rich content of ideas and proposals in response to the present crisis, which is not only economic, but also ecological, cultural, and moral (CV 32). Therefore, the Papal letter considers several particularly pressing problems of globalization ethics, such as human rights, development, poverty, unemployment, and ecological sustainability in light of the fundamental values and principles provided by the body of Catholic teaching.

## *Caritas in Veritate* within the Catholic social tradition

A proper understanding of *Caritas in Veritate* requires locating it within the modern social teaching of the Roman Catholic Church. The latter has its roots in the Bible and in the early Church, mainly through those ancient Christian writers known as Fathers of the Church, such as Clement of Alexandria, Basil of Caesarea, John Chrysostom, and Ambrose, among others. In this tradition, great Doctors of the Church, particularly Augustine of Hippo and Thomas Aquinas, have also had a great influence. In the Middle Ages, the monastic orders of the Benedictines and Cistercians, for example, found innovative practical approaches to incorporate a social dimension into business. Franciscan and Dominican orders, moreover, provided important theoretical contributions on moral aspects of economic activity. Theological reflections on economic ethics intensified in the 13th century and continued with particular vigor in the Late Scholasticism (mainly in the 15th and 16th centuries) (Charles 1998).[6] Thus, the tradition in which *Caritas in Veritate* can be located reaches back several hundred years and benefits from the criticism of the ages. Arguments that have found their way into the current social teaching of the

Church may prove pertinent in the present precisely because they have already stood the test of time.

A first milestone for the development of CST in modern times was the encyclical *Rerum novarum* (RN; 1891) by Pope Leo XIII who addressed the social problems created by the Industrial Revolution. Pope Leo's successors have since written seven encyclicals[7] on economic and business issues in order to provide moral and pastoral responses to specific contemporary problems in society. Taken together, these encyclicals constitute a systematic and comprehensive articulation of Catholic thinking on economic and business matters.[8] Thus, the Church seeks to lead people to their vocation as responsible builders of society (SRS 1).

## Values, virtues, and principles

### A Four Key Values on Which to Build a Better Future

Four ethical values are especially emphasized in *Caritas in Veritate*: freedom, truth, justice, and charity (love), along with the corresponding virtues which shape the moral character. In order "to build a better future" (CV 21), *Caritas in Veritate* calls and proposes these aforementioned values to elucidate the normative needs and deficits of the current ways of doing business, resulting in a catalog of interesting moral postulates applicable to economic activity.

#### *Freedom*

Catholic Social Teaching views the human being as radically free but at the same time requires the use of moral responsibility in the application of this freedom. CST propagates the idea of a "responsible freedom" (CV 17, 70), which conjoins the individual liberties with commitments to societal autonomy. In defense of the unconditional dignity of the always vulnerable human being, the liberty of one should be the enabler and protector of the freedoms of others. The use of our liberties ought to be conducive to both the spiritual and material well-being of humanity. Freedom, is, therefore, seen as more than freedom of choice (Friedman and Friedman 1962), that is, as essentially linked to integral human development. Freedom, so understood, demands a responsible behavior, which in the economic field leads to an engagement in activities in service to others and to contribute to the common good (CV 7). The encyclical, along with the whole body of CST, recognizes the importance of economic structures and institutions, but it stresses that these should be instruments of human freedom, and not elements of oppression (CV 17).

### *Truth*

In order to accomplish this goal, human freedom has to have access to truth. If human beings were unable to make rhyme or reason of their existence, how should they be able to act with adequacy to others and treat their environs correctly? Liberty is not license and freedom more than caprice because through an understanding of the deeper needs and true destination of life, people realize their interconnectedness with everything that surrounds them (Dierksmeier 2007). Personality, rightly understood, consists not only and not even foremost in individuality but in relationships. It is not independence but interdependence that characterizes the *conditio humana* – that is the truth to which human liberty must conform in order to fully realize the human potential. A focus on *truth* points to the need for a clear-headed analysis both of the malfunctions and underutilized options of the current economic system. First, economics should consider the essential truth of the human being (CV 18). This perspective commits us to advance integral human development, not a development understood in only economic terms (CV 8, 23), and, accordingly, to an ethically responsible use of technology (CV 70). Truth informs us that our freedom is profoundly shaped by our being, and by its limits. In the words of the encyclical, "no one shapes his own conscience arbitrarily, but we all build our own 'I' on the basis of a 'self' which is given to us" (CV 68).

### *Justice*

Responsible freedom, commitment to act truthfully in adequacy to others, requires justice, understood as the virtue which "disposes one to respect the rights of each and to establish in human relationships the harmony that promotes equity with regard to persons and to the common good" (CCC 1807). The virtue of *Justice* thus demands recognition and respect for the legitimate rights of individuals and peoples (CV 6). According to the encyclical, a sound society should be built with freedom and justice (CV 13), and this, obviously, includes economic activity. Justice must be seen as crucial in business and it should inform every phase of economic activity (CV 37). Justice not only involves fairness in contractual transactions but also a deep sense of respect for human dignity with some requisites of social justice, including decision-making, which do not cause disparities in wealth to increase in an excessive and morally unacceptable manner and to promote steady employment as much as possible (CV 32).

*Charity (Love)*

Charity, understood as generous and fraternal love, goes beyond justice, yet justice is the primary way of charity: "I cannot 'give' what is mine to the other, without first giving him what pertains to him in justice" (CV 6). Charity is the central value of Christian morality overall (CV 2). Charitable love is demanded from every Christian; not as a sentiment but rather as a devotion to the well-being of our fellows "understood, confirmed and practiced in the light of truth" (CV 2). Importantly, love and truth do not separate out as feeling versus rationality but instead are meant to go together (CV 30). Reason is to inspire all acts of charitable love, and charity is to enlighten the investigations of reason. Charity, transcends and completes justice in the logic of giving and forgiving (CV 6). From this idea, the encyclical proposes the "logic of gift" and the "principle of gratuitousness" for regular economic activity (CV 36). This is a challenge, since the mainstream theories of economics and business are based on a different logic; namely, on the "logic of exchange," and on legality and contractual justice.

## B Basic principles of CST

These four values, also included in other documents of CST, are interrelated with a number of principles which are proposed as a reference for a proper structuring of life in society (*Compendium* 197). We will consider four of these principles more closely. Particularly important is the respect of the transcendent *dignity* of the human person (*Compendium*, nn. 132ff). Another is the Principle of the Common Good,[9] to which every aspect of social life must be related if it is to attain its fullest meaning, and it stems from the dignity, unity, and equality of all people (*Compendium* 164ff). Besides the good of the individual, there is a good that is linked to living in society: the common good. Other than the notion of an aggregate good, constituted by and (only) for the benefit of contracting parties, the common good represents "the good of 'all of us', made up of individuals, families and intermediate groups who together constitute society" (CV 7). In other words, the truly common good also addresses itself to the benefit of persons outside "the social contract," for example, the members of future generations.

Two other crucial principles of social ethics emphasized by CST are the principle of *solidarity*, and the principle of *subsidiarity*. The former highlights the social dimension of the person and requires awareness as debtors of the society of which people have become part (*Compendium* 192ff). The latter establishes that "all societies of a superior order must adopt attitudes of help (subsidium) – therefore of support, promotion, development – with respect to lower-order societies" (*Compendium* 186). The focus here is on treating persons as *agents* of their own betterment and not solely as *patients* of outside assistance. The principle of solidarity is frequently cited in the encyclical of Benedict XVI (CV 35, 38, 39, 41–44, 47–54), as is the principle of subsidiarity (CV 47, 57–60, 68, among others). Both principles belong intrinsically together. As Pope Benedict explains "*The principle of subsidiarity must remain closely linked to the principle of solidarity and vice versa,* since the former without the latter gives way to social privatism, while the latter without the former gives way to paternalist social assistance that is demeaning to those in need" (CV 58; italics in original).

In this book, through its 12 chapters, our purpose is to interpret, comment on, and develop certain aspects of *Caritas in Veritate* that are significant for economic and business activity, in order to contribute to humanistic management. Some of these were initially presented at the 17th International Symposium on Ethics, Business and Society (May, 2010) held by IESE Business School, University of Navarra, Spain. The authors, specialists in their different fields, provide an interdisciplinary dialogue between their respective areas and the encyclical. The book has two parts. The first is more theoretical and focuses on the relationship between ethics and economics to advance toward a holistic view of business and managerial activity. The second part, oriented more toward practical-managerial aspects, discusses how the encyclical can contribute to more humanistic ways of management.

## Toward a holistic view of ethics and economics

Against the ever increasing specialization and compartmentalization of science, the encyclical invites us to a more holistic reflection, inspired by theological and philosophical perspectives, on business and its repercussions on our lives. The first part of this volume follows this suggestion.

*Caritas in Veritate* makes clear that the appropriate role for ethics in business cannot be found through external moralizing, oblivious to the specificities of the proprieties of the business world. Nor can business confine the demands of ethics to the margins of its practices, for example, in the form of mere legal side-constraints. Instead, the encyclical proposes that moral perspectives ought to inform the value proposition and the strategic directives of business. Therein the encyclical goes diametrically against many a tenet of former – namely neoclassical economics-, as Claus Dierksmeier discusses in the first chapter.

Instead of treating ethics as an intangible externality of economics, the Pope ponders what can be done in order to visualize and then internalize the positive as well as negative side effects of the current business model through a new economic hermeneutics. For that to happen, we must broaden the temporal and spatial scope of our economic observations and reject materialistic reductionism. To detect the human factors behind the economic facts and in order to see the constitutive role of human freedom in the laws of economics, it is imperative to approach business in a multidisciplinary way that includes and highlights the insights of the humanities and social sciences. Only once we can see the human being in the entirety of its relations with nature, culture, and society (not only material but also spiritual, esthetic, and moral), can we give a true, truly comprehensive account of the various outcomes of our economic activities.

Stefano Zamagni sees in the encyclical a specific interpretation of the financial crisis that began in summer 2007. According to this scholar, the encyclical identifies a triple divorce. First, he reconstructs the separation between the economic and the social spheres of society, driven by the idea that economic activity has no need to submit itself to ethical consideration or social assessment. Second, he focuses on the decoupling of labor and the origin of wealth, which legitimized greed as a more rational pattern of behavior. Third, light is shed on the separation between market and democracy, and its relation to the thesis about the self-referential and self-regulating nature of markets. Zamagni confirms the thesis advanced in *Caritas in Veritate*, according to which, only by reuniting what has been violently separated is it possible to cope with the many challenges stemming from the crisis.

The encyclical not only advocates in favor of reconciling the moral and the financial dimensions of economic activity but also stresses that the ontological connectedness of the economic and ethical dimensions of human action shows the intrinsic relationship of ethics and economics. In this sense, Benedict proposes overcoming the dualisms of old business models, for example, between individual morality and the legality of the state, between self-interest and the common good, between private and public concerns and between profits and people. The ontological connectedness of the economic and ethical dimensions of human action, along with the encyclical's proposal of an ethics centered upon the human person. This proposal includes as key elements the inviolable dignity of the human person and the transcendent value of natural moral norms (CV 45). Domènec Melé suggests that these and other insights provided by the encyclical permit rethinking current approaches to business ethics. He explores the suggestions of the encyclical for a moral foundation of business ethics based on natural law and a virtue-ethics centered on "love in truth." This proposal rejects approaches based on ethical rationalism or cultural relativism as incomplete (in the former case) or misguided (as in the latter).

The necessity of a holistic view of ethics and economics appears in considering business relationships, including those generated in labor and commerce. These relations involve persons, who are defined through interpersonal relations (CV 53). Seeing these relations as mere "transactions" is but a reductionist focus on their technical side, forgetful of the important truth that business "has a human significance, prior to its professional one" (CV 41). Labor and commercial relations are, first of all, human relations, and these have a great importance for human development. "The more authentically he or she lives these relations, the more his or her own personal identity matures. It is not by isolation that man establishes his worth, but by placing himself in relation with others and with God" (CV 53). This point is widely considered by Paul Dembinski, along with the social environment of business and the concern for the good of the other and the common good. In an in-depth critique of recent developments in the financial markets, he elucidates how increasing the anthropological and moral substance of financial activities has been lost, and forms of speculative enrichment have conquered ever more segments of business – to the detriment of solid and sustainable economic development.

Facing the challenges to the transactional logic pointed out by Dembinski, Francesc Torralba and Christian Palazzi investigate the logic of the gift proposed by the encyclical. They argue that this logic emanates from a broader concept of rationality than the narrow notion of rationality that has predominated much of management scholarship in the past twenty years through the predominance of rational-choice theories and game-theoretical approaches to economics. Benedict XVI discussed this point prior to the publication of *Caritas in Veritate*. A profound expansion and development of the notion of reason permits an understanding of the "logic of gift" as presented by the encyclical. Torralba and Palazzi also discuss some philosophical antecedents of the "logic of gift," and how understanding human relations from the perspective of Christian *agape* (fraternal love) changes the matrix of contemporary business rationales. Broadening the notion of economic rationality, they argue, is necessary for humanizing the globalization process through inspiring acts of generosity, hospitality, and inclusion, while its omission fosters inequality and injustice.

Michael S. Aßländer considers two principles mentioned above: solidarity and subsidiarity, and how these relate to Corporate Social Responsibility (CSR). He argues that the tenet of subsidiarity and its interpretation in *Caritas in Veritate* provide an interesting perspective for reframing the conception of CSR in contemporary business ethics theory. A perspective taken from CST focuses on a subsidiary co-responsibility of corporations and allows for the defining of corporate duties that go beyond good management practices and merely voluntary (e.g. philanthropic) engagements. In this sense, corporations are seen as intermediate instances that have to bear concrete duties in a system of subsidiary societal task-sharing, especially in cases of market failures and malfunctioning governments.

## Human development and humanistic management

Another objective of Benedict XVI's social encyclical is revisiting the teachings of Pope Paul VI in which the notion of integral human development was introduced, and to apply these to present problem constellations (CV 8). The Church's social doctrine is centered on the human person and of its unique value (CA 11), and *Caritas in Veritate* insists consequently on the necessity of enlightening the development of peoples from "an integral vision of man, reflecting the different aspects of the human person, contemplated through a lens purified by charity" (CV 32). This means looking at world developments through a lens other than the materialistic lens (focusing on aggregate gains and overall growth). Only through the perspective of genuine *benevolence* – that wishes each and every human being well – can human knowledge develop a more comprehensive vision of reality (Spaemann 2000). This approach to socioeconomic development can also claim to be more realistic in its critical assessments of ongoing developments. Instead of externalizing all moral, aesthetic, and spiritual concerns of humanity as marginal to economic calculi, a concentration on integral human development commits our policies to cater to *all* aspects of the human person. Devoted to the well-being of each global citizen, this theoretical angle cautions against sacrificing the welfare of some for the gains of many, and against trading-off idealistic aims for materialistic gains; "The truth of development consists in its completeness: if it does not involve the whole man and every man, it is not true development" (CV 18). It demands development of what constitutes one's more noble and spiritual capabilities as a human being (CV 18).

A realistically idealistic view of the human being is a key for a humanistic management; and that is in any management philosophy that tries to contribute to an authentic human development. Several authors focus on these topics in this volume. Robert Kennedy discusses the message of *Caritas in Veritate* on human development stressing its character of vocation, and connecting this with the principle of gratuitousness and the logic of gift. He argues that genuine human fulfillment, in Benedict's view, is only found in the gift of self, that is, in consciously and conscientiously serving the needs of others. As a practical consequence managers should commit themselves to addressing the needs of potential customers (especially the poor) through products and services, the needs of workers by organizing good and fruitful work, and the creation of genuine wealth for the community.

Gregory R. Beabout filters out the ideal profile of the humanistic manager as implied in *Caritas in Veritate*. He argues that Benedict XVI criticizes narrow-minded and short-term oriented management while praising the holistic, humanistic approach that understands the manager as a "far-sighted steward." After reviewing several key texts of the encyclical in dialogue with current managerial literature, he suggests that a "business humanities" approach should become part of management education, analogous to the development over the past several decades of the field of "medical humanities." The ideal humanistic manager treats workers with dignity and respect for their human rights and provides opportunities for everyone to make a personal contribution that develops his or her individual capacities (CV 41). Another is having concern for the responsible use of financial resources, focusing on long-term sustainability more than short-term profits, and an awareness of the profound links between the enterprise and the territory or territories in which it operates (CV 40). These goals require accepting ethics as constitutive to all the phases in the economic cycle, all of which inevitably have moral implications (CV 37). The "people-centered" ethics of the encyclical (CV 45) promotes a responsibility for all stakeholders (CV 40), manifested in virtues such as transparency and honesty (CV 36) but also in the voluntary assumption of a stewardship for the environment (CV 48, 50).

The encyclical espouses a Christian Humanism (CV 78) and highlights how the Gospel contributes to a broad and cosmopolitan view of the human being and of human development that *Caritas in Veritate* stresses that "adhering to the values of Christianity is not merely useful but essential for building a good society and for true integral human development" (CV 4). The Christian identity and ethics is meant to promote authentic human development on a global scale (CV 7, 18, 79), fostered by "Christian charity as the principal force at the service of development" and the Christian ideal of a humanity as a single family of peoples in solidarity and fraternity (CV 13). In light of these ideas, Álvaro Pezoa discusses how Christian Humanism can inspire humanistic management practices through (1) dignifying professional work, (2) strengthening family life, (3) giving reality and full meaning to social responsibility, and (4) developing humanistic business leaders.

Antonio Argandoña stresses that in the traditional theory of the firm, based on contracts, there is no place for love; and the economics of altruism and gift is taken within the self-interest paradigm, alien to the behavior ruled by love. However, he assumes the challenge by arguing that Benedict XVI's concepts of love, gift, and gratuitousness, along with the role of virtues can be incorporated into the theory of the firm. After an analysis of the concepts of love, gift, and gratuitousness and of the role of virtues in firms' management, Argandoña develops a parallel between acting in a virtuous way and "donating goods," either material or not, including developing virtues and "giving love." This is done in three ambits, market (exchange of equivalents), State (duty), and civil society (fraternity); the encyclical underlines that the "logic of gift" should be present in all of these, not only in the third.

Gratuitousness in business and entrepreneurship is not as rare as one might imagine. In this regards, Andre Habish and Christian R. Loza Adaui reflect on gratuitousness in entrepreneurial spirit. They analyze three historical examples inspired by Christian tradition: first, in pre-modern times, the focus is on St. Benedict of Norcia and St. Francis of Assisi. In a second part of their chapter, the authors discuss the role of an ethics of generosity during the industrialization, exemplified by the German textile entrepreneur Franz Brandts. Third, they provide an analysis of experiences of social entrepreneurs in current times. Across time and culture, their findings show that gratuitousness can be, and often is, an important driver of entrepreneurial spirit, as it fosters solid forms of cooperation that translate into sustainable corporate health.

Work and human development is considered by Jennifer Miller with a special focus on working mothers. She discusses problems and possible solutions, arguing that a negotiated flexible working time may best respond to the call for excellence within the sphere of the integral human development of the working mother. Human development is closely related to the realm of work. John Paul II developed this topic in his encyclical letter *Laborem excercens* (1981) by stressing the subjective dimension of work and affirming that "work is for man, not man for work" (LE 6). In continuity, the Church teaches that "in work, the person exercises and fulfills in part the potential inscribed in his nature" (CCC 2428). *Caritas in Veritate* refers to work organization and labor rights (CV 25, 32, 62), to *prioritize the goal of access to steady employment* for everyone (CV 32), managerial responsibility for employees (CV 40), and insists on the dignity of human work which deserves respect (CV 63). Benedict XVI defends the need for "decent work," which entails a number of requirements; one is that "the worker to be respected and free from any form of discrimination, other that the work makes it possible for families to meet their needs" (CV 63).

This short presentation of topics and authors will hopefully help the reader better understand the chapters included here. The challenge presented by the *Caritas in Veritate* is, we think, a stimulating one. Christian scholars began to tackle globally-common ethical problems several centuries before the present discourse on globalization ethics began. Whereas globalization is conceivable and has been practiced by some as a one-way street of cultural expansion, what our times truly require are multidimensional processes of reciprocal integration, informed by the constantly changing self-understandings of the manifold and widely divergent cultures that comprise the human family. As Pope Benedict XVI points out, while "society becomes ever more globalized, it makes us neighbours but does not make us brothers" (CV 19) and he tries to recover the sense of fraternity that has, in great measure, been lost. Sharing a world means, and demands, more than existing on the same planet; it requires mutual acknowledgment and understanding. It is the underlying thesis of this book that to arrive at such understanding, and hence for the entire ambit of current debates on globalization ethics, the moral arguments from the traditions of CST may be of immense value.

## Notes

1. An encyclical is a circular letter (*encyclical* comes from the Greek *egkyklios, kyklos* meaning a circle). Currently, the term encyclical is used to designate certain papal documents with important doctrinal or pastoral teachings addressed to Catholics and, in some cases like the Encyclical *Caritas in Veritate,* to all people of good will. Hereinafter, the encyclical letter *Caritas in Veritate* will be referred to as CV followed by the relevant number to cite a quotation or idea. The number corresponds with the official numeration of this Pontifical document. Similarly quoted are other documents of Catholic

Social Teaching and a list of abbreviations and sources can be found at the beginning of this book.

2. The media includes *The Financial Times* (Dinmore 2009a, Dinmore 2009b, Mychasuk 2009) and *The Times* (Gledhill 2009). Among politicians, German Chancellor Angela Merkel stated: "Pope Benedict has encouraged the state leaders to create rules so that this sort of worldwide economic crisis isn't repeated," and echoing the German social market economy, inspired to a great extent by Catholic social teaching, she added: "I also saw this as an order to work toward a social market economy in the world" (Reuters: www.reuters.com/article/2009/07/07/us-pope-encyclical-idUSTRE5662VM20090707?pageNumber=2&virtualBrandChannel=0 (accessed February 3, 2012)). Italy's Minister of Economy and Finance, Giulio Tremonti, said that *Caritas in Veritate* constitutes "a true guide for politics," as it reaffirms the centrality of the human person in society (www.catholicnewsagency.com/news/caritas_in_veritate_is_a_guide_for_politics_and_a_manual_for_the_economy_says_italian_minister/ (accessed February 3, 2012)). The encyclical was presented at the Italian Senate, and the European Parliament hosted a conference to discuss it in September 2010 (www.zenit.org/article-30369?l=English (accessed February 3, 2012)). The document, published only days before the *G8 Summit* held in Italy at the beginning of July 2009 may have had an influence on this meeting and on its decision to assign an additional US$5 billion to combat hunger (Dinmore 2009b).
3. Thus, a private seminar took place in London in October 2009 to discuss the relevance of *Love in Truth*, which was attended by guests such as Barclays chairman Marcus Agius, HSBC chairman Stephen Green, Lloyds chairman Sir Win Bischoff, Goldman Sachs vice-chairman Lord Brian Griffiths and CBI chairman Helen Alexander (Mychasuk 2009).
4. This includes introductory comments (Faux et al. 2009, Cordes 2009), conferences and monograph books (Schooyans et al. 2010, Melé and Castellà 2010), research papers such as Stormes (2010), Breen (2010), Grassl and Habisch (2011), and a forthcoming special issue of the *Journal of Business Ethics* edited by Melé and Naughton, and academic opinions (Gomez 2009, Laczniak and Klein 2010, and Zamagni 2011).
5. For example, a group of university leaders and professors, press editors, and presidents of various Evangelical Protestant institutions signed a message to "applaud" the Pope's encyclical *Caritas in veritate* (www.zenit.org/article-26706?l=English (accessed February 3, 2012)), and the Italian Muslim association *Comunità Religiosa Islamica* also welcomed the encyclical (http://blogs.reuters.com/faithworld/2009/10/28/italian-muslims-approve-popes-encyclical-caritas-in-veritate/ (accessed February 3, 2012)).
6. See also the section on Scholastic Thought and Business ethics, authored by D. Melé, D. Dierksmeier, M. Schlag, A. Alves and J.M. Moreira, and H. Alford, and Melé in the book *Handbook of the Philosophical Foundations of Business Ethics* edited by Christoph Lüetge. Heidelberg, Germany: Springer. (forthcoming).
7. These encyclicals are *Rerum novarum* (RN; 1891) by Pope Leo XIII; *Quadagessimo anno* (QA; 1931) by Pope Pius XI, written during the crisis which followed the 1929 crash; *Mater et magistra* (MM; 1961) by Pope John XXIII; *Populorum progressio* (PP; 1967) by Pope Paul VI, on the development of people; by Pope

John Paul II *Laborem exercens* (LE; 1981) on the human work, *Sollicitudo rei socialis* (SRS; 1987) on development, and *Centesimus annus* (CA; 1991) on several economic and social matters which followed the fall of the Berlin Wall in 1989; and *Caritas in Veritate* (CV; 2009) by Pope Benedict XVI.

8. In 2004, a *Compendium of Social Doctrine of the Church (Compendium)* was published by the Pontifical Council for Justice and Peace, which presents a valuable synthesis of Catholic Social Teaching (CST) for the present era.
9. The common good is understood as "the sum total of social conditions which allow people, either as groups or as individuals, to reach their fulfillment more fully and more easily" (GS 26).

## References

Adler, P.S. "Corporate scandals: It's time for reflection in business schools." *Academy of Management Executive*, Vol. 16, 2002: 148–149.

Bennis, W.G. and J. O'Toole. "How business schools lost their way." *Harvard Business Review*, Vol. 83, 2005: 96–104.

Breen, J.M. "Love, truth, and the economy: A reflection on Benedict XVI's *Caritas in veritate*." *Harvard Journal of Law & Public Policy*, Vol. 33, 2010: 987–1029.

Charles, R. *Christian Social Witness and Teaching. The Catholic Tradition from Genesis to Centesiums annus*. Herefordshire, UK: Gracewind, 1998.

Cordes, P.J. *Liebe in Wahrheit – Caritas in Veritate: Die Sozialenzyklika. Mit einer Einführung*. Herausgeber: Sankt Ulrich Verlag, 2009.

Dierksmeier, C. Qualitative oder quantitative Freiheit?, in *Rechtsphilosophische Hefte XII/2007*, 2007, 107–119.

Dierksmeier, C. "The freedom–responsibility nexus in management philosophy and business ethics." *Journal of Business Ethics*, Vol. 99, 2011a: 1–21.

Dierksmeier, C. *Humanistic Ethics in the Age of Globality*. New York: Palgrave Macmillan, 2011b.

Dinmore, G. "Pope condemns capitalism's 'failures'." *The Financial Times*, July 7, 2009a. Available at: www.ft.com/cms/s/0/cc9150d0–6af4–11de-861d-00144-feabdc0.html (accessed July 22, 2011).

Dinmore, G. "G8 to commit $20bn for food security." *The Financial Times*, July 10, 2009b. Available at: www.ft.com/intl/cms/s/0/b71a9052–6d2b-11de-9032-–00144feabdc0.html#axzz1SozEOMgE (accessed July 22, 2011).

Donaldson, L. "Damned by our own theories: Contradictions between theories and management education." *Academy of Management Learning & Education*, Vol. 1, 2002: 96–106.

Faux, J.-M., G.C. d. Maulde and M. Peltier. *Caritas in Veritate: Guide de lecture pour la Lettre encyclique*. Namur: Fidélité, 2009.

Ghoshal, S. "Bad management theories are destroying good management practices." *Academy of Management Learning & Education*, Vol. 4, 2005: 75–91.

Gioia, D.A. "Business education's role in the crisis of corporate confidence." *Academy of Management Executive*, Vol. 16, 2002: 142–144.

Gledhill, R. "Pope Benedict XVI calls for new economic system based on love in G8 message." *The Times*, July 7, 2009. Available at: www.timesonline.co.uk/tol/comment/faith/article6657155.ece (accessed July 22, 2011).

Gomez, P.-Y. "Le Pape et le gestionnaire. Pourquoi il faut lire l'encyclique *Caritas in veritate* [The Pope and the Administrator: Why you should read the encyclical letter *Caritas in veritate*]. *Revue des Sciences de Gestion*, 2009: 1–4.
Grassl, W. and A. Habisch. "Ethics and economics: Towards a new humanistic synthesis for business." *Journal of Business Ethics*, Vol. 99, 2011: 37–49.
Kimakowitz, E. von., M. Pirson, H. Spitzeck, C. Dierksmeier and W. Amann (eds.) *Humanistic Management in Practice*. New York: Palgrave-MacMillan, 2011.
Laczniak, G.R. and T.A. Klein. "Caritas in veritate: Updating Catholic Social Teachings for macromarketing and business strategy." *Journal of Macromarketing*, Vol. 30, 2010: 293–296.
Lüetge, C., ed. *Handbook of the Philosophical Foundations of Business Ethics*. Heidelberg, Springer, forthcoming.
Melé, D. "The challenge of humanistic management." *Journal of Business Ethics*, Vol. 44, 2003: 77–88.
Melé D. and J.M. Castellà. eds. *El Desarrollo Humano Integral. Comentatios interdisciplinares a la encíclica Caritas in Veritate de Benedicto XVI*. Barcelona: Editorial Iter, 2010.
Mintzberg, H. *Managers Not MBAs*. San Francisco: Berrett-Koehler Publishers, 2004.
Mitroff, I.I. "An open letter to the deans and the faculties of American business schools." *Journal of Business Ethics*, Vol. 54, 2004: 185–189.
Mychasuk, E. "Money and morals." *The Financial Times*, October 24, 2009. Available at: www.ft.com/intl/cms/s/0/51df1a16-c035-11de-aed2-00144-feab49a.html#axzz1SozEOMgE (accessed July 22, 2011).
Pfeffer, J. "Why do bad management theories persist? A comment on Goshal." *Academy of Management Learning & Education*, Vol. 4, 2005: 96–100.
Pirson, M. and P. Lawrence. "Humanism in business – towards a paradigm shift?" *Journal of Business Ethics*, Vol. 93, 2010: 553–565.
Rosanas, J. "Beyond economic criteria: A humanistic approach to organizational survival." *Journal of Business Ethics*, Vol. 78, 2008: 447–462.
Schooyans, M., R. Buttiglione and H. v. Rompuy. *Un développement humain intégral: La pensée sociale de Benoît XVI dans l'Encyclique Caritas in Veritate*. Namur: Fidélité, 2010.
Spaemann, R. *Happiness and Benevolence*. Notre Dame, IN: Notre Dame University Press, 2000.
Spitzeck, H., W. Amann, M. Pirson, S. Khan and E.V. Kimakowitz, eds. *Humanism in Business – State of the Art. A Reflection on Humanistic Values in Today's Business World*. Cambridge: Cambridge University Press, 2009.
Stormes, J.R. "Pope Benedict XVI's 'Caritas in veritate': A challenge to business ethics." *Journal of Religion & Business Ethics*, Vol. 1, 2010: 1–11.
Zamagni, S. "Caritas in veritate, market and firms. The Catholic Church's position on economy. An interview by Renato Mangano." *European Company & Financial Law Review*, Vol. 8, 2011: 65–69.

# Part I

# Ethics and Economics: Toward a New Humanistic Synthesis

# 1
# Deconstructing the Neoclassical Economic Paradigm

*Claus Dierksmeier*

> The Church has always held that economic action is not to be regarded as something opposed to society. In and of itself, the market is not, and must not become, the place where the strong subdue the weak. Society does not have to protect itself from the market, as if the development of the latter were *ipso facto* to entail the death of authentically human relations. Admittedly, the market can be a negative force, not because it is so by nature, but because a certain ideology can make it so. It must be remembered that the market does not exist in the pure state. It is shaped by the cultural configurations which define it and give it direction. (CV 36)

*Caritas in Veritate* enriches the international discussion on business ethics in the era of globalization with an innovative discourse on the epistemology and methodology of economics. In the long-standing tradition of Catholic Social Teaching, *Caritas in Veritate* defends the role of morals and metaphysics as integral to both the economy and economics. The encyclical argues against the "rejection of metaphysics in the human sciences" (CV 31) and for a reunification of "moral evaluation and scientific research" (CV 31). Economists are to study (again) "the integral good of man in its various dimensions" (CV 31) through a multifaceted methodology, enriched by the humanities, philosophy, and theology. Against "the excessive segmentation of knowledge" that, according to Benedict XVI, contributed to a reductionist understanding of economic realities and so (in a narrow-minded pursuit of ever more materialistic growth and gain) bred many of the current socioeconomic calamities, he recommends that "metaphysics and science come together in a collaborative effort in the service of humanity" (CV 31). The encyclical hence does not simply deliver a moral critique of the current state of the world economy from the sidelines. Instead it demands that ethics be moved from its hitherto marginal role in economics into the center of economic life and assumes an integral function for its direction. In order to accomplish this fundamental reorientation of the economy, the Papal letter undertakes an intellectual deconstruction of the prevalent mechanistic paradigm of economics; it rejects the *physicalism* underlying neoclassical economics and advocates for its replacement with a genuinely *humanistic* paradigm.[1]

In this chapter, I will elucidate the reasons behind this demand for a paradigm shift in economic thinking. In particular, the focus will be on the question how, through a metaphysics of *responsible freedom*, the materialism of neoclassical economics can be overcome in favor of a more *humanistic* conception of business. First, I reconstruct why the perspective of human freedom and morality was removed from the canon of economic teaching. Then I contrast this materialistic view of the economy with the humanistic emphasis on free human agency in *Caritas in Veritate*. Next, I highlight the practical outcomes of each perspective. The purpose of this contrastive reconstruction is to show how an edifice of freedom-based economic thought can contribute to a better balanced cognitive architecture for a future humanistic management education in pursuit of (more and better) corporate responsibility.

## 1 Freedom as a foundation for economics?

All moral responsibility presupposes freedom; and corporate responsibility requires managerial freedom. A freedom unknown, however, is a freedom unutilized (Dierksmeier 2009). Thus, the *practical* realization of corporate responsibility depends on the *theoretical* realization of the factual freedoms of management to pursue alternative courses of action, for example, to deviate from profit-maximization in favor of different objectives (Dierksmeier and Pirson 2010). Against the view that behavior in business is predetermined by certain laws to which each and every society must conform, *Caritas in Veritate* emphasizes the moral, cultural, and political *malleability* of economic life. Benedict XVI aims to replace the blind faith in allegedly inevitable economic laws with a theory of economic activity rooted in "responsible use of freedom" (CV 48). Indeed, the entire project of the encyclical depends of the defensibility of this alternative premise that the economy is but a product of free human agency.

### A The conventional wisdom

Thus far, managerial freedom has tended to be systematically neglected in economics (as inessential and/or powerless against market forces), or deprecated (as a deviation from rational efficiency rules). Exceptions to this trend, such as the eminent works of Amartya Sen, prove the rule (Sen 2002). As long as this state of affairs persists, the very premise of all corporate and managerial responsibility is in question and, consequently, efforts to make business more ethical are bound to appear as futile; as a naïve effort at best – and as an irresponsible waste of corporate resources at worst. For the mechanistic nature of neoclassical economics (where corporations are portrayed as "machines" for profit-maximization, subject to iron laws of competition) seems wholly impervious to considerations of free agency (Brodbeck 2000). The language of profit-maximization lives off a quantitative vocabulary and follows a strict mathematical grammar. Economic actors, within this linguistic scheme, are portrayed as in pursuit of managerial objectives which – ideally, albeit not factually – could be advanced by replacing human judgment by algorithms. Leeway in managerial decision-making thus appears to be something that – in the interests of better performance – ought to be reduced to zero. Within such parameters, managerial freedom is not viewed positively as an intellectual space for the exercise of responsibility, but negatively as something that, for the time being, cannot quite be eliminated; a tribute reluctantly paid – theoretically – to the uncertainties of a still imperfect science of econometrics and – practically – to the inevitable vagaries of human factors in business environments (Dierksmeier 2011a).

### B The perspective of *Caritas in Veritate*

Whereas a materialistic view of the economy rejects the moral responsibility of corporate actors, a humanistic reading of economic agency emphasizes that in responsible freedom we can and should discharge moral duties and obligations within business. "The economy" and "the market" are not natural products but social constructs, malleable by the cultures in which they are embedded. While the human being is certainly influenced, it is not conditioned by its surroundings, inspired but not predetermined by its environment (CV 36). "Human beings interpret and shape the natural environment through culture, given direction by the responsible use of freedom, in accordance with the dictates of the moral law" (CV 48). *Caritas in Veritate* holds that human freedom is not derivative of the choices proffered by the market but rather the very force that creates the former through governing (well or ill) the latter. Like *constitutional economics* (Buchanan 1990), the economic philosophy espoused by the Pontiff assumes human responsibility not only for *choices* made *within* given *constraints* but also for the (anterior) *choice of* those very *constraints*. A reflection not only on the *present* economic conditions but also on their *historical* formation and possible *future* transformation brings us to question the "conviction that the economy must be autonomous, that it must be shielded from 'influences' of a moral character" (CV 34). This long prevalent view presents in theory as *inevitable* what is in practice *alterable* and so has introduced an economic fatalism that has "led man to abuse the economic process in a thoroughly destructive way" (CV34).

While neoclassical economics is painting economic behavior in the reductionist colors of self-interest on a canvas of quasi-natural laws, exempt from all moral reasoning, the encyclical begs to differ: "The economic sphere is neither ethically neutral, nor inherently inhuman and opposed to society. It is part and parcel of human activity and precisely because it is human, it must be structured and governed in an ethical manner" (CV 36). The misguided nature of current economic affairs results, according to *Caritas in Veritate*, in no small part from the mistaken attempt of neoclassical economics to filter out any and all ethical aspects from the epistemology of economics. Instead the encyclical vindicates the Scholastic view that economic action cannot be expressed in extrinsic categories alone but must be seen as intrinsically oriented towards humane ends (Dierksmeier 2012). In line with that view, the encyclical rebukes the conventional wisdom that a logic of commutative symmetry and a quest for nothing but quantitative equivalence or the sheer striving for profit would suffice in order to explain and maintain economic relations (CV 36). Against this view, Benedict XVI reiterates and augments the Church's social doctrine which "holds that authentically human social relationships of friendship, solidarity and reciprocity can also be conducted within economic activity, and not only outside it or 'after' it" (CV 36).

## 2 Materialistic economics

In the 19th and 20th century, ever more scholars came to reject the unified vision of ethics and economics that had predominated in antique and medieval philosophy as "pre-modern" and "unscientific," based, as they came to believe, on an outmoded metaphysics that confuses norms with facts. How did this dramatic change in opinion occur?

Before trying to reunite economic thinking with moral principles (as so many management scholars currently propose) we need to understand whether the move of modern economists away from ethics was warranted. As the encyclical positions itself squarely against the mainstream of recent (Western) economic thinking, this opponent must be understood before it can be taken on. Let us therefore briefly reconstruct why over the past 200 years the idea of freedom was expunged from the canon of economics, before we examine whether and how today ethics could be reintegrated into the teaching of business and economics.

## A From objective to subjective values

From the Greek economists up to the moral philosophies of David Hume and Adam Smith it was commonplace to orient economic thinking morally (Heilbroner and Milberg 2008). However, in an effort to become just as "scientific" as their colleagues in the natural sciences, economists of the late 19th century cut their discipline off from the sociopolitical sciences and allied themselves instead with the methodological apparatus of physics and mathematics (Wieser 1884). Trying to analyze economic problems "purely," that is, without resorting to moral values or doctrines, more and more economists looked to physics, especially mechanics, in search of a new paradigm (Walras, 1909). The enormous success of Joseph Luis Lagrange's *Mécanique Analytique* (Paris, 1788) inspired John Stuart Mill (1806–1873), Auguste Comte (1798–1857), and numerous others to aim for the description of economic structures as *quasi-mechanical* laws in the language of mathematics.

While mechanics gave the new paradigm its *formal* aspect, utilitarianism contributed the *material* side, with the effect that the entire discipline of economics was now recast as a "mechanics of utility and self-interest" (Jevons 1871, p. 90). From dissatisfaction about the quarrels of metaphysics over the salient norms of political and economic decisions, Jeremy Bentham (1748–1832) and James Mill (1773–1836) decided to *subjectivize* the realm of values. Instead of asking what would be *objectively* right for human nature, they asked what might benefit given individuals. They pursued the enhancing of the utility of each in order to serve the happiness of all. Perhaps, utilitarians ventured, one could achieve social consensus, simply by measuring what people *actually* appreciated, instead of ranking what they *ought* to value (Spiegel 1971). Motivated by the forces of *pain* and *pleasure*, human behavior seemed to them a *natural* phenomenon like any other, open to *empirical* observation and technical manipulation. This view coincided with a strong emphasis on self-interest as the main driver of human action, which Bentham believed to be "predominant over all other interests put together" (1952, p. 421).

Bentham's utility theory, however, was not yet directly amenable to a mathematical treatment. At the root of his theory are different pleasures, "which cannot any one of them be resolved into more" (Bentham 1789, p. 42). Their *intra*personal incommensurability obstructs their *inter*personal comparison. For Bentham, moreover, the *subjective intensity* of a given pleasure or pain was *objectively inscrutable* and not susceptible of precise measurement. Thus this dimension of the pleasure/pain-assessment, too, remained inexorably *qualitative*. Consequently, social utility assessments had to result from (political) *judgment* rather than from (economic) *computation* (Warke, 2000). In order to make utility theory fit for *mathematical* treatment, William Stanley Jevons (1835–1882) changed Bentham's definition of utility as a function of an (immaterial) increase in personal happiness into denoting "the abstract quality whereby an object serves our purpose, and becomes entitled to rank as a commodity" (Jevons 1871, pp. 44–45). Having thus "materialized" utility into a function of (readily quantifiable) commodity consumption, Jevons's plan to "treat the Economy as a Calculus of Pleasure and Pain" (1871, p. vii) and to "treat pleasure and pain as positive and negative quantities" (1871, p. 38) proceeded unhampered. Freed from the intricacies of *qualitative evaluations*, the problem of utility *optimization* was translated into the simpler one of *quantitative maximization*. Later changes in the utility concept (such as Alfred Marshall's move away from *direct* commodity consumption towards the *indirect* willingness to pay for goods; Marshall 1890, pp. 15–16) did not change much in the outcome: economics had turned concerns of "better" versus "worse" into a calculus of "more" over "less."

The utilitarian shift to a subjectivist value theory in England joined forces with the move to "marginal utility" concepts in Austrian economics. Spearheaded by Carl Menger (1840–1921), the objective value of a good was no longer gauged in and of itself, nor to be derived from its moral quality or societal function, but from how given subjects value an additional unit of the commodity in certain situations (Menger 1871, p. 143). To the thirsty man in a desert (an additional unit of) water is more valuable than (an additional unit of) gold (Menger 1871, p. 113). Various technical differentiations in the works of Menger's followers aside, the general gist behind this notion was to move from *substantial value* estimates towards *procedural assessments* (expressed in prices), which reinforced the utilitarian turn from *objective* to *subjective* value theories (Hayek 1952). Only by discarding the idea of objective values, Menger believed, did economics have a chance to become an exact science (Menger 1871).

## B From normative to descriptive economics

With the departure from metaphysically founded value concepts came also a retreat from metaphysical freedom theories. Menger repudiated their importation into economics, as they threatened his program of describing human behavior with just as much precision as physical events in the natural sciences. Postulating a freedom to alter the very will that drives human behavior put into peril the mechanical regularity of transactions upon which the claim of economics to scientific exactitude was premised (Menger 1871, p. 8).

The utilitarians likewise gave the cold shoulder to the idea of a free will, as for their theoretical purposes "freedom of action" entirely sufficed. Why? Philosophers typically value the notion of free will in order to establish that we might alter our *first-order preferences* (e.g. a given desire for something) through *second-order preferences*, or meta-preferences (e.g. the wish not to be beholden to said desire), so as not be slaves to our wants. Since utilitarians, however, blithely endorse as a first-order preference whichever pursuit of pleasure, they have little need for such subtleties. Freedom for Bentham, as for numerous Anglo-American economists and social philosophers since, was henceforth defined solely against *outward coercion*, not against *inward inclinations* (Bentham 1970, p. 254). Theirs is a *quantitative* idea of freedom, aiming, as it does, for the *maximization of choices*, while discarding as useless all deliberations about the *quality of our options* (Dierksmeier 2007).

The relevance of these methodological shifts is patent: Up to Adam Smith (1723–1790) economic theories operated with the notion of objective values not only to *describe* reality but also *prescriptively*, with a view to correct aberrant evaluations. For instance, through criticizing the miser for hoarding too much, antique, medieval, and classical economists in unison rejected the value he subjectively ascribed to money as objectively too high. In contrast, theories that generate the value of given commodities exclusively from subjective appraisals cannot establish any such critical distance from their topics. The prescriptive and counterfactual use of economic value theory thus collapses.

The subjective turn in economics lead to the so-called *Methodenstret* between Carl Menger and Gustav von Schmoller (1838–1917). At issue in this important debate was the epistemology of economics (Bostaph 1978). In the eyes of the more *inductively* oriented "historical school" of economics, context co-defined the content of concepts so that Menger's search for *absolute* economic truth made little sense to them (Schmoller 1883). Basing theories on statistical and other forms of observation, the economist, they held, ought to view economic processes "holistically," that is, together with the constellations wherein they are embedded (Schmoller 1949[1893]). Menger's "axiomatic" or "isolationist" approach, however, supposes that through conceptual work one can ultimately arrive at the "simplest" elements and thus at the true "essence" of economic reality; and from there logical *deductions* (employing the laws of identity, contradiction, and the excluded third) can reveal further economic truths – of *absolute* epistemic status (Menger 1883). According to Menger, this method alone can provide the *explanatory* part of economics, relegating all observational methods to a secondary, merely *illustrative* status.

The lure of Menger's promise of exactitude and certainty won the day. The "historical school" – which at the time of the controversy was rather predominant – has never again regained its former standing in the discipline. In the wake of its demise followed the "Werturteilsstreit" between German economists and sociologists (Backhaus and Hansen 2000). Max Weber (1864–1920) and Werner Sombart (1863–1941) disputed over the proper role of *value judgments* ("Werturteile") in economics, that is, about the question of whether the discipline of economics should solely be *descriptive*, or should also contain critical and *prescriptive* elements. Ultimately, Weber's demand that economics refrain from an evaluation of the goals of economic activity prevailed; the discipline was to confine itself to explanations about how the economy worked, and leave its normative assessment and transformation to politics (Weber 1904, 1918). The non-empirical dimension of values thus being ostracized, economists turned to what was left: determining the most intelligent use of scarce resources. Embracing the idea of normative neutrality and versatile utility, this is the intented to import of the canonical formulation by Lionel Robbins (1898–1984): "Economics is the science which studies human behavior as a relationship between ends and scarce means which have alternative uses" (Robbins 1932, p. 16). Economics had, in short, become a value-free, *positivistic* science, whose policy advice rested in *hypothetical* imperatives alone: *If* a community wanted certain goods, *then* economists were to examine how to achieve those in the most cost-effective way (Friedman 1953). To date, a *categorical* discussion of the *moral* appropriateness of economic objectives has been staunchly rejected (Stigler and Becker 1977). Qualitative value and normative judgments are shunned in favor of ever more subtle quantitative descriptions (Lucas 1998).

## 3 Humanistic economics

When economic laws are deduced from axiomatic assumptions, without taking account of inductively gained empirical information about the agents and markets they concern, misjudgments are the upshot. Forgetting that the *factors* behind economic *facts* are free human beings, many economists projected the very rigidity of their methods onto the human being and society, perceiving these as being subjected to unalterable laws. Unlike the laws of gravity, which do apply no matter what we think about them, the structures of economic behavior are, however, influenced by our notions and ideals. As inductively oriented economists have shown time and time again, economic behavior changes with an alteration in human attitudes, thus eroding many an allegedly eternal "economic law" over time. Our freedom and the ideas about its responsible use do play an eminent role in the economy, albeit one that mathematical methods cannot always adequately conceptualize (Nguyen 2000). Simply carrying over methods and metaphors from the natural to the social sciences is hence quite problematic: A "scientific" terminology that suggests the predictability and computability of human action contrasts with an unbiased look at descriptive findings (Solow 1997). Economics does not have dead matter as its epistemic object but human life (Veblen 1898). Other than physical systems, human beings form theories about their contexts and act not simply driven by *material causes* but upon their *personal interpretations* of the world. The reflective reaction of economic actors on economic prognoses, for example, on stock markets, makes the limits of the physicalist approach to economics transparent (Brodbeck 2009).

Likewise the dogma of economics as a *value-free* science has to be subjected to critique (Dasgupta 2005). After all, the processes and procedures of science itself are quite *value-laden*: from problem-selection to the choice of hypotheses and methods, values (for determining what is pertinent, which criteria establish truth, etc.) play an immense role. In the interests of accountability therefore, economists should not try to hide the *implicit* value-dimensions of their discipline from the public, but rather *explicate* them so that they can be openly debated and criticized (Douglas 2009, pp. 70–73). This is borne out especially in current attempts to "internalize externalities." For environmental and social accounting, value choices are unavoidable (Endres 2011). We have to agree on how far to set the scope of our analysis and on the quantitative weighting of the respective qualitative phenomena. In short, we need to make qualitative and normative judgments before we can quantitatively estimate the fair value of future commodities, goods, or entities and their preservation (Dierksmeier 2011b).

For all these reasons, the shopworn belief that "quantitative" and "non-normative" equals "scientific" is woefully out of step with the march of time. Certain realities can only be described qualitatively, not quantitatively, but this makes them neither less real, nor less important (Marcuse 1964). Many arguments can only be formalized into algorithms very late in the scientific process, and some perhaps never – but that does not make them less reasonable or relevant (Chamberlain 1948). Since outside mathematically ideal worlds, algorithms for profit-maximization cannot be formulated, the "scientific" approach to management often proves inept in the real world: The maximization-oriented econometrist describes (ever more accurately) a world that does not exist instead of providing orientation for the one that does (Boettke 1997).

Moreover, quantitative reductionism can cause a self-immunization of economics against vital information which does not fit the paradigm. Once the counterfactual power of values and normative ideas is excluded from the scope of scientific rationality, the choice of values, by implication, is tainted as a merely subjective and largely arbitrary matter, deprived of all rational objectivity. Regard for the quantifiable alone creates a world in its own image: a world of matter in motion, devoid of qualities, ideas, and values (Marcuse 1964). Thus, the materialistic paradigm entraps us ultimately in a vicious circle: defining – first – economics as a merely quantitative science, its proponents – second – exclude all objective values (because of their non-quantifiable nature) from its domain, and conclude – third – that the counterfactual force of ethics is not amenable to scientific scrutiny. On this basis, the view is defended that it – fourth – would be illegitimate to engage economists in morally scrutinizing individual choices ("ends"), which helps – fifth – justify the current *instrumentalist* focus in economic research solely on the maximization of means (for unquestioned ends) that – sixth – lends itself to justifying the predominance of quantitative over qualitative categories in economics.

## A Responsible freedom

Economics would service society better were it to match the complexities of reality, frankly admitting that to do so requires, at times, "messy" procedures based on qualitative assessments resulting from following *democratic* instead of *technocratic* decision-making procedures (Sen 2002). Notwithstanding constantly improved quantitative measurements, today's economics is frequently oblivious to the qualitative impact of economic "success" or "progress" on human well-being. The latter, however, ought to be of central concern to economics, holds *Caritas in Veritate*. The encyclical argues, consequently, for a reversal of direction. Against the focus of conventional economics on the fictitious *homo economicus*, Benedict XVI recommends a concentration on the real *conditio humana*. Accordingly, *Caritas in Veritate* calls for "an orderly interdisciplinary exchange" of ideas and the "specific competence of every level of knowledge" in order to offer up a richer and more realistic anthropology to economic thinking (CV 30). Through an integration of the humanities as well as "new efforts of holistic understanding and a *new humanistic synthesis*" (CV 21, italics in original) economists are "to rediscover" both the "fundamental values" and the true nature of humanity (CV 21).

Whereas neoclassical economics has a behaviorist view of the human being and seeks to model and prognosticate economic action algorithmically, *Caritas in Veritate* insists on the pivotal role of human freedom. Although radically free against any form of conditioning, human action is not without normative orientation but, according to the encyclical, directed to the *common good*. The rationale for this position is rooted in a *relational* concept of the person that contrasts with the *atomistic* anthropologies of standard economics. The encyclical sees the individual as *naturally political*, that is, as a being that cannot thrive without society. Individual self-expression and personal fulfillment depend on access to and communication with others. "[T]he human creature is defined through interpersonal relations. The more authentically he or she lives these relations, the more his or her own personal identity matures.... Hence these relations take on fundamental importance" (CV 53). Everyone is co-determined by and indebted to his or her biological and cultural environs; no-one is, in matter of fact, "a self-made man." The encyclical points us to seek freedom therefore not in *abstract independence* from, but in *concrete interdependence* with, alterity. "*A person's development is compromised, if he claims to be solely responsible for producing what he becomes*.... In the face of such Promethean presumption, we must fortify our love for a freedom that is not merely arbitrary, but is rendered truly human by acknowledgment of the good that underlies it" (CV 68; italics in original).

Notwithstanding cultural differences and ethnic divergences, in "all cultures there are examples of ethical convergence, some isolated, some interrelated, as an expression of the one human nature," argues Benedict XVI (CV 59). This "natural law" of human life, epitomized in the *Golden*

*Rule*, "provides a sound basis for all cultural, religious and political dialogue, and it ensures that the multi-faceted pluralism of cultural diversity does not detach itself from the common quest" for the good that must serve as "the precondition for all constructive social cooperation" (CV 59). While natural reason suffices to recognize the said moral law (CV 68), it cannot explain why (in a world that, to the secular mind, is just mere matter in motion) there exists some such higher calling for the human being. The presence of the *natural law* in the human heart thus points the human being beyond the material dimensions of life towards a spiritual origin of being. It is from such deliberations that the encyclical concludes that, in the last instance, only openness to "*the spiritual dimension*" and a theory of the *conditio humana* "capable of *rising above a materialistic vision of human events*" can satisfy the quest for a meaningful life (CV 77; italics in original).

According to *Caritas in Veritate*, freedom is given to humanity both as an indestructible *potential* and as a permanent *calling* to moral responsibility. Humans can *neither acquire nor forfeit* their freedom and the concomitant imperative to its adequate use. In such freedom humanity realizes – theoretically as well as practically – its dignity. Human behavior ought to be, therefore, as protective as expressive of it. For this idea of unconditional dignity of the human being, without which "it is easy to fall into an empiricist and skeptical view of life" (CV 9), a metaphysical foundation is needed. The moral *prescription* that no-one must ever be used solely as a means to another's ends, rests after all not on a *descriptive* judgment of factual conditions but on an universal *ascription* of an inextinguishable potential for responsible freedom to each and every person. This is why, for Benedict XVI, a (theologically inspired) metaphysics of the human person "alone is the *guarantee of freedom*" (CV 9; italics in original). It wards off theories that reduce the value of human life to its material accomplishments and comforts by placing the origin of human dignity outside human reach.

Every sphere of human agency – including economic transactions – is called to guard the "inviolable dignity of the human person and the transcendent value of natural moral norms" (CV 45). Economics must not shield business from any and all normative influences, but rather consciously assume responsibility for the realization of human solidarity (CV 17), lest economics were to be "becoming subservient to existing economic and financial systems rather than correcting their dysfunctional aspects" (CV 45). The contemporary forms of "false freedom," based on an erroneous definition of liberty as license, have to be repudiated. Instead of the prevalent conception of *quantitative* freedom (maximization of arbitrary choices) that leads to "hedonism and consumerism" on part of the "haves" and "exploitation" on part of the "have-nots" (CV 51, 45), a *qualitative* idea of freedom (optimization of meaningful options) ought to be pursued (Dierksmeier 2007). That is to say, human liberty must never (neither intellectually nor practically) confine itself to the quantity of extant choices. The latter should always be superseded on behalf of the qualitative alternatives people desire (Marcuse 1964). Indeed, in transcending the ambit of its present instantiations from concern for future freedoms, the very idea of freedom appears intrinsically linked to the common good of humanity.

### B Social business

*Caritas in Veritate* reflects on the current discourse on globalization ethics. In part, the encyclical follows interpretations of globalization that emphasize the dangers of a "race to the bottom" in the social and environmental standards of business and its risks for our natural and cultural support systems (CV 24). Like much academic literature on the subject, Benedict XVI demands institutional improvements to halt and reverse these processes through increased democratic control on the national (CV 41) and on the global level (CV 67). The important and yet vastly unfulfilled role that *social justice* ought to play in the construction of any future global governance is underscored (CV 25), and Benedict XVI even raises such advocacy to a new pitch when demanding that henceforth social justice should govern *each* economic action and *every* economic transaction and business sector (CV 37). Even so, these pledges for a democratization of globalization pale besides the core doctrine of *Caritas in Veritate* that charitable *generosity* can and should permeate the economic sector.

While most humanistic and idealistic philosophies of the economy aspire to the globalization of social justice, Benedict XVI holds furthermore that only "a humanism open to the absolute can guide us in the promotion and building of forms of social and civic life" that answer fully to the essential needs of human existence (CV 78). For only a spiritual reading of life is open to the notion of *unconditional generosity*. As people become aware that the fundamentals of their life – their existence, freedom, and dignity – are neither earned, nor produced but received as a gift, the wish "to give back" arises. In acts of charity and care human beings express gratitude and reflect onto their neighbors the very gratuitousness they experience. Since in today's globalized world everyone is our neighbor (CV 19), hitherto localized communal relations of generosity should accordingly broaden into transnational, and global concerns for the welfare of all our fellow beings.

In the era of *globality* (Dierksmeier 2011b), the antagonistic logic of *private* versus *public* interests that leaves the private sector to the egotism of individuals and lets the public shoulder all alterity-oriented burdens, fails, the Pontiff notes (CV 41), for two reasons: *practically*, since the powers of nation states to bend business to public's interest are on the wane, and *theoretically*, because the abstract "distinction between profit-based companies and non-profit organizations" does not correctly describe the business reality of our era (CV 46). *Caritas in Veritate* consequently demands that also "in *commercial relationships* the *principle of gratuitousness* and the logic of gift as an expression of fraternity can and must *find their place within normal economic activity*" (CV 36; italics in original).

> In recent decades a broad intermediate area has emerged between the two types of enterprise. It is made up of traditional companies which nonetheless subscribe to social aid agreements in support of underdeveloped countries, charitable foundations associated with individual companies, groups of companies oriented towards social welfare, and the diversified world of the so-called "civil economy" and the "economy of communion". This is not merely a matter of a "third sector", but of a broad new composite reality embracing the private and public spheres, one which does not exclude profit, but instead considers it a means for achieving human and social ends. [...] [T]hey steer the system towards a clearer and more complete assumption of duties on the part of economic subjects. And not only that; *The very plurality of institutional forms of business gives rise to a market which is not only more civilized but also more competitive.* (CV 46; italics in original)

This is both a very clearheaded observation and a visionary prognosis. In recent years the *Social Business* sector has indeed grown rapidly. Enlarged economies of scale, enabled by the opening up of the global market, have afforded to *Social Entrepreneurs* novel ways of doing business. Transcending geographical boundaries with ever more ease, they have been able to find supportive clients and customers all over the globe. The increasing success of their humanistic management practices is fueled by a worldwide approval of business models which are, much more than those of conventional corporations, in harmony with the human interests that people bring to their workplace (Elkington and Hartigan 2008). The desire to contribute to the good, the wish to be useful, the need to find meaning in their work, the inspiration and energy drawn from shared visions and a common mission – in sum: the immanent dignity of service to the real needs of one's fellows (as opposed to the artificial creation of demand for contrived products) – all these and further moral as well as spiritual motives often find their realization in the non-traditional forms of Social Business (Kimakowitz et al. 2010). In other words, Social Entrepreneurs capitalize on the fact that "[b]usiness activity has a human significance, prior to its professional one" (CV 41).

Although improved systems of global governance are certainly needed, "institutions by themselves are not enough, because integral human development is primarily a vocation, and therefore it involves a *free assumption of responsibility* in solidarity on the part of everyone" (CV 11; italics added). What the experiences from micro-finance and credit-unions (CV 65), and ethical purchasing (fair trade products, etc.) and consumer cooperatives (CV 66) show is that through civic advocacy the degree of "economic democracy" and personal autonomy can be raised everywhere (CV 66). People in need thus do not feature as *patients* of outward assistance but as *agents* of their own development; they are not only the *ends* but also the *means* of economic emancipation, not only *recipients* but *producers* of economic benefits. *Solidarity* takes the form of *subsidiarity*. Hence space "needs to be created within the market for economic activity carried out by subjects who freely choose to act according to principles other than those of pure profit, without sacrificing the production of economic value in the process" (CV 37).

In addition, by their example social entrepreneurs can exert a beneficial influence on conventional business: making visible markets of unmet needs, exploring alternative (more socially sustainable) business models, and highlighting the heuristic benefits of a human-centered hermeneutics of economic behavior. "Alongside profit-oriented private enterprise and the various types of public enterprise ... commercial entities based on mutualist principles and pursuing social ends" can bring forth welcome "hybrid forms of commercial behavior" and foster an overall "attentiveness to ways of *civilizing the economy*" (CV 38; italics in original).

## 4 Practical outcomes

As methodologies pre-structure the questions and influence the answers of research, it is hardly surprising that the epistemological program of economic materialism renders different results to a management philosophy based on humanistic premises. Method matters; and hence business ethics and corporate responsibility cannot remain at the level of moral postulates but must proceed to a revision and reform of the intellectual foundations of our economic worldview. In order to overcome the staid dualism between an allegedly *quasi-physical* economic world devoid of moral resources and an ethical discourse far *removed* from and *marginal* to the concrete demands of business, a more *integrative* economic theory is needed: a *humanistic* theory of the economy that incorporates ethics from the outset and complements as well as orients quantitative measurements by qualitative criteria (Dierksmeier 2009).

## A Materialistic economics: quantitative maximization

A deductively generated belief in mechanical market forces that always restore a perfect equilibrium lends itself naturally to implications of *laissez-faire*. The neoclassical economist John Bates Clark (1847–1938), for example, suggested: "However stormy may be the ocean, there is an ideal level surface projecting itself through the waves, and the actual surface of the turbulent water fluctuates about it" (Clark 1899, p. 3). Given that belief, it may well seem best not to mess with the awesome natural forces which, in the long run, will put everything right (Mises 1931). Yet thus we fall prey to our own cognitive framework. The market is, after all, not a *natural* but a *social* product, not a *physical* object but a *cultural* construct. Hence Keynes quipped: "*In the long run* we are all dead. Economists set themselves too easy, too useless a task if in tempestuous seasons they can only tell us that when the storm is long past the ocean is flat again" (Keynes 1923, p. 65; italics in original).

Methodologies are not innocent devices. Whenever extra-economic, or non-quantifiable factors affect the economy, a method that blocks out such factors as irrelevant leads to false conclusions, which negatively impact the respective policy advice in turn. A solely deductive approach to markets, for example, based, as it typically is, on assumptions of perfect information, perfect competition, perfect rationality, and so forth will establish that markets are nothing but transaction platforms for human freedom. Ostensibly neutral to any and all human aspirations, the outcomes of market-based transactions will then appear as purely the result of free choices and mutually beneficial exchanges: spontaneously established orders of all-around fairness and reciprocal utility. Any interference with these resultants of individual liberty will consequently appear both ineffective and illegitimate (Waligorski 1990). Overlooked is thus, however, that market economies, under real conditions, favor the exchange of easily marketable goods and services. *Commodifiability* limits *practically* the entry of *phenomena* into the market economy as much as *quantifiability* restricts *theoretically* the entry of *noumena* into economics (Dierksmeier 2011a). Their purported neutrality to the contrary, both market economies and market economics have a *systematic* bias in favor of exchangeable and against non-substitutable goods (diZerga 1997).

The less economics recognizes itself as shaping the reality it observes through its descriptions, the less inhibited – that is, the more indifferent to the social consequences of its advice – its proponents tend to be (Galbraith 1986[1967]). The obdurately defended value-free character of economics is but an illusion (Ulrich 2008). Although modern economics forfeits explicit (categorical) orientations, it still employs implicit (hypothetical) objectives. Otherwise economists could neither unite their various sub-disciplines under a common research perspective, nor formulate tangible recommendations. Economics, simply put, needs a *common denominator* for (micro-economic and macro-economic) *success;* as soon as it foregoes the optimization of the *qualitative* direction of the economy, economic rationality must turn to *quantitative* parameters and will, by default, advocate the *maximization* of utilities. Imperceptibly at first, but ultimately very markedly, economics so arrives at ascribing to individuals and to economies as a whole a preference of "more" over "less," defining any and all economic agency as "maximization behavior" (Samuelson 1938). It is therefore by no means incidental that the broader business media typically measures macro-economic success through the Gross Domestic Product and micro-economic success by a brief look at the bottom line. In contrast, by rejecting any and all qualitative standards, contemporary economics has itself promoted quantitative growth as the supreme goal of the economy.

Starting out as an innocuous technical axiom, *maximization* has long since arrogated a normative role in neoclassical economics as the overarching goal of economic activity. When, for instance, economists subject certain policy options to *cost/benefit*-analyses, cautioning against anything that costs more than it earns, the recommendations so inferred, express *de facto* – despite all professed neutrality – a *value judgment* in favor of quantitative growth and gain. Commodity pricing is facile, yet the same cannot be said for the monetarization of values, ideas, and aesthetic phenomena (Putnam 2003). The latter demand more subtle forms of evaluation and often withstand quantitative assessment throughout. If that is not being factored into our cost/benefit-analyses, the outcome of these seemingly neutral, "scientific" decision-making procedures will, in fact, be wholly partisan, that is, forever supporting higher commodity production in the stead of alternative uses of collective resources. Thus, does removing the qualitative and normative objectives from economics surreptitiously drive a "progress toward the wrong goals" (Galbraith 1986[1967], p. 409)?

### B Humanistic economics: qualitative optimization

While standard economics and conventional management theories have long preached a "shareholder first" agenda, the sustainable growth of social enterprises all around the world indicates that firms with a "stakeholder first" approach are no less viable financially, while, at the same time, creating higher social value (Kimakowitz 2010). We therefore have to unlearn the lessons from our textbooks. Profit is not *eo ipso* good. "Profit is useful if it serves as a means towards an end that provides a sense both of how to produce it and how to make good use of it. Once profit becomes the exclusive goal, if it is produced by improper means and without the common good as its ultimate end, it risks destroying wealth and creating poverty" (CV 21). So, while modern economists typically plead for ever more economic growth and only differ in whether they want to spread the fruits of this growth *directly* (Neo-Keynsians) or *indirectly* via "trickle-down" effects (Chicago School), *Caritas in Veritate* questions the neoclassical logic altogether: "[T]he canons of justice must be respected from the outset, as the economic process unfolds, and not just afterwards or incidentally" (CV 37).

Submitting the quantitative economic success indicators to a qualitative evaluation the encyclical advocates *democratic* economic goal-setting over and against econometric *technocracy. Caritas in Veritate*, for example, mandates taking responsibility for all of humanity (including future generations) or assuming "stewardship over nature" (CV 50). While both environmental and social concerns have slowly but surely also entered into contemporary econometrics, neoclassical economics takes note of externalities only *secondarily*, that is, if and merely in so far as their (dis-)regard translates into ups or downs in costs. Instead, they are of *primary* interest and primordial rank in the ethically grounded economics of *Caritas in Veritate*. The comprehensive regard for the contexts of life that Benedict XVI calls for rests upon the conviction that the "*way humanity treats the environment influences the way it treats itself, and vice versa*" (CV 51; italics in original). The encyclical therefore stipulates that if the conventional econometric tools do not account adequately for the factual externalities of our actions and omissions, then, because of the *human* importance of said externalities, our econometric toolkit must be revised to improve the internalization of these externalities into business rationales.

Herein lie the novelty and pertinence of *Caritas in Veritate* – in positioning ethics not as a corrective or additive to ordinary business conduct but at its core. "Locating resources, financing, production, consumption and all the other phases in the economic cycle inevitably have moral implications. *Thus every economic decision has a moral consequence.*" Which is why moral principles *"must be applied to every phase of economic activity"* (CV 37; italics in original). Instead of merely amending the old *physicalist* economic paradigm with moral council and mending the extant economy with charity-driven business endeavors, "Benedict XVI calls for a profoundly new way of understanding the business enterprise" (CV 40), in which managers should assume responsibility for all *"who contribute to the life of the business*: the workers, the clients, the suppliers of various elements of production, the community of reference" (CV 40; italics in original). This leads to think on the necessity of a *humanistic* paradigm of economics in which ethics to be central.

*Caritas in Veritate* consequently advocates for an ethical pincher movement. On one hand, the encyclical underlines the importance of an "institutional path" to worldwide social progress (CV 7) and reinforces the call for a democratic transformation of the global economic order so as to provide every human being fair access to and equitable participation in the worldwide exchange system. On the other hand, Benedict XVI sees that the structural prodding of monetary incentives alone does not suffice in order to assure the economic development of the entire human family. The voluntary assumption of individual and collective responsibility is also required. This is why the encyclical argues at length for transcending the symmetry-based calculi of utility-maximizing agents through conscious and conscientious attempts at generosity that aim to bridge the asymmetries of culture, status, and purchasing power that almost everywhere still undermine human solidarity. "In the global era, economic activity cannot prescind from gratuitousness, which fosters and disseminates solidarity and responsibility for justice and the common good among the different economic players.... Solidarity is first and foremost a sense of responsibility on the part of everyone with regard to everyone, and it cannot therefore be merely delegated to the State" (CV 38).

Benedict XVI repeatedly reminds us "that the *primary capital to be safeguarded and valued is man, the human person in his or her integrity*" (CV 25; italics in original). Nothing is gained, if in the pursuit of quantitative growth the dignity of the human being is jeopardized (Melé

2003); not even money, because at long last the "economy needs ethics in order to function correctly" (CV 45). Only through a shift from the *one-dimensional* quantitative matrix of yesterday to qualitative and *multidirectional* governance systems can tomorrow's socioeconomic needs be met. The way forward is premised on a departure from the dogma of utility *maximization* and oriented toward the *optimization* of business outcomes through innovative forms of social and environmental accounting, managing, and auditing (CV 22).

## 5 Conclusions

*Caritas in Veritate* addresses and buttresses the present discourse about triple-bottom-line (planet, people, and profit) standards, shared value criteria, stakeholder orientations, and so forth by emphasizing the need to adapt our econometric measurements to human needs and values. The encyclical makes clear, moreover, that only through alternative incentive and promotion systems based on a renewed management philosophy can we create a qualitative and sustainable growth instead of merely more of the "same economic growth [that] has been and continues to be weighed down by *malfunctions and dramatic problems*" (CV 21; italics in original). Yet this is not all, nor the most important merit of the encyclical. The true innovation of the document lies in its deconstruction of the physicalist axioms of the neoclassical paradigm. Realizing that efforts in business ethics and corporate social responsibility will continue to be hampered, as long as conventional economics presents the economy as a realm of *necessity*, wherein human *freedom* and *responsibility* have neither place nor function, *Caritas in Veritate* boldly stakes out territory for a future *humanistic economics* based on the idea of *responsible freedom*. The much noted "convergence between economic science and moral evaluation," Benedict XVI reminds us, owes its existence ultimately to the often overlooked verity that ultimately *human factors create economic facts* (CV 32). Responsibility, that is, can be the guiding principle of management because freedom is its true source (Dierksmeier 2011a).

Business success depends on human development (CV 32). Business must never forget the "wider network of relations within which it operates," lest in the pursuit of "short-term profits" it destroys the "reciprocal enrichment and the dynamics of cooperation" upon which it is premised (CV 32). In other words, "if the market is governed solely by the principle of the equivalence in value of exchanged goods, it cannot produce the social cohesion that it requires in order to function well. *Without internal forms of solidarity and mutual trust, the market cannot completely fulfill its proper economic function*" (CV 35; italics in original). That is, this rehabilitation of economic ethics is "also demanded by economic logic" (CV 36). With this poignant diagnosis, a new era of humanistic economics and humanistic management scholarship is ushered in.

## Executive summary

*Caritas in Veritate* demands that ethics be moved from its hitherto marginal role in economics into the center of economic life and assumes an integral function for its direction. In order to accomplish this fundamental reorientation of the economy, the Papal letter undertakes an intellectual deconstruction of the prevalent mechanistic paradigm of economics; it rejects the *physicalism* underlying neoclassical economics and advocates for a new humanistic synthesis, which suggests to shift the convectional paradigm for another genuine *humanistic*. The foundation of this new, humanistic economics lies in a metaphysics of *responsible freedom*.

First, the question of why (in the 19th century) the perspective of human freedom and morality was slowly but surely removed from the canon of economic teaching has been investigated. Second, the resulting materialistic paradigm of neoclassical economics has been contrasted with the emphasis in *Caritas in Veritate* on free human agency, and the practical outcomes of either perspective compared. Eventually, through this reconstruction, it is shown how an edifice of freedom-based economic thought can lead to a better balanced cognitive architecture for a humanistic management education in pursuit of corporate responsibility.

## Note

1. Neoclassical economics is understood here to mean economic theory in the version represented by and after Alfred Marshall (1842–1924). The concept "neoclassical" was coined by Thorstein Veblen (1898) in order to express the fusion of "classical" economics (Smith, Ricardo) with the teachings worked out by the Austrian marginal utility school (Menger, etc.) to form a more or less uniform credo. (See Niehans 1980 for more on the history of the concept.)

## References

Backhaus, Jürgen and Reginald Hansen. "Methodenstreit in der Nationalökonomie." *Journal for General Philosophy of Science*, Vol. 31, 2, 2000: 307–336.

Bentham, Jeremy. *Economic Writings*. Vol. 3. London: Published for the Royal Economic Society by Allen & Unwin, 1952.

Bentham, Jeremy. *Of Laws in General*. In H. L. A. Hart. London: University of London, Athlone Press, 1970.

Bentham, Jeremy. *An Introduction to the Principles of Morals and Legislation*. In J. H. Burns and H. L. A. Hart. Oxford: Clarendon Press, 1996[1789].

Boettke, Peter J. "Where did economics go wrong? Modern economics as a flight from reality." *Critical Review*, Vol. 11, 1, Winter, 1997: 11–64.

Bostaph, Samuel. "The methodological debate between Carl Menger and the German historicists." *Atlantic Economic Journal*, Vol. 6, 3, December, 1978: 3–16.

Brodbeck, Karl-Heinz. *Die fragwürdigen Grundlagen der Ökonomie, Eine philosophische Kritik der modernen Wirtschaftswissenschaften, Darmstadt*. Wissenschaftliche Buchgesellschaft, 2000 (reprint 2007).

Brodbeck, Karl-Heinz. *Die Herrschaft des Geldes, Darmstadt*. Wissenschaftliche Buchgesellschaft, 2009.

Buchanan, James. "The domain of constitutional economics." *Constitutional Political Economy*, Vol. 1, 1990: 1–18.

Chamberlain, Edward. "An experimental imperfect market." *Journal of Political Economy*, Vol. 56, 1948: 95–108.

Clark, John Bates. *The Distribution of Wealth*. New York: Macmillan, 1899.

Dasgupta, Partha. "What do economists analyze and why: Value or facts?" *Economics and Philosophy*, Vol. 21, 2005: 221–278.

Dierksmeier, Claus. "Quantitative oder qualitative Freiheit?" Paolo Becchi u. a. (Hrsg.), *Nationen und Gerechtigkeit, Rechtsphilosophische Hefte XII*, Frankfurt am Main, 2007: 107–119.

Dierksmeier, Claus. "A requisite journey: From business ethics to economic philosophy, in Humanism in Business." In *The Humanistic Management Network*. Cambridge: Cambridge University Press, 2009.

Dierksmeier, Claus. "The freedom–responsibility nexus in management philosophy and business ethics." *Journal of Business Ethics*, Vol. 101, 2011a: 263–283.

Dierksmeier, Claus. *Humanistic Ethics in the Age of Globality*. New York, Palgrave Macmillan, 2011b.

Dierksmeier, Claus. "Scholastic business ethics. Thomas Aquinas versus William of Ockham." In Lüetge, C. (ed.) *Handbook of the Philosophical Foundations of Business Ethics*. Heidelberg: Springer, forthcoming 2012.

Dierksmeier, Claus and Michael Pirson. "The modern corporation and the idea of freedom." *Philosophy and Management*, Vol. 9, 3, 2010: 5–25.

diZerga, Gus. "Market non-neutrality: Systemic bias in spontaneous orders." *Critical Review*, Vol. 11, No. 1, Winter, 1997: 121–144.

Douglas, Heather E. *Science, Policy, and the Value-Free Ideal*. Pittsburgh: University of Pittsburgh Press, 2009.

Elkington, John and Pamela Hartigan. *The Power of Unreasonable People. How Social Entrepreneurs create Markets that Change the World*. Boston, MA: Harvard Business School Publishing, 2008.

Endres, A. *Environmental Economics: Theory and Policy*. New York: Cambridge University Press, 2011.

Friedman, Milton. *Essays in Positive Economics*. Chicago: University of Chicago Press, 1953.

Galbraith, John Kenneth. *The New Industrial State*. Boston: Houghton Mifflin, 1986[1967].
Hayek, Friedrich August von. *The Counter-Revolution of Science*. Glencoe: Free Press, 1952.
Heilbroner, Robert and William S. Milberg. *The Making of Economic Society*. Upper Saddle River, NJ: Pearson Prentice Hall, 2008.
Jevons, William Stanley. *The Theory of Political Economy*. London/New York: Macmillan, 1871.
Keynes, John Maynard. *A Tract on Monetary Reform, Collected Writings, IV*. London: Macmillan, 1923.
Kimakowitz, Ernst v., Michael Pirson, Claus Dierksmeier, Heiko Spitzeck, and Wolfgang Amann, eds. *Humanistic Management in Practice*. London/New York: Palgrave Macmillan Publishers, 2010.
Lucas, Robert. "On the mechanics of economic development." *Journal of Monetary Economics*, Vol. 22, 1998: 3–42.
Marcuse, Herbert. *One-Dimensional Man. Studies in the Ideology of Advanced Industrial Society*. Boston: Beacon Press, 1964.
Marshall, Alfred. *Principles of Economics*. London: Macmillan and Co., 1890 (quotations follow the 8th edition from 1920).
Melé, Domenec. "The challenge of humanistic management." *Journal of Business Ethics*, Vol. 44, 2003: 77–88.
Menger, Carl. *Grundsätze der Volkswirtschaftslehre. Erster Allgemeiner Theil*. Wien: Willhelm Braumüller, 1871.
Menger, Carl. *Untersuchungen Über die Methode der Sozialwissenschaften und der Politischen Ökonomie insbesondere*. Leipzig: Duncker and Humblot, 1883.
Mises, Ludwig von. *Die Ursachen der Wirtschaftskrise*. Tübingen: Mohr, 1931.
Nguyen, Huy. "Do humanistic values matter?" *Academy of Management Best Paper Proceedings* ODC, 2000: A1–A6.
Niehans, Jurg. *A History of Economic Theory. Classic Contributions 1720–1980*. Baltimore: Johns Hopkins University Press, 1980.
Putnam, Hilary. "For ethics and economics without the dichotomies." *Review of Political Economy*, Vol. 153, 2003: 395–412.
Robbins, Lionel. *An Essay on the Nature and Significance of Economic Science*. New York: New York University Press, 1932.
Samuelson, Paul. "A note on the pure theory of consumers' behaviour." *Economica*, Vol. 5, 1938: 61–71.
Schmoller, Gustav von. *Die Volkswirtschaft, die Volkswirtschaftslehre und ihre Methode*. Frankfurt: Klostermann, 1949[1893].
Schmoller, Gustav von. "Zur Methodologie der Staats- und Sozialwissenschaften." *Schmollers Jahrbuch für Gesetzgebung, Verwaltung und Volkswirtschaft*, 7, 1883.
Sen, Amartya. *Rationality and Freedom*. Cambridge: Harvard University Press, 2002.
Solow, Robert. "How did economics get that way, and what way did it get?" *Daedalus*, Vol. 134, 4, 1997: 39–58.
Spiegel, Henry William. *The Growth of Economic Thought*. Englewood Cliffs, NJ: Prentice Hall, 1971.
Stigler, George and Gary Becker. "De Gustibus Non Est Disputandum." *American Economic Review*, Vol. 67, 2, 1977: 76–90.

Ulrich, Peter. *Integrative Economic Ethics. Foundations of a Civilized Market Economy.* Cambridge: Cambridge University Press, 2008.

Veblen, Thorstein. "Why is economics not an evolutionary science?" *Quarterly Journal of Economics*, Vol. 12, 1898: 373–397.

Waligorski, Conrad. *The Political Theory of Conservative Economists.* Lawrence: University of Kansas Press, 1990.

Walras, Léon. "Économique et méchanique." *Bulletin de la Société Vaudoise de Sciences Naturelles*, Vol. 45, 1909: 313–324.

Warke, Tom. "Mathematical fitness in the evolution of the utility concept from Bentham to Jevons to Marshall." *Journal of the History of Economic Thought*, Vol. 22, N. 1, 2000, 5–27.

Weber, Max. "Die 'Objektivität' sozialwissenschaftlicher und sozialpolitischer Erkenntnis." *Archiv für Sozialwissenschaft und Sozialpolitik*, Vol. 19, Band, 1904.

Weber, Max. "Der Sinn der "Wertfreiheit" der soziologischen und ökonomischen Wissenschaften." *Logos*, Vol. 7, 1918. Reprinted in M. Weber. *Gesammelte Aufsätze zur Wissenschaftslehre.* In J. Winckelmann, ed. Tübingen: Mohr, 1988.

Wieser, F. von. *Über den Ursprung und die Hauptgesetze des wirthschaftlichen Werthes.* Wien: Hölder, 1884.

# 2

# *Caritas in Veritate*'s Interpretation of the Nature of the Financial Crisis

*Stefano Zamagni*

> The intention to do good must not be considered incompatible with the effective capacity to produce goods. Financiers must rediscover the genuinely ethical foundation of their activity, so and not to abuse the sophisticated instruments which can serve to betray the interests of savers. (CV 65)

This chapter defends the thesis that the encyclical *Caritas in Veritate* (CV), published by Pope Benedict XVI on June 29, 2009, contains a specific interpretation of the financial crisis which began in summer 2007 in the United States and then spread throughout the rest of the world. At its core, the interpretation is that the crisis is systemic in nature, not merely cyclical. It is the inevitable result of a process that, over a period of more than thirty years, has fundamentally changed the way finance is carried out. This has generated the phenomenon known as the financialization of society. At the root of the many causes of the crisis, the encyclical identifies a triple divorce: first, the separation of the economic and the social spheres of society; second, a decoupling of labor and the origin of wealth; and third, a divorce between the market and democracy. Taken together, these three separations point to the common and general consideration made here.

It is an acknowledged fact that in our time the market and the culture of contract, on which the market is based, have become progressively more important in our life. There are those who believe that nowadays the global market will recreate social obligation and rebuild human relationships, and they want everything in our social, political, and cultural life to be directed to enhance the efficiency of mechanisms and the effectiveness of procedures. The "good news" of competition and globalization seem to have become, in recent years, a sort of new ideology of the post-industrial society. Christians, instead, believe that a new human perspective is needed, seeing this as good not only for efficiency but also for the three dimensions of all human beings; the material, the socio-relational, and the spiritual – without discrimination. However, while the encyclical underlines this aspect in its subtitle ("On integral human development in Charity and Truth") it does not, as some would wish, reject the market, the social role of private enterprises, profit, finance, and so on.

Instead, the encyclical holds that everyone can help generate the rules and build institutions, to select the aims and priorities by which the economy is governed. If in the teachings of the Church there is critical reference to the prevailing model of development, this is not because its enormous potential and the benefits it has brought to humankind are not acknowledged, but because such potential is too often exploited to create inequalities rather than to enhance solidarity; to increase what is superfluous rather than to redistribute necessities; to impose the dominance of one particular model of development rather than to acknowledge the resources of the many diverse models. "*The world's wealth is growing in absolute terms, but inequalities are on the increase.* In rich countries, new sectors of society are succumbing to poverty...In poorer areas some groups enjoy a sort of 'superdevelopment' of a wasteful and consumerist kind which forms an unacceptable contrast with the ongoing situations of dehumanizing deprivation" (CV 22; italics in the original).

A doubt, from a hasty reading of *Caritas in Veritate*, might arise: is it not perhaps true that the criterion to be used to choose the legal and economic institutional set-up of society has to be efficiency? Isn't it therefore true that when in a given moment in history certain rules are followed instead of others, it is because these rules have proven to be more efficient than the alternatives? For brevity, I would like to give two main reasons why the answer to both questions is no. First of all, the concept of efficiency, as it is used in economics, is not a primitive concept – it derives from Bentham's utilitarian principle, which is a normative principle and not an economic one. Therefore, efficiency cannot be said to be value-neutral, and consequently cannot be an objective assessment criterion to evaluate alternative states of affairs. Rather, it is a "positionally objective" criterion in the sense of Amartya

Sen (1992). In other words, efficiency acquires an objective meaning only after the researcher (or the manager) has openly declared the vision of the world – that is, the position – sustaining his/her discourse or action.

Second, in calculating efficiency, the social externalities (positive or negative, as the case may be) of economic activity are never fully taken into account. Let's consider the situations, of which there are many, where efficiency is opposed to freedom in its positive sense. If in order to achieve a more efficient allocation of resources positive freedom must be sacrificed, what then guarantees the sustainability of the market institution over time? True, in the short-term perspective economists can abstract from this concern, but this would defeat the very purpose of their argument since the market cannot function properly, nor for long, without freedom. On the other hand, economic development is the result of factors that do not belong solely to the economic sphere. The famous French sociologist Emile Durkheim warned that the values of society are not mere means at the disposal of economic calculation, given that society can always "oblige" or compel its members to act so as to neutralize the injunctions originated by that calculation.

The message sent by Benedict XVI to the economic world is that the renowned thesis of the market, as the place where agents are free to choose is self-legitimizing and therefore not subject to moral constraints, has to be critically reconsidered. The point is, in brief, the following: The market is the place where the coordination of economic decisions is carried out through voluntary cooperation. This is fundamentally because "both parties in an economic transaction benefit from it, provided that the transaction is bilaterally voluntary and informed" (Friedman 1962, p.13). As a consequence, when two (or more) parties, with no fraud or coercion, freely originate an economic transaction, they also agree to any consequences stemming from it. The concept of consent based on freedom of choice is well explained by Richard Posner when he writes: "I personally believe that he who buys a lottery ticket and loses, agrees to the loss if there was no fraud or coercion" (1981, p. 94).

Therefore, choosing freely means giving one's consent and agreeing the means to legitimize. As pointed out by Fabienne Peter (2004) the market does not need to ask for a certificate of ethical legitimacy, because it is capable of legitimizing itself on its own. This is not the case of the State which, on the contrary, in order to be able to use coercion – which is the main means it uses in attaining its goals – needs the approval of the electorate, as it is only the electorate that can legitimate the State. What is the weak point in this reasoning? Basically, that it is almost never true that freedom of choice postulates consent. It would be so if the subject of the choice took part in the creation of the choice menu – which is never the case in real life. As Peter (2004) notes, the parent voluntarily offering, under no obligation of any kind, to sell one of his organs to alleviate the poverty of his family certainly does not agree to the consequences of his act. Free choice of an option has the power to legitimize it only if the set of alternatives is somehow part of the subject's choice menu. If this set is *given*, this prerequisite is by no means fulfilled.

It is known that the key role played by the category of consent is typical of the social contract tradition of political thought, starting with Hobbes. The idea is that if I signed a contract with you to do something I now no longer want to do, your answer could be "but you agreed to do it at the time, now you have to abide to the terms of the contract." That is, consent generates obligation. Among those scholars who embrace social contract theory, none surpassed John Rawls. Rawls (1971) was able to show that in order for consent to produce obligation the constraints under which the parties to the contract take their decisions must be shared by everyone. Only if it can be proved that the parties to the social contract agreed (or intended to agree) to the rules of the game they are in, can it be legitimately claimed that the agreement reached through consent implies obligation.

It is common knowledge that in our market economies this condition is practically never fulfilled. Indeed, freedom of choice describes the absence of coercion by others. It has to do with the *possibility* of choice, that is to say with the existence of a domain or space within which the subject can exercise his/her sovereignty. This still says nothing about the *ability* to choose, in other words about the real exercise of the choice. Having a large number of alternatives is not enough if one doesn't know how to choose among them or if one lacks the capability to actually choose. As Benedict XVI reminds us, the *use* of freedom is essential to its own *definition*. Someone who is virtually free to put into practice his or her action plan, but who does not possess the capacity to do so, cannot be said to agree to the consequences of his or her actions. Therefore, trying to justify the present economic and financial architecture on the grounds of the efficiency criterion *only*, would simply be a mere tautology.

## 1 The economic and social spheres being kept separate

I come now to the first of the remote underlying causes of the present economic crisis. One of the negative legacies from modernity is the notion that the only eligible members of the "economic club," that is, of the market are those entrepreneurs who are profit-seekers. This is tantamount to affirming that if one does not pursue exclusively the maximization of profit, one cannot be considered a real entrepreneur. As a consequence, one must resign to belonging to the social sphere, where social enterprises, cooperatives, non-profit organizations, and the like operate. This absurd conceptualization – itself the offspring of the theoretical error that confuses the market economy, which is the *genus*, with its major *species*, namely the capitalist system (Zamagni 2010b) – is responsible for the well-known dichotomous model of social order. According to this model the economic sphere is the locus of the production of wealth (a locus whose governing principle is efficiency) and the social sphere the locus of its redistribution (a locus where the fundamental canon of behavior is solidarity). (It may be of interest to recall that John Stuart Mill (1987[1848]) was the first economist to distinguish between the laws of production and the laws of distribution of income). *Caritas in Veritate* states: "Perhaps at one time it was conceivable that first the creation of wealth could be entrusted to the economy and then the task of distributing it could be assigned to politics. Today that would be more difficult (...) Hence the canons of justice must be respected from the outset, *as the economic process unfolds*, and not just afterwards or incidentally" (CV 37; italics added).

The consequences of this separation are before our eyes. As the economic historian Angus Maddison (2001) has shown, in the past thirty years the indicators of social inequality, both within and between nations, have risen to scandalously high levels, even in those countries where the welfare state administers a substantial share of resources. Indeed, while it is certainly true that globalization is a positive sum game that increases aggregate wealth, it is also true that it exacerbates the contrast between winners and losers. This fact is linked to the emergence of a new form of competition, unknown until recently: positional competition, according to which the "winner takes all and the loser loses everything" – the so-called superstar effect. Why is it that the literature on this subject is so hotly divided? A credible answer comes from the work by Milanovic (2006) who distinguishes between *world* (or global) and *international* inequality. The latter considers the differences in the average incomes of various countries, unweighted ("Concept 1 inequality" in Milanovic's sense) and duly weighted to account for the size of the population ("Concept 2 inequality"). The former, in contrast, also takes into account the inequalities in income distribution within individual countries ("Concept 3 inequality"). It is world (or global) inequality which is increasing as a consequence of globalization; not so much international inequality.

In fact, in order for "Concept 3 inequality" to diminish, two conditions have to be met: (i) poor and densely populated countries must grow at a faster rate than rich countries; and (ii) this must occur without an increase in inequality within the country. Now, while the first condition is more or less satisfied, progress on the second condition is virtually absent. In fact, over the past quarter of a century, the growth rate of the poorest countries has been higher than that of the richest countries (4 percent versus 1.7 percent, as indicated by Maddison, 2001). Since it is a principal cause of conflict and ultimately of civil war the question arises: why should one worry about the growth of global inequality? As wisely indicated by Polachek and Seiglie (2006) conflict can be defined as "trade gone awry": if a country's gains from trade are not as high as it thinks it should receive, this becomes a major determinant of conflict, which might in the end jeopardize peace itself. That is why the search for a socially responsible trade integration regime, capable of taking into consideration the "pains from trade" (Verdier 2005), is a duty that economists cannot escape from or forget about.

The conclusion one can draw from the above is that the well-known aphorism that "a rising tide lifts all boats" and its neo-liberal corollary, the "trickle-down" effect, according to which wealth, like rain, eventually benefits all, even the poorest, is untenable in most cases. Such a belief is wrong because it does not take into consideration the explosion of pecuniary externalities following globalization.[1] Only technological externalities (e.g. environmental degradation) receive significant consideration and this cannot be accepted on ethical grounds. To understand the nature of pecuniary externalities, it might be of interest to recall what Adam Smith wrote in *The Wealth of Nations* on the consequences of the discovery of America and the passage of the Cape of Good Hope – "The two greatest and most important events recorded in the history of mankind" (1950[1776], p. 141). Dealing with the consequences of these events, Smith remarked: "What benefits or what misfortunes to mankind may hereafter result from those great events, no human wisdom can foresee. By uniting, in some measure, the most distant parts of the world...their general tendency would seem to be beneficial. To the native, however, both of the East and West Indies, all the commercial benefits which can have resulted from those events have been sunk and lost in the dreadful misfortunes which they have occasioned... At the particular time when these discoveries were made, the superiority of force happened to be so great on the side of the Europeans, that *they were enabled to commit with impunity every sort of injustice in those remote countries.* Hereafter, perhaps, the natives of those countries may grow stronger, or those of Europe may grow weaker and the inhabitants of all the different quarters of the world may arrive at that equality of courage and force which ... can alone overawe the injustice of independent nations into some sort of respect for the rights of one another" (1950[1776] p. 141; italics added). I consider this passage a remarkable anticipation of the argument according to which we now require a more prudent (and wise) approach in order to acknowledge both the gains and losses from globalization. Indeed, if it is true that today we enjoy enormous "gains from trade," it is also the case that we are facing "pains from trade." It is not acceptable that only the first component is taken into consideration in the public debate.

*Caritas in Veritate* makes it clear that the solution to the problem of an endemic increase of inequality consists of putting back together what has been astutely separated. Endorsing the conception of the market typical of the civil economy tradition of thought,[2] according to which social bonds cannot be reduced to the mere "cash nexus," the Pope suggests that we can fully experience human sociability within normal economic life, not outside it as it happens in the dichotomous model of the social order. The challenge to accept is neither to see the economy as in ontological conflict with the good life, as if it were but a locus of exploitation and alienation, nor to view it as the only solution for all the problems of society, as the anarchic-neoliberal school of thought would have it. In other words, the challenge is to go beyond the two main conceptions inherited from modernity about the relationship between the economic and social spheres. The first conception – the neo-liberal one – considers the market as a basically *asocial* institution whose main duty is to produce wealth irrespective of the modes and ways employed. Government – according to this conception – should take care of the redistributive function. According to the other conception – that of the neo-structuralists – the market is essentially an *antisocial* institution. As the famous words of Karl Polanyi taken from *The Great Transformation* illustrate: "the market advances on the desertification of society." As such, the market is nothing but a necessary evil.

The perspective adopted by the Encyclical rejects the reductionist stance of the two streams of thought. It shows that the market is capable of hosting, within its own institutions, not only the principles of exchange of equivalents and of redistribution, but also the principle of reciprocity:

> What is needed, therefore, is a market that permits the free operation, in conditions of equal opportunity, of enterprises in pursuit of different institutional ends. Alongside profit-oriented private enterprise (...) there must be room for commercial entities based on mutualist principles and pursuing social ends to take root and express themselves. It is from their reciprocal encounter in the marketplace that one may expect hybrid forms of commercial behavior to emerge, and hence an attentiveness to ways of *civilizing the economy*. (CV 38; italics in the original)

## 2 The financial ethos versus the ethics of work

Let me go on to the second type of separation. For centuries humankind held on to the idea that the origin of wealth lay in human labor – one kind of labor or another, the type didn't matter. In fact, Book I of Adam Smith's *Wealth of Nations* (1950[1776]) is devoted precisely to "the improvement of the productive powers of labour." What novelty has the financialization of the economy that began about three decades ago ultimately brought? It is the idea that speculative finance creates much more wealth, and much faster, than work. Countless episodes confirm this thesis. Consider the phenomenon of de-industrialization which has negatively affected so many countries that have literally changed their productive structure. In the past few decades the world's greatest universities have seen the explosive growth of study areas such as business finance, financial markets, financial econometrics, and the like, crowding out and impoverishing other fields of economic study, observable in the distribution of funds by research area, the professional choices of the majority of economics students, and so on. The spread of the financial ethos, with the complicity of the media, has helped establish the belief that getting rich does not take work – better to fly high, gamble, and above all eschew moral scruples. As I have shown previously (Zamagni 2010b) the ethos of finance has led to the legitimation of greed – a specific form of avarice – as a sort of civic virtue: "Greed is good; greed is right," cried Gordon Gekko, the protagonist of the 1987 movie *Wall Street*. The result has been a movement from the notion of *free market* to that of *greed market*. At the same time, the ethos of superiority of finance has led to a systematic alternation between greed and panic. As more than one commentator has explained, panic is no more than euphoria with the minus sign; therefore, if euphoria is rational, so is panic. (The fact is that it is the economic theory supporting the ethos of finance which is aporetic, as demonstrated in Zamagni 2010a).

The consequences of this cultural revolution are now glaringly evident. One is the maladroit attempt to displace the concept of "worker" within the social order in favor of that of "citizen-consumers." Today, for instance, we no longer have a broadly shared notion of labor that can help us understand the transformations under way. We know that starting with the commercial revolution of the eleventh century the idea of craft work gradually gained ascendancy, with its combination of knowledge and activity, of production process and *mestiere* – a term which itself refers to the mastery of the master craftsman. With the advent of the industrial revolution and then of the Ford-Tayloristic mode of production, what gained currency was the idea of "tasks" (the mark of parcellized labor) and not craft and with it came the notion of freedom *from* work as emancipation from the "realm of necessity." In the Fordist era, workers on a production line performed specialized tasks repetitively, as illustrated by Frederick W. Taylor in his fundamental book on the scientific organization of labor published in 1911. Today, in the post-Fordist era, what idea do we have of labor? Some propose the idea of *skill* in terms of professional capabilities, but they are unaware of the perilous implications, signaling the confusion of meritocracy with meritoriousness, as if these terms were synonyms. Western civilization is based on a powerful idea, the idea of the "good life," whence comes the right-cum-duty of each person to plan his or her life with a view to happiness. What possible starting point toward this objective can there be, if not labor as the central category of the good existence? The flourishing of the human spirit – Artistotle's *eudaimonia* – must not be sought *after* work, because men and women encounter their human condition *while* they are working. Hence the urgent need to elaborate on the concept that work is not only pain and effort, a concept that on the one hand overcomes the hypertrophy of labor typical of our times (work filling an expanding anthropological void) and on the other declines the idea of liberty *at* work (the freedom to choose those activities that can enrich the heart and mind of the person engaged in work – an idea that was already anticipated by Adam Smith in his critique of alienating labor).[3]

Clearly, the acceptance of the eudaimonic paradigm implies that the purpose of an enterprise – whatever its legal form – cannot be reduced to profit alone, though of course not excluding profit.[4] That is, accepting this paradigm implies the possible birth and development of enterprises with a civil vocation, capable of transcending self-referentiality and thereby expanding the scope for people's effective ability to choose their type of work. "The very plurality of institutional forms of business" – one reads in the encyclical – "gives rise to a market which is not only more civilized but also more competitive" (CV 46). It may be of interest in this regard to quote from a recent essay by Michael Porter: "A big part of the problem lies with companies themselves, which remain trapped in an outmoded approach to value creation that has emerged over the past few decades. They continue to view value creation narrowly, optimizing short-term financial performance in a bubble...The solution lies in the principle of *shared value*, which involves creating economic value in a way that *also* creates value for society by addressing its needs and challenges. Business must reconnect company success with social progress" (Porter 2011, p. 4).

Our having forgotten that no human society is sustainable where everything is, on the one hand, reduced to improving transactions based on the principle of exchange of equivalents and, on the other, to increasing public paternalistic transfers explains why it is so hard to advance from the notion of labor as activity to that of labor as work (*opus*). It also explains the tremendous spread, in the past quarter of a century, of greed in our societies as a cultural habit. In the Judean-Christian tradition, greed as a form of avarice is the capital vice held responsible for the many forms of (secondary) scarcity and the consequent distributive conflicts (Zamagni 2009). There is a two-way link between avarice and scarcity: on the one hand, scarcity prompts more and more self-interested conduct, as the possession of scarce goods heightens one's prestige, on the other hand, avarice aggravates scarcity through its adverse effect on the availability of goods and the difficulty in distinguishing, in practice, between needs and wants (or desires). Interestingly, the Hebrew word for money – the main object of avarice – is *damin*, which in the Talmud and the Cabalist tradition is the plural of "blood." And blood sustains life only if it circulates: if it stagnates, death is certain. The analogy with the metaphor of the well used by Basil of Caesarea in his famous homily "On the good use of riches" delivered in 370 AD could not be a better fit: "The wells that are drawn from most often are those from which water gushes most readily; left unused, they go putrid. And riches kept idle too are useless, while if they circulate they are useful to the common good and bear fruit." Avarice keeps the blood from circulating, as it keeps us from drawing water from the well.

The doctrine that intended to minimize the role of ethics in financial activity is based on two fallacious tenets. First, the assumption of perfect competition would make agents' moral responsibility superfluous, that is, irrelevant. The second is that self-interest and greed are necessary conditions for market efficiency. However, the discovery – so to speak – of the enduring incompleteness of markets and the existence of substantial market failures empties these tenets of any empirical basis. Given what markets are in reality, agents' greed – along with their bounded rationality – entails opportunistic and moral hazard behavior that generate negative externalities for the whole economy and are also self-defeating for the agents themselves. It is worth noting the encyclical's text:

> Finance, therefore (...) now needs to go back to being an *instrument directed towards improved wealth creation and development*... Above all, the intention to do good must not be considered incompatible with the effective capacity to produce goods. Financiers must rediscover the genuinely ethical foundation of their activity, so and not to abuse the sophisticated instruments which can serve to betray the interests of savers. (CV 65, italics in the original)

To conclude this section on a positive note it can be said that very recently, after a long period of disfavor, the notion of virtue is witnessing a vital revival of interest. Thanks to persuasive interventions of contemporary moral philosophers such as Philippa Foot, Alasdair McIntyre, Martha Nussbaum, Bernard Williams, Charles Taylor, and others, the virtue ethics, originally formulated by Aristotle, is gaining new ground in the debate on ethical finance. It is certainly true that there are different versions of virtue ethics. However, what is common to all versions is to oppose those ethical approaches that appraise actions atomistically, either in terms of consequences, as in utilitarianism, or in terms of compatibility with deontological codes of behavior. In other words, where the basic unit of moral evaluation for rival frameworks is individual action, the basic unit for virtue ethics is the human person, in its entirety (Zamagni 2011).

## 3 When the market divorces from democracy

Finally, the present crisis results from a third major separation, that of market and democracy. Economic theory – especially the neo-Austrian school of thought – has always maintained that a society's success and progress depend crucially on its ability to mobilize and manage the knowledge and know-how dispersed among its members. The principal merit of the market as a socio-economic institution, in fact, is that it offers the best solution to the problem of knowledge. As Friedrich A. Von Hayek made clear in his renowned essay *The Use of Knowledge in Society* (1945) to effectively channel local knowledge – the one that is possessed by individuals – a decentralized mechanism of coordination is needed, and the price system exactly serves this purpose.

Yet this point of view, very common among economists, tends to conceal an element of central importance. That is, the operation of the price mechanism as an instrument for coordination presumes that economic agents share, and consequently understand, the "language" of the market. This suggests that the market needs not one but two types of knowledge in order to perform its appointed task. The first type is lodged in every individual and, as Hayek noted, can be managed by ordinary market mechanisms. The second type is the knowledge that circulates between and among the various groups that make up society, which has to do with the common language that enables a multitude of individuals to agree on and share the meaning of the categories of discourse that are used and to understand one another when they come in contact (Tognato 2005).

Every society involves the coexistence of many different languages, and the language of the market is just one of them. If it were the only one, there would be no problem. All you would need to efficiently mobilize individual local knowledge would be the standard market instruments. But this is not so, for the simple reason that contemporary society is a multicultural framework in which individual knowledge must cross linguistic borders, which raises formidable obstacles. The neo-Austrian school of economic thought could abstract from this difficulty by implicitly postulating that community knowledge does not exist because, say, all the members of society share the same value system and accept the same principles of social organization. But where this is not the case – as in reality we must acknowledge – it follows that in order to govern a "multi-language" society another institution apart from the market is necessary, to bring out the language of contact in which members belonging to different "linguistic" communities can conduct a dialogue. This institution, basically, is deliberative democracy. This helps us to see why the problem of knowledge management in today's society, which is in the end the problem of human development itself, posits the need for two institutions – democracy and market – to be able to work jointly, side by side. Instead, the separation of market from democracy that has taken place over the past quarter of a century, on a wave of exaltation of a certain type of cultural relativism and an extreme individualistic ideology has convinced many, including many thinkers and scholars, that it is possible to expand the area of the market without worrying about the need to strengthen democracy.

Two main consequences have followed. First, the pernicious idea that the market is "some kind of morally neutral zone" – to use the famous expression of Gauthier in (1984) – that is not subject to ethical judgment, because its core already contains the moral principles needed for its social legitimacy. However, this is simply not true. The reason lies in a particular interpretation of the celebrated Böckenförde's paradox: the market economy lives and constantly feeds itself with presuppositions – sympathy, trust, benevolence, to use Adam Smith's trilogy – that it is not capable of generating and guaranteeing by itself (Böckenförde 2007). It follows that when the market cuts off its vital link with democracy – that is, with the locus where those presuppositions are cultivated and spread among citizens – it becomes self-referential and its degeneration becomes inevitable (Bruni and Sugden 2008).

The second consequence has to do with the wrong idea that democracy, once in existence, will continue to remain forever. The Aristotelian notion of fragility of the good comes to mind in this regard. The fact is that democracy is a fragile good that needs to be protected and managed with care. Since if the fragile good of democracy is subject to a slow deterioration, because of a lack of educational investments, it may come about that the market will be prevented from gathering and managing knowledge efficiently; so society may cease to progress not because of some defect in the market mechanism but because of a deficit of democracy. The current economic and financial crisis strongly suggests the empirical validity of this proposition. Just think of the domination in present-day culture of short-termism in both economics and politics, while democracy necessarily presupposes a long-term time horizon. Essentially, we need to rejoin market and democracy to cope with the many threats of the present epoch. The warning of Pope Paul VI that "The world is in trouble because of the lack of thinking" (CV 53) seems to me to be significant. It must be remembered that there are two types of thought: calculating and thinking. We need both, yet, it is a well-known fact that in recent times the first type has smothered the second. We need to restore the balance. We can remember here the Chariot Allegory in the Plato's dialogue *Phaedrus* (sections 246a–254e). The charioteer is driving a chariot pulled by two winged horses, and tries to stop the horses from going different ways, and to proceed towards enlightenment. One can say: "The furrow will be straight [and the crop will be abundant] if the two horses dragging on the plough proceed at the same speed."

Before leaving the present argument, a final point deserves some attention. In section 66 of *Caritas in Veritate* it is stated that: "global interconnectedness has led to the emergence of a new political power, that of *consumers and their associations*... It is good for people to realize that purchasing is always a moral—and not simply economic—act. Hence the *consumer has a specific social responsibility,* which goes hand-in- hand with the social responsibility of the enterprise... A more incisive role for consumers, as long as they themselves are not manipulated by associations that do not truly represent them, is a desirable element for building economic democracy."

The quoted excerpt marks the first mention, in a Pontifical document, of the social responsibility of consumers. It symbolizes an important step and must be given due weight. Specifically, it is important to stress that Benedict XVI urges all "men of good will" to accelerate the transition from a *consumption society* where consumers' freedom of choice is theoretical rather than real to a *consumers' society* in which consumers are entitled to "steer" production in a given direction. As Alfred Marshall had foreseen in his *Principles of Economics* (1890), by applying the principle of substitutes and complements in consumption, consumers choose among different companies, in the same way as the producer chooses the best combination of productive inputs. Let us not forget that consumers are first and foremost buyers that collect information and narratives associated with goods.

What is the connection between the above and consumer social responsibility? In order to reply to this question, it is crucial to focus on the two options we are faced with in the present time. The first option entails feeling satisfied with the state of things and embraces the slogan "buy more, pay less." The motto of the second option, on the other hand, is "buy more, be happy." It is common knowledge that our society tends to diminish spare time, as it deems consumption a "classic" economic activity. However, this creates a problem: in order to foster happiness, consumption requires time. In the past quarter of a century, the formation of so-called complex societies, generated lifestyles based on densification, where the idea of ostentatious consumption recedes in favor of a consumption that has a deeper significance thus increasing the consumer's experience. In this sense, the ultimate aim of consumption is not to show off but, rather, to live symbolically. This is why marketing tends to increasingly focus on selling "events" or "experiences" rather than goods. In the latter set of observations lies the potential to create something positive and truly innovative. If we use as a starting point the Latin etymon *cum-sumere* – where *cum* means "together, together with" and *sumere* means "to take without depriving" – consumption can be experienced as a form of interpersonal communication.

The strong relational role played by consumption in our present society poses a great challenge: a balance must be struck between work and spare time, between *negotium* and *otium*. Indeed, the way the social surplus is allocated between leisure time and money time constitutes a real challenge for advanced societies. In the past, on the contrary, the key challenge concerned the division of social surplus between consumption and savings. How to overcome the *negotium–otium* dichotomy is one of the major challenges of the present generation.

## 4 Conclusion

The central message stemming from the argument laid out above is to call for a deep rethink of the issue concerning the anthropological foundation of economic discourse. This issue is attracting a growing interest among economists. This is partly motivated by the recognition that a viable and effective strategy that copes with the problem of integral human development requires a move away from the reductionist stance of a great deal of contemporary economic theory. Such a reductionism expresses itself in the fact that in modern economics relations among human beings are reduced to relations of exchange of equivalents, as if these were the only ones worthy of economic interest. As is well-known, the economic universe is made up of various economic worlds, each characterized by the prevalence of a specific type of relations. Yet, the (ontological) assumption still prevailing in economics is that all types of social relations should be modeled as some variant or another of exchange relations. In so doing, the discipline is imposing upon itself a constraint that prevents a thorough investigation of economic relations which are of great economic relevance in our societies. Think of the relations of reciprocity. It is the compound figure of relational individuality (i.e. personalism), as stemming from Christian Social Teaching that, while allowing the apories of individualism on the one side, and collectivism on the other side to be overcome, would enable economic theory to be reconstructed on more solid bases (Zagmani 2010a).

It is now a well-recognized fact that market systems are compatible with many cultures (defined as tractable patterns of behavior). In turn, the degree of compatibility of market systems with cultures is not without effect on the global efficiency of the systems themselves: in general, the final outcome of market-coordination will vary from culture to culture. Thus, one should expect that a culture of extreme individualism will produce different results from a culture where individuals, although motivated by self-interest, entertain a sense of solidarity. However, cultures are not to be taken as given and beyond analysis. Cultures respond to the investment of resources in education, so much so that in many circumstances it may be socially beneficial to engage in cultural engineering. For, how good the performance of an economic system is also depends on whether certain conceptions and ways of thinking have achieved dominance. I posit that a society that provides opportunities for virtuous behavior is one that is more conducive to virtuous individuals. Not only this but the practice of effective virtuous behavior leads more people to adopt virtuous behavior through the process of imitation. That is why the presence in a system of economic agents basing their actions on intrinsic as well as transcendent motivations offers not only a remarkable way of overcoming many social scarcities, but serves as a context for positive character formation (Argandoña 2008).

As in all human endeavors, it would be naive to think that radical processes, like those hinted at above, do not entail high rates of conflict. Indeed, the interests – scientific and political – involved are enormous. Understandably distress concerning the future of economic life, and in particular the possibility of humanizing market economy, is, today, spreading in many circles. This concern is being used by some, in the name of a "culture of crisis," as a device to produce a sort of market Machiavellism – fundamentalism – that lies at the heart of the many forms of market. It is precisely against this neo-Machiavellian culture and its underlying ethical relativism that those who, like the Christians, are the bearers of a specific message of hope should put up a fight. Catholic Social Thought would acquire significance and credibility, even with the non-believer, when it is accompanied by actual experiences which do not merely represent traditions of moral reflection, but turn into laboratories for innovating practices of life.

## Executive summary

Various interpretations of the present financial crisis have been offered. The majority focus, albeit from different angles, on its proximate causes. This chapter takes a different route by considering the remote causes of the crisis, which are basically systemic rather than cyclical. It would be practically impossible to escape an entropic (i.e. systemic) crisis unless one considers the ultimate factors responsible for it. In this regard, the chapter assumes the encyclical *Caritas in Veritate* by Pope Benedict XVI as a sort of special glasses, employed to read and to interpret the *res novae* of the present times. The encyclical identifies a triple divorce that has occurred in the past few decades in the Western world. First, the divorce between the economic sphere and the social sphere, which justified the idea that economic activity has no need to submit itself to ethical consideration or social assessment. Second, the decoupling of human labor and the origin of wealth, which legitimized greed as a more rational pattern of behavior. Third, the separation between market and democracy, which provided the foundation of the thesis about the self-referential and self-regulating nature of markets. The chapter defends the thesis advanced in *Caritas in Veritate* according to which only by reuniting what has been violently separated it is possible to cope with the many challenges stemming from the current economic crisis. Needless to say such a perspective makes clear the urgency of a reconsideration of the anthropological foundation of economic discourse, whose reductionist stance is nowadays perceived by many scholars and businessmen as one of the major impediments to both the economic and moral progress of our societies.

## Notes

1. On the notion of pecuniary externality see Barrera (2011).
2. This topic has been developed by Bruni and Zamagni (2007).
3. On this question, see the penetrating argument developed by Illanes (2003).
4. On this specific point see Dierksmeier and Pirson (2009).

## References

Argandoña, A. "Integrating ethics into action theory and organizational theory." *Journal of Business Ethics*, Vol. 78, 2008: 435–446.

Barrera, A. *Market Complicity and Christian Ethics*. Cambridge: Cambridge University Press, 2011.

Böckenförde, E.W. *Cristianesimo, libertà, democrazia*. Brescia: Morcelliana, 2007.

Bruni, L. and R. Sugden. "Fraternity: why the market need not be a morally free zone." *Economics and Philosophy*, Vol. 24, 1, 2008: 35–64.

Bruni, L. and S. Zamagni. *Civil Economy*. Oxford: Peter Lang, 2007.

Dierksmeier, C. and M. Pirson. "Oikonomia versus Chrematistike. *Aristotle on wealth and well-being*." *Journal of Business Ethics*, Vol. 88, 3, 2009: 417–430.

Friedman, M. *Capitalism and Freedom*. Chicago: Chicago University Press, 1962.

Gauthier, D. *Morals by Agreement*. Cambridge: Harvard University Press, 1984.
Illanes, J.L. *The Sanctification of Work*. New York: Scepter, 2003.
Maddison, A. *The World Economy: A Millenial Perspective*. Paris: OECD, 2001.
Milanovic, B. *Worlds Apart: Measuring Global and International Inequality*. Princeton: Princeton University Press, 2006.
Mill, J.S. *Principles of Political Economy*. Fairfield, NJ: A. Kelley, 1987[1848].
Peter, F. "Choice, consent and the legitimacy of market transactions." *Economics and Philosophy*, Vol. 20, 1, 2004: 1–18.
Plato. *Phaedrus*. Plato in Twelve Volumes, Vol. 9 translated by Harold N. Fowler. Cambridge, MA, Harvard University Press; London, William Heinemann Ltd. 1925. Available at: http://www.perseus.tufts.edu/hopper/text?doc=Perseus%3Atext%3A1999.01.0174%3Atext%3DPhaedrus (accessed March 5, 2012).
Polachek, A. and B. Seiglie. "Trade, peace and democracy: an analysis of a dyadic dispute." IZA, DP, June 2006.
Pope Benedict XVI, *Encyclical Letter Caritas in Veritate*. Vatican City, 2009.
Porter, M. "Capitalism under siege." *Harvard Business Review*, February 2011.
Posner, R. *The Economics of Justice*. Cambridge: Harvard University Press, 1981.
Sen, A. *Objectivity and Position*. Lawrence: University of Kansas, 1992.
Smith, A. *The Wealth of Nations*. London: Edwin Cannon, 1950[1776].
Rawls, J. *A Theory of Justice*. Cambridge, MA: Harvard University Press, 1971.
Tognato, C. *Enculturating Political Economy*. Los Angeles: UCLA Center for Governance, 2005.
Verdier, T. "Socially responsible trade integration." *NBER*, October 2005.
Von Hayek, F. "The use of knowledge in society." *American Economic Review*, Vol. 35, 4, 1945: 519–530.
Zamagni, S. *Avarizia. La passione dell'avere* (*Avarice. The Passion of Having*). Bologna: Il Mulino, 2009.
Zamagni, S. "Catholic social thought, civil economy, and the spirit of capitalism." In D. K. Finn, ed. *The True Wealth of Nations*. Oxford: Oxford University Press, 2010a: 63–95.
Zamagni, S. *The Proximate and Remote Causes of a Crisis Foretold: A View from Social Catholic Thought*. Vatican City: Pontifical Academy of Social Sciences, 2010b.
Zamagni, S. "The dialogue between economics and ethics." In H. Opedebeeck and L. Zsolnai, eds. *Spiritual Humanism and Economic Wisdom*. Antwerp: Garant, 2011.

# 3
# Foundations for Business Ethics: Exploring *Caritas in Veritate*

*Domènec Melé*

> Much in fact depends on the underlying system of morality. On this subject the Church's social doctrine can make a specific contribution, since it is based on man's creation "in the image of God" (Gen 1:27), a datum which gives rise to the inviolable dignity of the human person and the transcendent value of natural moral norms. (CV 45)

In the past few decades Business Ethics (BE) has been developed considerably (De George 2006), it has become an academic discipline (Enderle 1996) and is present in many business schools. Voluminous handbooks on Business Ethics are now available (e.g., Bowie 2002, Epstein and Hanson 2006, vol. 2, Brenkert and Beauchamp 2010), as is the case of Corporate Social Responsibility (CSR) (Epstein and Hanson 2006, Crane et al. 2008, Kolb 2008). From a practical perspective, many companies are attentive to business ethics and corporate social responsibility and include these concepts in their activities. In this context, several ethical theories have been proposed as moral foundation for BE (Frederick 2002).

The encyclical *Caritas in Veritate* (CV) explicitly addresses Business Ethics (BE) (CV 45) and Corporate Social Responsibility (CSR).[1] It praises certain initiatives in these fields[2] (CV 40, 45) but, at the same time, warns about possible abuses of the adjective "ethical," and the necessity "to develop a sound criterion of discernment" (CV 45). It also shows concern for certain systems of morality which underlie some business ethics approaches (CV 45). Similarly, the encyclical points out that not all the ethical considerations that currently inform debate on the social responsibility of the corporate world are acceptable from the perspective of the Church's social doctrine (CV 40). Benedict XVI defends the position that the economy needs ethics in order to function correctly, yet not any ethics whatsoever, but "an ethics centered upon the human person"[3]: a "person-friendly" ethics (CV 45). The aim of this chapter is to explore this proposal along with some relevant insights of the encyclical *Caritas in Veritate* for foundations of BE and CSR, in contrast with some current moral systems employed in BE. Certain problems regarding BE which the encyclical explicitly or implicitly affronts will also be object of our inquiry.

## 1 Current moral systems for business ethics

In the early years of the contemporary business ethics movement, at the end of the 1970s and beginning of the 1980s, there appeared proposals mainly based on Deontology (Kantianism, Moral Rights Theories), Utilitarianism, and Contractualism (De George 1982, Velazquez 1982, Donaldson 1982).

Some years later, the development of virtue ethics also made itself felt in business ethics (Solomon 1992, Koehn 1995, Hartman 1998, and Sison 2003, among others). In contrast with the rationalist self-legislation and freedom of Kantian deontology, and the calculation of happiness employed by Utilitarianism, virtue ethics proposes the cultivation of virtues as the basis for BE.

Some approaches based on natural law, realistic personalism, and the human virtues can also be found in the literature of business ethics (Whetstone 2002, Alford and Naugthon 2001, Melé 2009) but, for the present, these are still in the minority. Nevertheless Benedict XVI seems to tend toward this latter focus, as we will see below.

In certain cases, procedural theories are also employed in BE; in them substantive ethical norms are replaced by procedural norms to determine when an action is correct. Other theories, with a postmodern character have also tried to establish themselves in the field of business ethics. These include, ethics of care (Held 2006), and the ethics approach of Emmanuel Lévinas based on intersubjective responsibility (Knights and O'Leary 2006), although certain limitations of these approaches have been expressed for both ethics of care (Koehn 1998), and the approach inspired by Levinas (Bevan and Corvellec 2007).

### A Decision-making and stakeholder management

Ethical theories can enter business ethics in two different and often complementary ways. One is being an instrument for moral reasoning in order to make judgments about the ethical acceptability of certain actions or to solve ethical dilemmas. The second is integrating theories of ethics into stakeholder management.

The utility of ethical theories for making moral judgments, and thus introducing certain constraints to decision-making came first. The 1980s saw the publication of various textbooks putting forward normative ethical theories which dealt with various ethical issues and could be used as instruments to solve ethical dilemmas (De George 1982, Velazquez 1982). It was supposed that the reader should make a choice from a diversity of theories. Some authors, however, offered models integrating several theories, for example Utilitarianism, theories of moral rights, and theories of justice (Cavanagh et al. 1981).[4] Most recently a pragmatic approach has been championed that consists of using a variety of normative observations coming from different theories to resolve ethical dilemmas (Crane and Matten 2007, p. 120). However, there have also been authors who have published on business ethics based on a single theory. This is the case of Bowie (1999), who takes Kant's ethical theory as a reference, and of Donaldson and Dunfee (1999) who have proposed the "Integrative Social Contract Theory," a theory with a contractualist bent.

Stakeholder management, which became popular following R. Edward Freeman's *Strategic Management: A Stakeholder Approach* published in 1984, offered the opportunity to integrate theories of ethics into management. Contrasting with conventional "shareholder management," that holds that the corporation should be managed toward the interests of shareholders, "stakeholder management" focuses on the interests of individuals or groups with a "stake" in or claim on the company. In a very general sense, stakeholders are groups and individuals who benefit from or are harmed by corporate actions, including customers, suppliers, owners, employees, and local communities, in a way compatible with the survival of the firm. Initially, this approach was presented in strategic terms: "The stakeholder concept – wrote Freeman – provides a new way of thinking about strategic management – that is, how a corporation can and should set and implement direction. By paying attention to strategic management executives can begin to put a corporation back on the road to success" (1984, p. vi). However, at the core of stakeholder management there is the *duty* to protect the legitimate interests of all stakeholders. In Evan and Freeman's words: "management, especially top management, must look after the health of the corporation, and this involves balancing the multiple claims of conflicting stakeholders" (1988, p. 151).

Some normative theory is indeed required in order to *justify the legitimacy* of stakeholder interests and to solve the "multiple claims of conflicting stakeholders." Only legitimate interests should be considered in stakeholder theory, otherwise every interest including what could be reasonably considered as demagogic interests would be taken into account. In considering stakeholder interests or claims, a sound theory of ethics seems even more necessary *to solve conflicting stakeholder interests*. According to Freeman (1994) every normative theory can be integrated into stakeholder management. Thus, stakeholder management admits a pluralistic set of interpretations (e.g. feminist, ecological, fair contracts). This makes the stakeholder theory a great umbrella practically for every theory of ethics, although one can expect that the resulting approaches can differ one to each other.

*Caritas in Veritate* pays attention to stakeholder management by recognizing that there is "a growing conviction that *business management cannot concern itself only with the interests of the proprietors, but must also assume responsibility for all the other stakeholders who contribute to the life of the business*: the workers, the clients, the suppliers of various elements of production, the community of reference"[5] (CV 40; italics in original). The encyclical stresses that responsibility for the management of the company towards these groups in the particular case of outsourcing of production, which "can weaken the company's sense of responsibility towards the stakeholders — namely the workers, the suppliers, the consumers, the natural environment and broader society — in favor of the shareholders, who are not tied to a specific geographical area and who therefore enjoy extraordinary mobility" (CV 40). But it is in this context where the encyclical states that "ethical considerations that currently inform debate on the social responsibility of the corporate world are not all acceptable from the perspective of the Church's social doctrine" (CV 40). Sound moral foundations of stakeholder management therefore seem necessary.

Going back to the reservation of the encyclical for certain ethical approaches, one wonders which could be these, inasmuch as the encyclical does not mention any particular theory. It simply defends a "person-friendly" or, if you prefer, "a person-centered ethics" (CV 45). However, elsewhere, Benedict XVI has openly expressed objections toward ethical rationalism and relativism. We will analyze these two problematic approaches to BE next.

## 2 Facing ethical rationalism and relativism

In a speech given just a few weeks after the publication of *Caritas in Veritate*, Benedict XVI (2009) said that 150 years ago there was a "dictatorship of rationalism" while in the current epoch a sort of "dictatorship of relativism" is evident in many contexts. According to the Pope, both rationalism and relativism seem inadequate responses to the human being's justifiable request to use his reason as a distinctive and constitutive element of his own identity. "Rationalism was inadequate because it failed to take into account human limitations and claims to make reason alone the criterion of all things, transforming it into a goddess; contemporary relativism humiliates reason because it arrives de facto at affirming that the human being can know nothing with certainty outside the positive scientific field. Today however, as in that time, man, 'a beggar for meaning and fulfillment,' is constantly in quest of exhaustive answers to the basic questions that he never ceases to ask himself" (2009).

## A Ethical rationalism in business ethics

Rationalism emerged from the movement of the eighteenth-century "Enlightenment." According to ethical rationalism, ethics should be based on aprioristic principles of morality provided by human reason. These principles are considered knowable *a priori*, without any sensorial contribution. Typically, the representative of this ethical rationalism is Immanuel Kant, with his Categorical Imperative. Utilitarianism, in spite of the empirical evaluation of consequences of an action generally in terms of satisfaction, is also founded on an aprioristic principle ("the greater happiness for the greater number"). Similarly, "Integrative Social Contract Theory" also has ethical rationalism as one of its founding principles in assuming that morality derives of social consent, but also includes an empirically-based acceptance of empirical norms – termed hyper-norms and authentic norms. These theories are focused on determining whether or not an action is ethically acceptable and on solving ethical dilemmas. They operate, however, without any reference on how morality contributes to the human flourishing of the moral agent or on the role of character in making moral judgments.

Benedict XVI is not alone in his reservations on Rationalism. In the second half of the 20th century, ethical rationalism was severely criticized, by Elizabeth Anscombe (1958), Philippa Foot (1978), and Alasdair MacIntyre (2008 [1981]), among others, about the failure to consider the agent and his or her moral character and how the action shapes virtues and vices of the agent. MacIntyre suggested as an alternative an ethical approach which considers the Aristotelian concept of teleology, focused on the human ends that human reason can discover from the innate human tendencies. According to MacIntyre (2008 [1981]), the philosophers of the Enlightenment because their theories were shorn of teleological elements and used an incomplete framework for the moral foundation of ethics as did their successors. MacIntyre is also contrary to Emotivism and other theories aligned with David Hume[6] who proposed a morality based on sentiments, and consequently opposed ethical rationalism. The position of Anscombe, Foot, and MacIntyre brought about a great development of "virtue ethics," which stresses the relevance of the decision-maker's moral character. This development then entered business ethics, as noted above.

The integration of normative theories in managerial thought could be considered an advance if you compare them with the view of value-free business. However, when normative theory comes from rationalistic ethics, ethics appears exclusively as a constraint of economic activity: "you should avoid actions which are not ethically right." But, what is right? The answer is not any action other than that which is in accordance with the rationalistic ethical principle adopted.

### B Ethical relativism

Apart from ethical rationalism, the other problem mentioned is relativism. In addition to traditional relativism which understands the individual or the society as the source of morality (subjectivism and cultural relativism, respectively). In business ethics another type of relativism derives from the variety of normative theories of ethics which compete to serve as theoretical support for business ethics (Crane and Matten 2007, pp. 85ff), and the lack of a sound criterion of truth for a sound discernment among them. These theories are presented as a matter of a pure subjective choice. Offering models which integrate several theories; or proposing pragmatic approaches by using a variety of normative observations are also forms of relativism. When there is no objective reference it is not difficult to arrive at a relativist posture – you can use any theory – and even positions of skepticism as regards business ethics.

The integration of different theories of ethics into stakeholder management introduces a variety of interpretations and the consequent ethical relativism. As Hummels pointed out, "each interpretation provides us with a different set of stakeholders and stresses the importance of specific values, rights and interests. Hence, different stakeholder interpretations lead to different distribution of benefits and burden, of pleasures and pain, of values, rights and interests" (1998, p. 1404). This could be a more serious problem if stakeholder theory did not adopt a sound ethical theory and if the manager did not act uprightly. He or she could then simply seek the theory which best "justifies" or provides reasons for bettering his or her interests.

Ethical relativism can be even more pronounced in CSR than in BE, when ethics is substituted by social or cultural values. This approach was present at the very beginning of CSR movement, in the mid-1950s, when Howard R. Bowen wrote his book *Social Responsibility of Businessman*. He assumed that the social responsibility of businessmen "refers to the obligation of businessmen to pursue those policies, to make decisions, or to follow those lines of action which are desirable in terms of the objectives and values of our society" (1953, p. 6). Nowadays, theories of ethics may support CSR, but often such responsibility is based on values and norms provided by each society. Sometimes, ethics is put aside and what really matters is the satisfaction surveyed from the stakeholders of the firm. No doubt that both social values and stakeholder satisfaction are important, but this does not guarantee an ethics-based CSR.

## 3 Ethics and its relationship with business

Business ethics posits as the first problem the nature of the relationship between ethics and business, but an even more crucial problem is what perspective should be adopted in considering ethics. Regarding the latter the "First-Third Person" question emerged, and the encyclical has a clear position on both topics. We will analyze these, beginning with first-person ethics.

### A A "first person" ethics

Abbà (1995, 1996) has pointed out two different perspectives in considering the point of view of the observer who makes moral judgments, which lead to two different manners of understanding ethics. In the "first person" perspective it is the decision-maker or the acting subject who seeks the "good" in deciding or performing an action. In doing so he or she is aware of this action contributes to a virtuous life, or vice versa. In the "third-person" ethics the perspective moves to an external and impartial observer who tries to determine whether an action is "right" and for this end seeks principles and norms. This is the case of the above-mentioned rationalist ethics. In this way, the internal effects of the action on the acting person and its contribution to human flourishing are ignored. Under this perspective, this latter concept has no sense. Managing one's own life is a matter of personal preferences, a purely private and subjective question where ethics has nothing to say. A set of rules or principles provide some constraints to human activity, but guarantee the satisfaction of individual wishes if they are within the limits of these rules. Abbà stresses this point adding that the aim of the "third-person" ethics is "creating a social order where man as a being of desires or as autonomous subject can do what he wants, but without hurting others, or maybe hurting them only with a better end in mind, but silence reigns concerning the meaning of the life of these free subjects." But then a question emerges: "Why be moral? Why, should the utilitarian rules of justice, for example, be observed?" These questions remain without an answer in third-person ethics. Abbà concludes by saying: "The principle of the intelligibility of a normative ethics of the third person must be located in the ethics of the first person. Human conduct, in fact, in as much as it is constructed and produced by the acting subject, contains an original, practical knowledge that is not reducible to the knowledge of the legislator, the judge, or the critic; an operative knowledge that has its own logic" (1995, p. 105).

We should recognize that the "third-person" perspective is quite common in moral systems employed in business ethics, and the answer to the motivation for a moral behavior is only based on utilitarian motives (ethics is profitable) or on the moral duty without further justifications: "You should act rightly because this is your duty!" or "you have to do this because this is the right thing!" In contrast, the encyclical takes a "first-person" stance. This is evident in the central theme of the encyclical: integral human development which is achieved through love in truth, and the role of the personal conscience (CV 34, 36, 68). Definitively, this focuses on the first person and gives reason to the question: "why be moral?"

## B Ethics at the core of business

Regarding the nature of the relationship between ethics and business, some approaches hold a complete separation. This is the case of theories derived from Logical Positivism, as that presented by Herbert Simon (1976[1945]), an influential author in management. According with this stream of thought ethics is reduced to subjective values, and "values" and "facts" should be carefully separated. Thus, it arises what is termed as "facts-values dichotomy". Facts should be treated scientifically while values are a matter of preferences. This approach severally criticized nowadays (e.g. Putman 2002) is not accepted by most business ethics theorists. However, normative ethics is often offered as an added to economic thought as a constraint in decision-making. In this way, BE and similarly CSR appear to be extrinsic to business. It is like saying: "try to maximize the bottom line but also be responsible by complying with some ethical code or by paying attention to a number of social issues related to corporate activity as theories of ethics determine. In addition, you should provide some money to corporate philanthropy or other activities of social responsibility." This brings about a dichotomy; ethics is not seen as being at the core of business, but as a limitation or, maybe a complement of business, which can be profitable in the long term.

In *Caritas in Veritate* we find the position of ethics is neither a matter of preferences nor added to economic decisions as a constraint. The encyclical affirms that "the notion of 'efficiency' is not value-free" (CV 50), and also that "the object that is known always conceals something beyond the empirical datum" (CV 77). The Pope rejects "the conviction that the economy must be autonomous, that it must be shielded from 'influences' of a moral character," which "has led man to abuse the economic process in a thoroughly destructive way" (CV 34). On the contrary, Benedict makes clear that economic activity is not ethically neutral, "it is part and parcel of human activity and precisely because it is human, it must be structured and governed in an ethical manner" (CV 36).

According to the encyclical, ethics is not limited to a number of prohibition issues such as fraud, bribery, and insider trading. Actually, "*every economic decision has a moral consequence*" (CV 37; italics in original), and consistently with this, every phase of the economic activity has a content of justice, "because this is always concerned with man and his needs" (CV 37).

If my interpretation is correct, the encyclical suggests that there is not an extrinsic relationship between ethics and business; ethics is intrinsic to business. In other words, ethics is at the core of business. That is why ethical requirements are, to financial and economic activities, "intrinsic to its very nature" (CV 45).

Overcoming the dichotomy of business and ethics also has consequences in living virtues within economic activity. They are required within the economic activity, and not after or outside it. In this sense, the encyclical affirms that "authentically human social relationships of friendship, solidarity and reciprocity can also be conducted within economic activity, and not only outside it or 'after' it." (CV 36)

This being said, let us now turn to the encyclical's proposal on moral foundations for business ethics, when it suggest an ethics centered upon the human person or a "person-friendly" ethics (CV 45), as noted in the introduction.

## 3 An ethics centered upon the human person

According to *Caritas in Veritate* a "person-friendly" ethics is an ethics which leads to a striving "to meet the deepest moral needs of the person," and "the authentic human good"[7] (CV 45). In these words, the Pope advocates an ethics oriented at human development or growth through the act; based on what is really good for the human being, and not only desirable. As Mauri suggested, "a person-friendly type of ethics is an ethics which aids personal growth, which accompanies the human being on the individual and the shared journey of life, which charts the path that runs between possibility and excellence" (2010, p. 95). Consequently "any attempt to govern human life by norms which are contrary to human nature, or which overlooks human nature, in part or completely, cannot be called person-friendly ethics. Neither, by the same token, can an ethics "whose norms only aspire to regulate the co-existence of human beings and ignore personal and social moral development" (Mauri, 2010, p. 95).

Benedict XVI asserts the necessity for an ethics that includes norms derived from the biblical reference of the Creation of man as *imago Dei*, "image of God," which involves "the inviolable dignity of the human person, as well as the transcendental value of natural moral norms" (CV 45). In the context of CSR the dignity of the human person and natural moral norms, although they can be discovered by reason, have their ultimate value in the authority of God-the-Creator, author of the human nature. For believers, the creation of man "in the image of God" is a solid foundation for the dignity and rights of the human being. Nevertheless, respect for the dignity, natural moral norms, and human rights is quite a reasonable disposition in and of itself. These are respected by many non-Christians, be it due to arguments of reason or to the wide consensus reached around these matters. Although not everyone will come to accept the transcendent rationale indicated by the Pope, sharing the recognition and respect for every person and natural moral norms is a crucial reference for ethics.

Pope John Paul II said that the main thread and, in a certain sense, the guiding principle of all the Church's social doctrine is, a correct view of the human person and of his unique value (CA 11). Benedict XVI confirms such unique value and dignity of the human being in several passages of *Caritas in Veritae* (15, 18, 25, 41, 45). "Christian vision – he affirms – has the particular characteristic of asserting and justifying the unconditional value of the human person and the meaning of his growth (CV 18). It is on this growth that the encyclical puts a special emphasis talking in term of "human development," defending the necessity of "authentic development of every person and of all humanity." (CV 1) The encyclical sees such development as a calling, or an innate orientation to develop one's own humanity. In this sense, we can read: "the man is constitutionally oriented towards 'being more'" (CV 14).

The question is what, in practice, does "being more" mean and what reference can be found for this end. According to the encyclical, human development *"concerns the whole of the person in every single dimension"* (CV 11; italics in original) and must *include both material and spiritual growth* (CV 76). Regarding the latter love and truth are seen as primordial. These two crucial values appear as an interior impulse, which in some way, is made evident in everyone. The encyclical stresses this, adding that "love and truth never abandon them completely, because these are the vocation planted by God in the heart and mind of every human person" (CV 1). Seeking the truth and loving in accordance with that truth leads one to discover moral norms in human nature.

It is logical to think that flourishing as a human being requires discovering what we are and the tendencies inherent in human nature: man "cannot prescind from his nature" (CV 21), says the encyclical; and in similar terms, it states that "we all build our own 'I' on the basis of a 'self', which is given to us... we must fortify our love for a freedom that is not merely arbitrary, but is rendered truly human by acknowledgment of the good that underlies it" (CV 68). In other words: you should act well because this contributes to integral human development: the development of the acting person and the others; or because this is the answer to your human vocation to become better as a human being, and ultimately to respond to the will of God. That is why the moral norms should be coherent with this end, and each person "needs to look inside himself in order to recognize the fundamental norms of the natural moral law which God has written on our hearts" (CV 68). This leads to discuss what is known as the Natural Moral Law, or simple natural law.

## 4 The moral natural law

Is it possible to find in human nature certain tendencies whose end can be apprehended and understood as a human good by human reason? Those who defend what is called Moral Natural Law agree that some basic human goods and a series of fundamental moral norms can be rationally discovered; and their authority can be attributed to the ultimate author of human nature, God, the Creator. The predecessor of Benedict XVI, Pope John Paul II explained this capacity of the human reason in these words:

> The person, by the light of reason and the support of virtue, discovers in the body the anticipatory signs, the expression and the promise of the gift of self, in conformity with the wise plan of the Creator. It is in the light of the dignity of the human person – a dignity which must be affirmed for its own sake – that reason grasps the specific moral value of certain goods towards which the person is naturally inclined. And since the human person cannot be reduced to a freedom which is self-designing, but entails a particular spiritual and bodily structure, the primordial moral requirement of loving and respecting the person as an end and never as a mere means also implies, by its very nature, respect for certain fundamental goods, without which one would fall into relativism and arbitrariness. (VS 48)

Benedict XVI's reference to moral natural norms, links to the realistic moral natural law rooted in the tradition of Thomas of Aquinas (S Th, II-II, q. 94) – which differs from the rationalistic natural law proposed by John Locke[8] and others. The Aquinite's fundamental presupposition is of a certain rational capacity of the human being that permits them to discern between good and bad by grasping the moral message contained in human nature, together with the imperative to act consequently. In this sense, Thomas Aquinas affirmed that the first precept of the natural law is: "good is to be done and pursued, and evil is to be avoided" (S Th, II-II, q. 94, a.2). This principle appears as self-evident, along with some basic human goods appropriate for human development, such as life, procreation and education of children, the seeking of the truth, and what contributes to living together in harmony and peace (justice, benevolence, friendship, love,...), which should be done and pursued. A natural law then, is not a norm imposed from outside man, but is part of his very being.

It is not only Thomas of Aquinas that affirms the human capacity to know moral order, at least in a basic way – the entire Christian tradition does the same as do other religions and wisdom traditions. The universal character of natural law is made evident in the Bible itself. St. Paul confirmed the existence of a moral law which affected the Gentiles too; those who "have not the law, do by nature the things contained in the law, these, having not the law, are a law unto themselves" (*Romans* 2:15).

As noted, Christian tradition is not alone in defending the existence of moral norms which are not "invented" but "discovered" in the rational human nature. In the pre-Christian world too certain outstanding writers, for example Sophocles and Cicero, referred to an unwritten law which was above the positive laws.[9] Another manifestation of the existence of natural law is the "Golden Rule," which has you put yourself in the place of the other, and avoid (doing) the ill which you would not want for yourself, and treating people as you yourself would want to be treated – a maxim found in all the world's great religions.

Speaking before the General Assembly of the United Nations, Benedict XVI reminded an audience of the existence of moral norms beyond the point that consensus has been reached: "respect for human rights is principally rooted in unchanging justice," he affirmed, and appealed to "the fruit of a commonly held sense of justice built primarily upon solidarity among the members of society, and hence valid at all times and for all peoples." His words also recalled the Golden Rule, following the formulation of St. Augustine:

> Since rights and the resulting duties follow naturally from human interaction, it is easy to forget that they are the fruit of a commonly held sense of justice built primarily upon solidarity among the members of society, and hence valid at all times and for all peoples. This intuition was expressed as early as the fifth century by Augustine of Hippo, one of the masters of our intellectual heritage. He taught that the saying: *Do not do to others what you would not want done to you* "cannot in any way vary according to the different understandings that have arisen in the world." (*De Doctrina Christiana*, III, 14). (Pope Benedict XVI 2008)

*Caritas in Veritate* says that "*the decisive issue is the overall moral tenor of society*" (CV 51) and that it is necessary to look to the "book of nature" which is one and indivisible (CV 51). The encyclical does this in referring to ecology, but from a wider perspective: "Our duties towards the environment are linked to our duties towards the human person, considered in himself and in relation to others" (CV 51).

With a little more detail, Benedict XVI (2008) recalls that from the first and foremost principle of natural law "do good and avoid ill," the logic of which would immediately be plain to anyone, sprouts the other more individual principles that regulate ethical judgment over the rights and duties of each person. Among these are respect for human life, the duty to search for the truth, freedom shared with everyone else, and the respect for the truth of the human being – "the truth of the human being, the fundamental message of being itself, exactly the *lex naturalis*" together with justice and solidarity. He adds that "in these values are expressed unbreakable and contingent norms that do not depend on the will of the legislator and not even on the consensus that the State can and must give. They are, in fact, norms that precede any human law: as such, they are not subject to modification by anyone" (Pope Benedict XVI 2008).

Pope Benedict XVI is not only in favor of the natural law, he also insists on the importance of recovering natural law as a common ethics, pointing out the urgent necessity "to reflect upon the theme of natural law and to rediscover its truth common to all men" (2007).

## 5 Love in truth

As noted, a person-friendly ethics includes the good (CV 45), which should be done and pursued, in accordance with the above-mentioned first principle of the natural law. In this principle, virtues are not explicitly mentioned, but virtues are implicit in the precepts of natural law, at least in the Thomas Aquinas' approach. This affirms that, "precepts are given about acts of virtue" (S Th, II-II, q. 44, a. 2, ad 1; a. 1). In other words, doing good entails acquiring virtues, which are expression of interior growth. Thus, it is no surprise at all that together with natural moral law, presented as universally common ethics, the social doctrine of the Church emphasizes the importance of the virtues, especially the virtue of charity, understood as fraternal love. This is easily understandable, since love to God and to neighbor, according to the teaching of Jesus, is the synthesis of the entire Law (cf. *Matthew* 22:36–40). Love includes all other virtues. As St. Paul points out: "Charity is patient, is friendly, is not envious, does not work with arrogance, does not boast, is not ambitious, does not seek its own interest, does not get irritated, does not take ill suffered into account, does not delight at injustice, is content in the truth, can bear anything, it expects everything and bears everything" (*1 Corinthians* 13: 4–7). Aquinas affirms in different ways that charity is "root and mother," of all other virtues. Virtues depend on charity in some way (S Th, I-II, q. 62, a. 2 ad 3) and moral virtues cannot be without charity (love) (S Th, II-II, q. 65, a. 2).

The encyclical stresses the necessity of love in truth, "*Caritas in Veritate* is the principle around which the Church's social doctrine turns, a principle that takes on practical form in the criteria that govern moral action" (CV 6). The encyclical emphasized that love and truth should go together: "Intelligence and love are not in separate compartments: *love is rich in intelligence and intelligence is full of love*" (CV 30; italics in original). We could say that what the Pope proposes is an "intelligent love." Without truth, love can become sentimentalist or an empty attitude hardly applicable in the business context. "*Only in truth does charity shine forth,* only in truth can charity be authentically lived. Truth is the light that gives meaning and value to charity" (CV 3; italics in original).

In the business context, the truth leads to the recognition that economic activity is first of all a human activity (CV 36), and this requires seeking "the fully human meaning of human activities" (CV 70). This means seeing the person as an end and the instrumental character of an efficient use of means. It happens that "when the sole criterion of truth is efficiency and utility, development is automatically denied" (CV 70).

### A Justice, the first demand of love

Love in truth has in the first place a demand for justice, as the encyclical itself makes clear. Justice is inseparable from love, intrinsic to it, and the primary way of love (CV 6). Justice entails "recognition and respect for the legitimate rights of individuals and peoples" (CV 6). Business, likewise the whole of society, should be built, first of all, according to law and justice; and justice, which leads us to give each his or her what is due (rights) should be applied to every decision and in *every phase of economic activity,* including locating resources, financing, production, and consumption (CV 37; italics in original).

Along with justice, "traditional principles of social ethics like transparency, honesty and responsibility cannot be ignored or attenuated, but also that in *commercial relationships* the *principle of gratuitousness* and the logic of gift as an expression of fraternity can and must *find their place within normal economic activity*" (CV 36; italics in original). Following this idea, the logic of gift and the principle of gratuitousness, as an expression of fraternity, need a space within normal economic activity, and within BE. Without excluding justice, the logic of gift and the principle of gratuitousness are necessary to make authentically human economic, social, and political development (CV 34–36). Seeing others – employees, colleagues, clients – as persons worthy of respect, deserving of reciprocal treatment and even of gratuity, overcomes a purely transactional vision or a consideration of others as mere resources or means to economic or power-objectives.

On the moral foundations of BE there is the concern and effective orientation and strive toward the *common good* as a requirement of justice and charity. (CV 7) It is just to contribute to the common good of the communities to which one belongs. One receives from the community and in reciprocity one should contribute. But such contribution is not only a matter of justice but also of charity (love). In this sense, the Pope explains that charity (love) must not be limited to these *micro-relations*, but must also be extended to *macro-relations*, "like social, economic and political relations." In the firm there are both micro- and macro-relations. The first in small work-groups or in professional relations from which fellowship and even genuine friendship can appear. Macro-relations exist at all levels in the firm and in its various divisions too if the firm is sizeable, and also in the relations between the firm and society (CV 2).

### B The pursuit of the common good

The consideration of the common good should be a permanent reference for economic activity, where the application of *commercial logic* "needs to be *directed towards the pursuit of the common good*" (CV 36). Likewise, the common good should be the ultimate end in business. This contrasts with the approaches in which profit becomes the exclusive goal of business. "Once profit becomes the exclusive goal," the encyclical notes, "if it is produced by improper means and without the common good as its ultimate end, it risks destroying wealth and creating poverty" (CV 21). Economic and business activity with real growth, which benefit everybody, and genuinely sustainable is highly desirable (CV 21). On the contrary, management should avoid favoring short-term profits which in the long term impede reciprocal enrichment and the dynamics of cooperation (CV 33).

Last, but not least, the virtue of prudence or practical wisdom is also considered in the encyclical (CV 41) and of great important in Christian tradition. Practical wisdom makes natural law operative in practice and allows one to evaluate each situation in search of the true moral good as a dimension inherent in reality. This brings about acting with love and justice in accordance with the truth.

## 5 Conclusion

The encyclical *Caritas in Veritate* entails a number of relevant insights for business ethics. First of all, the concept of business ethics itself, in which it differs from others that see ethics as extrinsic to business. On the contrary, ethics is intrinsic to any economic activity which is first of all a human activity.

The moral foundation of business ethics is an ethics centered upon the human person in which pursuing and doing human good is crucial. This develops virtues and virtues contribute to human flourishing. This contrasts with moral systems based on ethical rationalism, in which what is sought is simply doing "the right thing" which is no other than conformity with certain aprioristic principle provided by the theory of ethics adopted.

The encyclical proposes as key elements for a sound system of morality: the inviolable dignity of the human person and the transcendent value of natural moral norms (CV 50). The former emphasizes the primacy of the persons and their innate rights, as well as the necessity to contribute to the common good and the instrumental value of profits. The latter leads one to focus on the moral natural law or, what is the same, to see in human flourishing a crucial reference for determining moral norms. The transcendent value of these norms derives from the Creator, author of the human nature. Acting in accordance with these moral natural norms develops human virtues. The encyclical emphasizes love (charity) with includes justice, and truth; a love which requires truth.

The Pope's proposal is a challenge, inasmuch as the dignity of the human person, natural moral law, and virtues taken together are rarely mentioned in literature on business ethics. While respect for human dignity, on the one hand, and virtues on the other are now quite common, natural law is a lacuna. The reason can be found in the loss of the sense of the metaphysic. Then nature is seen in an empirical sense, with which it is not possible to capture its moral message. Natural law is then interpreted as a physicism or naturalism. With the physicism, moral laws are reduced to biological laws, while in naturalism moral law derives exclusively from the spontaneous tendencies of human nature, without the mediation of the rational knowledge of the human good. From these perspectives, natural law is labeled a "naturalist fallacy," an expression popularized by the philosopher George Edward Moore (1951 [1903]) at the beginning of the 20th century. *Physicism* and *naturalism* run against the traditional concept of natural law that cannot in any way be qualified as fallacious. In contrast to physicism and naturalism which solely express empirical descriptions, natural moral law expresses rational prescriptions, the universal, and permanent.

There are hopeful advances in recovering the moral natural law in line with Thomas Aquinas' approach (Rhonheimer 2000, Murphy 2001, and 2006, Gómez-Lobo 2002, Schockenhoff 2003, Dierksmeier and Celano 2012, among others). A recent and authoritative attempt is the document *The Search for Universal Ethics: A New Look at Natural Law* (2008) by the International Theological Commission, which reviews and answers some misunderstandings and objections to the natural law, opens new horizons for a better understanding of natural law, and emphasizes the necessity of common values in a global world along with the fact that there are many values which people from different cultures and religions share.

## Executive summary

This chapter explores some relevant insights of the encyclical *Caritas in Veritate* for the foundations of business ethics and corporate social responsibility in contrast with some current moral systems. It also discusses some problems inherent to business ethics. One of the problems is the abundant use of ethical rationalism in many current approaches of business ethics. There is also an abusive use of the adjective "ethical" for certain business activities. A third problem examined here is the role of relativism within business ethics and corporate social responsibility, which includes a pluralistic use of ethical theories which are often presented without any sound criterion of discernment, nor any reference to their contribution to human flourishing. A fourth question is the concept of business ethics itself. Frequently business and ethics are presented as two separate realms and ethics is seen as an extrinsic constraint to business, focused on the analysis and determination of ethical issues and dilemmas.

The encyclical defends a "first person" ethics and holds that ethics is inherent to economic activity, which is first of all a human activity that requires one to strive to meet the deepest moral needs of the person. Regarding the moral foundations of business ethics, *Caritas in Veritate* speaks for a person-centered ethics in which the two key elements are the inviolable dignity of the human person and the transcendent value of natural moral norms. These have their grounding in the capacity of the human reason to discern good from bad which is the basis of Moral Natural Law. Virtues are connected with Moral Natural Law in which love (Christian charity) is preeminent. Love, whose first requirement is justice, requires the light of the truth; or as the encyclical says, "love in truth."

## Notes

1. Literally, the encyclical refers to "*social responsibility* on the part of business" (CV 40), "responsibilities of business towards society" (CV 45), and the "social responsibility of the enterprise" (CV 66).
2. Benedict XVI mentions a number of activities in teaching and research on business ethics as part of the movement of ideas associated with the responsibilities of business toward society, along with investments based on ethical funds and ethical financing through micro-credit and, more generally, micro-finance (CV 45).
3. This is my own translation, which differs from the translation presented at www.vatican.va ("not any ethics whatsoever, but an ethics which is people-centered). It seems that "ethics centered upon the human person" is closer to the Latin (*ethica personae amica*) and also Italian (*un'etica amica della persona*) and German (*menschenfreundliche Ethik*). I am indebted to Jennifer Miller for her help in this translation. A "person-friendly" ethics or even a "person-centered" ethics seems also appropriate.
4. Cavanagh et al. (1995) added another theory: the ethics of care.
5. Italics in original.
6. See, especially in *A Treatise of Human Nature*, Book 3 (Hume 2000[1739]) and in *An Enquiry Concerning the Principles of Morals* (Hume 1998 [1751]).
7. See note 4.
8. The rationalistic theory of natural law is incorporated by John Locke into many of his theories and philosophy, but particularly in *Two Treatises of Government*, first published in 1689 (Locke 1989[1689]).
9. Sophocles, in his famous tragedy *Antigona*, had the main character reproach the attitude of Creon, the tyrant who denied burial to the corpse of Antigona's brother. She said to Creon that a man cannot change the unwritten and unchanging laws of heaven because eternity is beyond the bounds of time, beyond today or yesterday, beyond forever (Sophocles, *Antigona* vv. 563 ss). Cicero, on his part, affirmed: "For there is a true law: right reason. It is in conformity with nature, is diffused among all men, and is immutable and eternal; its orders summon to duty; its prohibitions turn away from offense.... To replace it with a contrary law is a sacrilege; failure to apply even one of its provisions is forbidden; no one can abrogate it entirely" (Cicero, *De Republica* III, 22, 33).

## References


Abbà, G. *Felicità, vita buona e virtù. Saggio di filosofia morale*, 2nd edn. Rome: LAS, 1995.

Abbà, G. *Quale impostazione per la filosofia morale? Ricerche di filosofia morale – 1*. Rome: LAS, 1996.

Alford, H.J. and M.J. Naugthon. *Managing as if Faith Mattered. Christian Social Principles in the Modern Organization*. Notre Dame: Notre Dame University Press, 2001.

Anscombe, E. "Modern moral philosophy." *Philosophy*, Vol. 33, 1958: 1–19. Reproduced in R. Crisp and M. Slote, eds. *Virtue Ethics*. Oxford: Oxford University Press, 1997.

Bevan, D. and H. Corvellec. "The impossibility of corporate ethics: For a Levinasian approach to managerial ethics." *Business Ethics: A European Review*, Vol. 16, 2007: 208–219.

Bowen, H.R. *Responsibilities of the Businessman*. New York: Harper and Brothers, 1953.

Bowie, N.E. *Business Ethics: A Kantian Perspective*. Oxford: Blackwell, 1999.

Bowie, N.E., ed. *The Blackwell Guide to Business Ethics*. Oxford: Blackwell, 2002.

Brenkert, G.G. and T.L. Beauchamp, eds. *The Oxford Handbook of Business Ethics*. Oxford: Oxford University Press, 2010.

Cavanagh, G.F., D.J. Moberg and M.G. Velasquez. "Making business ethics practical." *Business Ethics Quarterly*, Vol. 5, 1995: 399–418.

Cavanagh, G.F., D.J. Moberg and M.G. Velasquez. "The ethics of organizational politics." *Academy of Management Review*, Vol. 6, 1981: 363–374.

Cicero, *The Republic and the Laws*. Translated by Niall Rudd and edited by Jonathan Powell. Oxford: Oxford University Press, 1998.

Crane, A. and D. Matten. *Business Ethics*. Oxford: Oxford University Press, 2007.

Crane, A., A. Williams, D. Matten, J. Moon and D.S. Siegel, eds. *The Oxford Handbook of Corporate Social Responsibility*. Oxford/New York: Oxford University Press, 2008.

De George, R.T. *Business Ethics*. New York: Macmillan, 1982.

De George, R.T. "The history of business ethics." In M.J. Epstein and K.O. Hanson, eds. *The Accountable Corporation, Vol 2 Business Ethics*. Westpoint: Praeger 2006.

Dierksmeier, C. and A. Celano. 'Thomas Aquinas on Justice as a Global Virtue in Business', *Business Ethics Quarterly* Vol. 22, 2012: 247–273.

Donaldson, T. *Corporations and Morality*. Englewood Cliff, NJ: Prentice-Hall, 1982.

Donaldson, T. and T.W. Dunfee. *Ties That Bind: A Social Contracts Approach to Business Ethics*. Boston: Harvard Business School Press, 1999.

Enderle, G. "Towards business ethics as an academic discipline." *Business Ethics Quarterly*, Vol. 6, 1996: 43–65.

Epstein, M.J. and K.O. Hanson, eds. *The Accountable Corporation*. London: Praeger Publishers, 2006.

Evan, W.M. and R.E. Freeman. "A stakeholder theory of the modern corporation: Kantian capitalism." In T. Beauchamp and N. Bowie. *Ethical Theory and Business*. Englewood Cliffs: Prentice-Hall, 1988.

Foot, P. *Virtues and Vices*. Oxford: Blackwell, 1978.

Freeman, R.E. *Strategic Management: A Stakeholder Approach*. Boston: Pitman, 1984.

Freeman, R.E. "The politics of stakeholder theory: Some future directions." *Business Ethics Quarterly*, Vol. 4, 1994: 409–429.

Frederick, R.E., ed. *A Companion to Business Ethics*. London/Oxford: Blackwell, 2002.

Gómez-Lobo, A. *Morality and the Human Goods: An Introduction to Natural Law Ethics*. Washington, DC: Georgetown University Press, 2002.

Hartman, E.M. "The role of character in business ethics." *Business Ethics Quarterly*, Vol. 8, 1998: 547–559.
Held, V. *The Ethics of Care: Personal, Political, Global*. Oxford: Oxford University Press, 2006.
Hume, D. *An Enquiry Concerning the Principles of Morals*. Edited by Tom L. Beauchamp, Oxford/New York: Oxford University Press, 1998[1751].
Hume, D. *A Treatise of Human Nature*. Edited by David Fate Norton and Mary J. Norton. Oxford-New York: Oxford University Press, 2000[1739].
Hummels, H. "Organizing ethics: A stakeholder debate." *Journal of Business Ethics*, Vol. 17, 1998: 1403–1419.
International Theological Commission. "Alla ricerca di un'etica universale: nuovo sguardo sulla legge naturale." Vatican City, December 2008. Available at: www.vatican.va/roman_curia/congregations/cfaith/cti_documents/rc_con_cfaith_doc_20090520_legge-naturale_it.html (accessed August 5, 2011). Unofficial translation into English by Joseph Bolin is available at: www.pathsoflove.com/universal-ethics-natural-law.html (accessed August 5, 2011).
Knights, D. and M. O'Leary. "Leadership, ethics and responsibility to the other." *Journal of Business Ethics*, Vol. 67, 2006: 125–137.
Koehn, D. "A role for virtue ethics in the analysis of business practice." *Business Ethics Quarterly*, 5, 1995: 533–539.
Koehn, D., 'Virtue ethics, the firm, and moral psychology', *Business Ethics Quarterly*, Vol. 8, 1998: 497–513.
Kolb, R. W. ed. *Encyclopedia of Business Ethics and Society*. Los Angeles: Sage, 2008.
Locke, J. *The Two Treatises of Civil Government*. London: Routledge, 1989[1689].
MacIntyre, A. *After Virtue*. Notre Dame, IN: Notre Dame University Press, 2008[1981].
Mauri, M. "Hacia una recuperación de la ley moral natural como ética común." In D. Melé and J. M. Castellà, eds. *El Desarrollo Humano Integral. Comentarios Interdisciplinares a la encíclica 'Caritas in veritate' de Benedicto XVI*. Barcelona: Iter, 2010.
Melé, D. "Integrating personalism into virtue-based business ethics: The personalist and the common good principles." *Journal of Business Ethics*, Vol. 88, 2009: 227–244.
Moore, G.E. *Principia Ethica*. Cambridge: Cambridge University Press, 1951[1903].
Murphy, M.C. *Natural Law and Practical Rationality*. New York: Cambridge University Press, 2001.
Murphy, M. C. *Natural Law and Jurisprudence in Politics*. Cambridge/New York: Cambridge University Press, 2006.
Pope Benedict XVI. "Address to the participants in the International Congress on Natural Moral Law." Pontifical Lateran University, Rome, February 12, 2007. Available at: www.vatican.va/holy_father/benedict_xvi/speeches/2007/february/documents/hf_ben-xvi_spe_20070212_pul_en.html (accessed August 5, 2011).
Pope Benedict XVI. "Address in the Meeting with the Members of the General Assembly of the United Nations Organization." New York, April 18, 2008. Available at: www.vatican.va/holy_father/benedict_xvi/speeches/2008/april/

documents/hf_ben-xvi_spe_20080418_un-visit_en.html (accessed August 5, 2011).

Pope Benedict XVI. "General audience." Castelgandolfo, August 5, 2009. Available at: www.vatican.va/holy_father/benedict_xvi/audiences/2009/documents/hf_ben-xvi_aud_20090805_en.html (accessed August 5, 2011).

Pope John Paul II. Encyclical letter *Veritatis splendor.* Vatican City, August 6, 1993. Available at: www.vatican.va/edocs/ENG0222/_INDEX.HTM (accessed August 5, 2011).

Putnam, H. *The Collapse of the Fact/Value Dichotomy and Other Essays.* Cambridge, MA: Harvard University Press, 2002.

Rhonheimer, M. *Natural Law and Practical Reason: A Thomist View of Moral Autonomy.* New York: Fordham University Press, 2000.

Schockenhoff, E. *Natural Law and Human Dignity: Universal Ethics in an Historical World.* Washington, DC: Catholic University of America Press, 2003.

Simon, H. A., *Administrative behavior.* New York: Free Press, 1976[1945].

Sison, A. J. G. *The Moral Capital of Leaders. Why Virtue Matter.* Cheltenham, UK/ Northampton, MA, USA: Edward Elgar, 2003.

Solomon, R. C., *Ethics and Excellence. Cooperation and Integrity in Business.* New York: Oxford University Press, 1992.

Sophocles. *Antigone.* Translated by M. Townsend. London: Longman, 1962.

Velasquez, M.G. *Business Ethics: Concepts and Cases.* Englewood Cliffs, NJ: Prentice-Hall, Inc., 1982.

Whetstone, J.T. "Personalism and moral leadership: The servant leader with a transforming vision." *Business Ethics: A European Review,* Vol. 11, 2002: 385–392.

# 4
# Broader Rationality and the "Logic of Gift" in Economics

*Francesc Torralba and Cristian Palazzi*

> Charity and truth confront us with an altogether new and creative challenge, one that is certainly vast and complex. It is about *broadening the scope of reason and making it capable of knowing and directing these powerful new forces*, animating them within the perspective of that "civilization of love" whose seed God has planted in every people, in every culture. (CV 33)

The current economic and financial crisis may offer the ideal opportunity to rediscover essential values if we are able to reflect on its causes and the imbalances of market logic that govern the world. As articulated in the document *Global Economic Ethic. Consequences for Global Businesses* (Global Ethic Foundation 2009), launched during a business ethics symposium at UN Headquarters on October 6, 2009 and signed in 2009 by Michel Camdessus, Hans Küng, Mary Robinson, Jeffrey Sachs, and Desmond Tutu, among others, the crisis that we are going through is not independent of the oversight of certain ethical principles. Greed and the lack of integrity, transparency and distributive rationality are some of the structural causes of this crisis. So, in short, the crisis offers a chance to rethink the link between economics and ethics, a necessary hiatus between market logic and ethical principles. As expressed in the latest encyclical letter by Benedict XVI, the crisis may awaken the need for a new "humanistic synthesis," the foundation of an economy that includes the fundamental principles of ethics.

"The different aspects of the crisis, its solutions, and any new development that the future may bring," says Benedict XVI, "are increasingly interconnected, they imply one another, they require new efforts of holistic understanding and a *new humanistic synthesis*" (CV 21). The complexity and gravity of the present economic situation rightly cause us concern, but we must adopt a realistic attitude as we take up with confidence and hope the new responsibilities to which we are called by the prospect of a world in need of profound cultural renewal, a world that needs to rediscover fundamental values on which to build a better future.

The present chapter aims to show how it is possible to think of economic practice in another manner; without contradicting market logic, but transcending it. We will try to show that the objective proposed by Benedict XVI both in this encyclical letter and in other documents broadens the sense of reason and widens its meaning, particularly that of economic reason. Benedict XVI tries to include within it the *logic of gift*. This widening of the concept of reason and the opening up of market logic to the logic of gift are proposals upheld in *Caritas in Veritate* that we are invited to explore and build upon.

## 1 Broadening the notion of rationality

Reason, like being, can be expressed in many ways. In this sense, the one-dimensional and simplistic view of this ability should be overcome and reason should be understood holistically, open to emotional life, to the life of beliefs, and to mystery. It is only possible to carry out this intellectual operation if we broaden the concept of reason that has been inherited by modern capitalism, a unilateral and impoverished idea of rationality.

The vision of rationality that stems from economicism severely reduces the field of meanings of rationality. The reason is reduced to pure instrumental rationality (*instrumentelle Vernunft*). Instrumental reason, as conceived by the philosophers of the first generation of the Frankfurt School, Theodor Adorno and Max Horkheimer, referred to in particular in Benedict XVI's second encyclical letter, *Spe salvi* (2007, nn. 42–43), is a device that aims to gain maximum benefit from all objects.

Instrumental reason does not have truth, harmony, or contemplation, as its objective.[1] Its aim is to obtain the maximum benefit, and it is always geared towards commercial interest. When instrumental reason becomes the only way of thinking, thinking is calculation; weighing up pros and cons and motivated always by interest. Instrumental reason in the realm of science and technology has yielded great benefits, but when we lose sight of other uses and models of rationality, the human condition becomes impoverished.

Thinking cannot be reduced to pure calculation. Martin Heidegger (1966), in "Conversations on a country path about thinking published" in *Discourse on Thinking* contrasts meditative thinking with calculative thinking and urges the application of reason that is open to the truth and not just to pure interest. Instrumental reason applied within the economic sphere is useful for competing and gaining the maximum benefit from resources at the lowest cost, but without the balancing effect of other forms of rationality, this entails severe injustices and environmental problems.

Benedict XVI says: "The 'broadening of our concept of reason and its application'[2] is indispensable if we are to succeed in adequately weighing all the elements involved in the question of development and in the solution of socio-economic problems" (CV 31). In effect, it is essential that we widen the concept of progress and social and economic development. It is not about changing the concept of reason, but rather about broadening its use. From instrumental reason, the concept of progress ends up being unilateral, as at its heart it does not include vital dimensions of progress.

"It is about," writes the Pope, "*broadening the scope of reason and making it capable of knowing and directing these powerful new forces*, animating them within the perspective of that 'civilization of love' whose seed God has planted in every people, in every culture" (CV 33; italics in original).

The idea of the *civilization of love* comes from the idea that as well as a rational being, a human being is *ens capax amoris* (capable of love). The creation of this civilization is a real possibility of the human being, to the extent in which he wants to love and be loved and is capable of widening the concept of instrumental reason, and holding communicative reason and cordial reason in his heart. In his first encyclical letter *Deus caritas est* (2005, nn. 1–39), Benedict XVI analyzes the essence of love and shows, with an Augustinian approach, that love does not contradict rationality, nor does it oppose it, but rather that reason, transformed by *Eros*, the creator, divine power, is capable of completely new dynamics. The civilization of love is a work of love, but it is not distanced from reason, rather the expression of a love that transfigures rationality.

The gift is a free act, something that might not have taken place. In the evangelical tale, the Good Samaritan is paradigm of goodness, literary incarnation of the ethical archetype, who stops to give his time, his money, and his consolation to a stranger who has been beaten. He stops as a result of love. Previously, two others passed by and neither stopped. The Good Samaritan stops when he might not have; hence the greatness of his behavior. He could have walked on past, as his predecessors had done, but instead he breaks with all expectation, and stops. This giving is the universal expression of goodness, more so because it is done freely.[3]

When, colloquially speaking, we say that someone is good, a good friend, a good professional, a good citizen, we are referring to a being who gives of themselves, gives what they have, what they know, who gives of their time, who does not deny others their presence, who gives consolation to those who need it, and silence when requested. Giving words as expected; ultimately, they give of what and who they are.

We deem someone to be good if they give of themselves completely, not keeping anything back for themselves; throwing themselves into alleviating the needs of others and developing their possibilities. They give without expectation; they give without compensation. We say someone is an excellent friend when we believe that they give themselves to us, that they do not hide their being, that they reveal themselves transparently, without needing to play the crude game of simulation and hypocrisy.

The practice of goodness requires love, but also requires a previous rational analysis of the situation, an identification of needs and possibilities. That is why the gift requires a logic, a labor of *logos*. The gift is the fruit of love, of *agape*, but to be efficient and fruitful, it requires the exercise of rationality.

## 2 Rationality and the "logic of gift"

If we expand upon the notion of reason, aspects and dimensions of human life can be recognized that are impossible to envisage through instrumental reason. Instrumental reason is blind to gratuitousness, as from this standpoint it is understood that all processes, from an everyday operation to a major financial transaction, are controlled by the calculation of interests. Nevertheless, when we expand upon the notion of reason, this broadens the field of vision, and lifestyles, unique events and group behavior obeying the principle of gratuitousness can be glimpsed.

"Gratuitousness," writes Benedict XVI, "is present in our lives in many different forms, which often go unrecognized because of a purely consumerist and utilitarian view of life. The human being is made for gift, which expresses and makes present his transcendent dimension." And he adds: "Charity in truth places man before the astonishing experience of gift" (CV 34).

In the same way that, in the Catholic perspective, faith does not contradict rationality, nor does love come into conflict with reason, but they rather mutually enrich and complement one another, the logic of love does not oppose social justice, but instead transcends it. "We must make it clear," declares Benedict XVI, "on the one hand, that the logic of gift does not exclude justice, nor does it merely sit alongside it as a second element added from without; on the other hand, economic, social and political development, if it is to be authentically human, needs to make room for the *principle of gratuitousness* as an expression of fraternity" (CV 34; italics in original).

This thesis, which we will find in works by philosophers like Paul Ricoeur, is part of the anthropological supposition that beyond his egocentric tendencies, the human being is capable of acting based on a model of the principle of gratuitousness. Only the gift that is free is truly a gift. It is that which is given selflessly, not to be recovered, without seeking repayment. This was expressed by St. Thomas Aquinas: "A gift is literally a giving that can have no return ... it is not given with the intention of being repaid" (*donum proprie est datio irreversibilis ... id est quod non datar intentione retributionis*) (S Th q. 38, a. 2, c.).

Benedict XVI does not reject economic logic, but he maintains that it is essential to expand upon it with two further forms of logic: political logic and that of the unconditional gift. He writes: "The economy in the global era seems to privilege the former logic, that of contractual exchange, but directly or indirectly it also demonstrates its need for the other two: political logic, and the logic of the unconditional gift" (CV 37).

The expression *logic of gift* refers both to a way of understanding reality and a way of approaching the challenge of existing; it includes an ontology and an ethics. It is both descriptive and prescriptive.

Our purpose here is not only to describe reality from the perspective of the gift; we also propose an *ethos*, a life ethic rooted in the logic of gift. Describing the phenomenon of being is the fundamental mission of the philosopher, along with proposing a mode of existence, an ethic, an orientation in the arduous exercise of existing.

We start from the anthropological assumption that we are made to reveal what we carry inside to the world and to others. We are constitutively a gift and we are aimed to be a gift for others. This teleology of the gift is inscribed within the human condition itself because we are a gift that can be conscious of its existence and live in accordance with the logic bestowed upon it by its being and its life.

We are made for the gift and we want to begin with the thesis that happiness can only lie in this movement of externalization. The person who can give what they carry inside, who can express their richness, and interior creativity in the world, is free.

Perceiving reality as gift entails understanding it as something that has been given, that is there, that might not be there, but which does not belong to us as if it were an object or a thing. Reality is not placed by the subject. It is manifested, it is expressed, it is given in multiple ways. We understand something of it, but it is not created by the mind of the person. There are different possible ways to react to it. The plurality of ways in which to receive the gift of reality is manifest in life. One can adore the gift, contemplate it, venerate it, but also act on it, cultivate it, transform it, develop it. And there is no doubt that the gift received can also be an object of corrosion, dissolution, or exploitation.

Understanding existence itself from the logic of gift means realizing that the essential purpose of living is to give of oneself, externalizing what one is, since only in this way can reality be qualitatively enriched, made more beautiful, more plural, continuing the creative process in the world. Hence, examining what one is becomes essential; finding out one's gifts and capacities.

In this philosophy, the Delphic "know thyself" which, later, Socrates made his own, acquires its full meaning. I can only give what I am destined to give if I understand who I am and what my talents are. We begin with the thesis that happiness lies essentially in being able to give of oneself, in projecting one's own talents and, thereby, transforming reality.

According to Benedict XVI, we will only overcome the reductionism of reason (which is not to deny the impressive development of scientific and technical knowledge, but on the contrary to accept it with all its fabulous conquests and its great risks) if we can attain a broader notion of reason.

In his conclusion at Regensburg (Benedict XVI 2006), he affirmed: "The intention here is not one of retrenchment or negative criticism, but of broadening our concept of reason and its application. While we rejoice in the new possibilities open to humanity, we also see the dangers arising from these possibilities and we must ask ourselves how we can overcome them. We will succeed in doing so only if reason and faith come together in a new way, if we overcome the self-imposed limitation of reason to the empirically falsifiable, and if we once more disclose its vast horizons."[4]

He returns to this thesis on June 27, 2008 as a central proposal to his pontificate, when he gave his inaugural speech at the VI European Symposium of University Professors relating to this issue: *Broadening the Horizons of Rationality – Perspectives for Philosophy.* "The proposal to 'broaden the horizons of rationality' – said the Pope – must not simply be included among the new lines of theological and philosophical thought, but rather should be understood as a request for a new openness towards the reality to which human beings in their uni-totality are called, overcoming old prejudices and reductive viewpoints in order to open the way to a new understanding of modernity"(Benedict XVI 2008).

Ultimately, he is exhorting the need to broaden the horizons of modern rationality, a broadening-out which includes the rationality of faith and, thereby, metaphysical reason purified by faith itself. One of his principal interlocutors, before he became Pope, was Jürgen Habermas, author of the well-known book *The Theory of Communicative Action* (1984–87[1981]).

Joseph Ratzinger (Pope Benedict XVI) returned to the issue of reason, in particular ethical reason, and raised the question of what reason is; how a rational statement that constitutes a moral norm can be proved to be reasonable. When doing so, he quotes John Rawls who, although he denies that global religious doctrines possess the quality of public reason, sees nonetheless in their non-public reason a reason that, in spite of the secularist point of view, cannot be unknown.[5] He also approaches Jürgen Habermas, taking his notion of a sensibility to the truth as a necessary element in the process of political argumentation, thus restoring the concept (beyond what Jürgen Habermas understands by truth) to the philosophical and political debate.[6]

In modern times, new dimensions of knowledge have opened up, both in the natural sciences, which have developed on the basis of the link between experimentation and the presumed rationality of matter, and in the historical and humanistic sciences, in which man seeks to understand himself better. This development has opened to mankind not only an immense quantity of knowledge and power, but it has also developed the knowledge and acknowledgment of human rights and human dignity. However, man's journey can never be said to be complete or free from risk, and he says in this regard that the danger (especially for the Western world) is that man, especially considering the greatness of his knowledge and power, *surrenders when faced with the question of truth*. This would mean that reason ultimately folds from the pressure of interests and the attractiveness of utility, being forced to recognize it as the ultimate criterion.[7]

## 3 Is the logic of gift credible?

The logic of gift, as conceived by Benedict XVI, is related, as we have seen, to the principle of gratuitousness, which rules most of our reciprocal choices. If we were to cease to be generous, to give without expecting something in return, history would come to an end. Symbolical means of exchange cannot be reduced to money and power, as this would therefore cause an entropic drift and the relationship between these magnitudes does not work. Closer to power and money is solidarity, which is the decisive means of exchange, in which the oversimplification of quid pro quo no longer rules.

The logic of gift can also be found, although from quite different approaches, in some thinkers. Throughout the 20th century and the beginning of the 21st century a great deal of thought has been put into the spirit of the gift and its practice (Mauss 1950, Lévi-Strauss 1950, De Certeau 1986, Rabaté and Wetzel 1992, Caillé 1994, Benoist 1996, Godelier 1998, Marion 1998, Godbout 2000, Caputo and Scanlon 2000, Ricard 2001, Horner 2001, Ricoeur 2004). Although the philosophical precedents of this logic are not quoted in the encyclical letter, the classic *Essay on the Gift* by Marcel Mauss (1872–1950), published in 1923–24, should be cited.

Faced with the proposal of a logic of gift, a whole host of questions emerges. One might ask: Is the logic of gift credible? Is it possible to come up with a non-economistic view of the economy and to desacralize market logic, that is, to consider it dialectically with the logic of gift? Do truly selfless actions exist where selflessness does not turn out to be a mask of veiled interests?

As championed by philosophers of the gift, the logic of gift exists, beyond market logic, exacerbated individualism, the pure culture of ownership and display, and beyond the fragmented society. Although present in family, social, and work dynamics, it is very often hidden. In effect, there is a concealment of the gift that makes one think that this logic is folly and, nevertheless, social life is full of examples and moments of giving. We give blood, we donate organs, we give our time, we give our work, we give space, we give our own skills to others by volunteering, we create networks to help each other out, especially in the face of economic crisis. The practice of the gift is not residual, or irrelevant. It has a strong presence in family structure. The act of procreation is a donation that cannot solely be interpreted in terms of interest and the calculation of yield. Also the community is a constituent dimension of the individual and, therefore is necessary for survival. Without the gift it is not possible to become oneself. Life is a gift, but without the gifts that we have received from others, we cannot develop ourselves as people, or follow through with our own personal project.

As has been shown by Marcel Mauss, the greatest exponent of the anthropology of gift, the practice of gift, of the generous exchange of goods and mutual assistance is a basic tenet of primitive societies. Nevertheless, the gift survives in our societies as a result of certain ideologies; it is hidden, but it is there. Man, says the French thinker, is not a calculating machine, rather a being who is made for gift and who gains satisfaction from giving of himself.

For Mauss, exchange is the common denominator in many social activities. In traditional societies, exchanges are not financial; rather they are continuous exchanges that permit the symbolization of group life. These exchanges do not divide and separate the point of view of interests; instead, their selflessness offers cohesion to the society. Mauss shows how in traditional societies, this type of exchange can be seen through three obligations: the obligation to give, the obligation to receive (this was socially threatening, given that a donation could not be rejected), and the obligation to return (reciprocation).

Marcel Mauss writes: "Although marked by their experiences, individuals in these groups were less sad, less serious, less miserly and less personal than we are. At least externally, they were or are more generous, more liable to give than we are" (Mauss 1968, p. 104). As opposed to commercial exchange, a gift does not respect the rule of economic equivalence between what is received and what is returned, nor does it tend to promote material wealth, because the most important thing about the gift is not that it is exchanged from the point of view of its use, but rather for its symbolic value and the social relationship established by the gift. In Mauss' opinion, the gift is nothing more than *"a social contract used by primitive peoples"* (1990, p. 5). The network of reciprocal gift relationship places people within a system of uninterrupted relationships, so it works as a social asset and a basis of sociability.

The system of the gift is truly one of the essential foundations of society, as it revolves around the notion of a social being: the state of relative freedom to which the individual should be subjected in order to live in a group. There are rules, such as that of returning gifts, but everyone is free to become involved, as he or she can choose the time, place and way of giving.

Benedict XVI takes a wider perspective. He writes: "We are a gift" (CV 68). In effect, existence is a gift, but so is the essence. Nobody has given himself his own existence. Nobody has gained his own nature. One finds oneself existing, being given (*Étant donné*), to put it in the style of Jean-Luc Marion (1998).

Marion developed his perception of the gift based on an interpretation of the notion of *Gegebenheit*, as seen in a lecture course from 1907 by Edmund Husserl entitled *The Idea of Phenomenology*. Among the disciples stands out the figure of Edith Stein (1891–1942) who has developed this same concept in her philosophical anthropology, published under the title *Finite and Eternal Being* (Stein 2002, MacIntyre 2007).

Jean-Luc Marion writes: "The gift arises from itself without being inscribed in the economic circle where exchange would in advance orient it, prompt it, and consume it. The singular appearing of the gift must therefore be described such as it shows itself of itself insofar as it gives (itself)" (1998, p. 83).

The logic of gift has, according to Marion, two meanings. It describes, on one hand, the act itself of giving and, on the other, what has been given is what makes up the gift. The gift shows certain generosity, a generosity with no other objective than that of generating generosity. It consists of giving more than we receive, in overcoming the logic of calculation or of reciprocity. The gift shows concern for the other person, an interest in the other person. Giving is coming out of oneself (*sortir de soi*), as expressed by Marcel Mauss, giving what one is to others.

## 4 Conclusions

In *Caritas in Veritate*, the expression *logic of gift* is used in contrast with commercial logic. Throughout, Benedict XVI considers it essential to include this logic in economic reason, thereby broadening the traditional concept of economic rationality and propounding, in addition, the need to rethink the financial world order based on capitalism from the standpoint of what he calls the principle of gratuitousness.

According to the pontiff, this form of logic does not necessarily contradict the market system, given that the gift is part of the essence of being human and giving and receiving is part of the essence of society. But *"development is impossible without upright men and women, without financiers and politicians whose consciences are finely attuned to the requirements of the common good"* (CV 71, italics original).

The logic of gift transforms the concept of freedom and justice. Freedom is no longer understood as free will, but rather as liberation of the *ego*. Justice is no longer interpreted purely as equity, but rather as the creation of the minimum conditions needed to apply the gift. Love, as written by Alain Finkielkraut in *La sagesse de l'amour* (1997, p. 39), transcends justice, but does not oppose it. The gift does not reject equity, but it transcends pure commutative justice as distinguished by Aristotle.

Frémeaux and Michelson write the following on the matter: "giving for its own sake with 'no strings attached' presents an opportunity to provide deeper and more enduring meaning to a wide range of social and business relations" (2011). The logic of gift is a deep-rooted opportunity within the human being not only in a particular point of view but also for business. It's a power which radiates from his very being, as he is gift; he is made for the gift and his plenitude stems from the act of giving of himself. So, economic reason should be broadened and pure personal interest and the instrumental view of the world transcended (Melé 2003, Rocha and Miles 2009, Giovanola 2009), because transcending instrumental reason does not mean denying the value that it has in itself, but rather to open it up to new perspectives and fill it with new meanings.

As an *ens rationale*, the human being is able to calculate, plan, and program, not just for the benefit of himself or his interest group, but rather for the common good. The logic of gift is first and foremost logic, and not an irrational movement. Giving of oneself is not contradictory to human nature, or to rationality. Reason, enriched by the principle of gratuitousness, boosts the ability to think to its maximum potential, and means that human beings are able to give more and better, giving the best of themselves to others.

## Executive summary

In Benedict XVI's most recent encyclical letter, *Caritas in Veritate*, the expression *logic of gift* is used – in contrast to commercial logic. Throughout, Benedict XVI considers it essential to include this logic in economic reason, thereby broadening the traditional concept of economic rationality and propounding, in addition, the need to rethink the financial world order based on capitalism from the standpoint of what he calls the *logic of gift*.

The chapter examines in detail the meaning of this logic and its philosophical foundation. To do this, the notion of the gift is explored by taking the work of Marcel Mauss as a starting point, his intellectual precedent and the later philosophy of the gift, comprising of French thinkers of the 20th century like Jean-Luc Marion, Claude Lévi-Strauss, Paul Ricoeur, Jacques T. Goudbout, Maurice Godelier, and Claude Bruaire.

According to the pontiff this form of logic does not necessarily contradict the market system, given that gift is part of the essence of being human and giving and receiving is part of the essence of society. Benedict XVI states that the omission of this logic brings about serious inequality and injustice. From his point of view, humanizing the globalization process requires the necessary introduction of this logic of gift and, consequently, to broaden the notion of rationality.

## Notes

1. Adorno and Horkheimer 2002, pp. 94–136; Horkheimer 1947, pp. 40–62.
2. Benedict XVI, Address at the University of Regensburg, September 12, 2006.
3. Torralba (2010) examined this issue.
4. Benedict XVI 2006.
5. Cf. Benedict XVI 2008.
6. Benedict XVI 2008.
7. Benedict XVI 2008.

## References

Adorno, T. and M. Horkheimer. *The Dialectic of Enlightenment*. Stanford: Stanford University Press, 2002: 94–136.

Benedict XVI. Encyclical letter *Deus caritas est*, 2005. Available at: www.vatican.va/holy_father/benedict_xvi/encyclicals/documents/hf_ben-xvi_enc_20051225_deus-caritas-est_en.html (accessed July 28, 2011).

Benedict XVI. "Faith, reason and the university. Memories and reflections." Speech at University of Regensburg, September 2006.

Benedict XVI. Encyclical letter *Spe salvi*, 2007. Available at: www.vatican.va/holy_father/benedict_xvi/encyclicals/documents/hf_ben-xvi_enc_20071130_spe-salvi_en.html (accessed July 28, 2011).

Benedict XVI. Speech at La Sapienza University, Rome, January 2008. Available at: www.vatican.va/holy_father/benedict_xvi/speeches/2008/january/documents/hf_ben-xvi_spe_20080117_la-sapienza_en.html (accessed July 28, 2011).

Benoist, J. "Qu'est-ce qui est donné? La pensée et l'événement." *Archives de Philosophie*, Vol. 59, 4, 1996: 629–657.

Caillé, A. *Don, intérêt et désintéressement, Bourdieu, Mauss, Platon et quelques autres*. Paris: La Découverte, 1994.

Caputo, J.D. and M.J. Scanlon. *God, the Gift and Postmodernism*. Indianapolis: Indiana University Press, 2000.

De Certeau, M. *Heterologies; Discourse of the Other*. Minneapolis: University of Minnesota Press, 1986.

Finkielkraut, A. *La sagesse de l'amour [The Wisdom of Love]*. Paris: Gallimard, 1984. Lincoln: University of Nebraska Press, 1997].

Frémeaux, S. and G. Michelson. "'No strings attached': Welcoming the existential gift in business." *Journal of Business Ethics*, Vol. 99, 2011: 63–75.

Giovanola, B. "Re-thinking the anthropological and ethical foundation of economics and business: Human richness and capabilities enhancement." *Journal of Business Ethics*, Vol. 88, 2009: 431–444.

Global Ethic Foundation. *Global Economic Ethic. Consequences for Global Businesses.* New York: UN Headquarters, 2009.

Godbout, J.T. *Le don, la dette et l'indentité. Homo donator vs homo oeconomicus.* Paris: La Déocuverte, 2000.

Godelier, M. *L'Énigme du don [The Enigma of the Gift].* Paris: Fayard, 1996.

Habermas, J. *The Theory of Communicative Action,* 2 vols. Cambridge: Polity, 1984–87[1981].

Heidegger, M. "Conversation on a country path about thinking." *Discourse on Thinking.* New York: Harper and Row, 1966.

Horkheimer, M. *The Eclipse of Reason.* Oxford: Oxford University Press, 1947.

Horner, R. *Marion, Derrida and the Limits of Phenomenology.* New York: Fordham University Press, 2001.

Lévi-Strauss, C. "Introduction à l'oeuvre de Marcel Mauss." In M. Mauss, *Sociologie et anthropologie.* Paris: Presses Universitaires de France, 1950.

MacIntyre, A. *Edith Stein: A Philosophical Prologue.* Lanham, MD: Rowman and Littlefield, 2007.

Marion, J.-L. *Étant donné: essai d'un phénoménologie de la donation [Being given: toward a phenomenology of givenness].* Paris: PUF, 1998 . Palo Alto: Stanford University Press, 2002.

Mauss, M. *Sociologie et anthropologie.* Paris: Presses Universitaires de France, 1950.

Mauss, M. *Essai sur le don. Forme et raison de l'échange dans les sociétés primitives [The gift. The form and reason for exchange in archaic societies].* Paris: PUF, 1968[1923]. London: Routledge, 1990[1923].

Melé, D. "The challenge of humanistic management." *Journal of Business Ethics,* Vol. 44, 2003: 77–88.

Rabaté, J.-M. and M. Wetzel, eds. *L'éthique du don: Jacques Derrida et la pensée du don.* Paris: Métailie-Transition, 1992.

Ricard, M.-A. "La question de la donation chez Jean-Luc Marion." *Laval Théologique et philosophique,* Vol. 57, 1, 2001: 83–94.

Ricoeur, P. *La lutte pour la reconaissance et l'économie du don.* Paris: UNESCO, 2004.

Rocha, H. and R. Miles. "A model of collaborative entrepreneurship for a more humanistic management." *Journal of Business Ethics,* Vol. 88, 2009: 445–462.

Stein, E. *Finite and Eternal Being. The Collected Works of Edith Stein,* Vol. 9. Washington: ICS Publications, Institute of Carmelite Studies, 2002.

Torralba, F. *No pasar de largo. La experiencia ética.* Barcelona: Proteus, 2010.

# 5
# Fecundity vs. Efficiency: Rediscovering Relations

*Paul H. Dembinski*

> ...a new trajectory of thinking is needed in order to arrive at a better understanding of the implications of our being one family; interaction among the peoples of the world calls us to embark upon this new trajectory, so that integration can signify solidarity rather than marginalization. Thinking of this kind requires a *deeper critical evaluation of the category of relation.* (CV 53; italics in original)

In these words the encyclical *Caritas in Veritate* calls on us to give our thinking a "new trajectory." This new trajectory is expected to bring us closer to a deep understanding of the bonds of solidarity, which is essential for thinking and living humanity as one single family. The prerequisite for a successful journey along the new trajectory, says the Pope, is the critical evaluation of the "category of relation" in the light of what is essential in the Christian message, namely "man's transcendent dignity." Although the Pope expects that the contribution of social sciences to this task will be of importance, in his opinion they ought to be complemented by theology and metaphysics.

As to the contribution of social sciences, they will really contribute to the "new trajectory" only if they successfully supersede their disciplinary walls and boundaries so as to progressively build a transdisciplinary understanding of the "category of relation." Once developed, such a conceptual framework will usefully serve as an anchor for further analysis and action.

This chapter is a contribution, mainly from the economic perspective, to the endeavor of mapping this "new trajectory." It aims to compare and investigate two basic forms of social, financial, and economic interaction: namely the category of "relation" on one hand, and of "transaction", on the other. Although, transaction is not mentioned in the encyclical as a "category" worth studying, it is used here as a contrapuntal tool that is very helpful for a better understanding of relations. The starting point for this investigation is provided by mounting tide of financial transactions experienced in the past three decades, whose impact on the landscape and functioning of the OECD economies (and societies) has proved deep and lasting. In the second part of the chapter, the categories of transaction and relations are investigated in broader, more philosophical terms while the third and final part deals with the consequences of the mounting tide of transactions that expands well beyond finance and has tangible social and economic consequences. It also provides a systemic diagnosis of the present crisis. To do so, the last section draws on the manifesto "Finance that Serves the Common Good" made public in 2008 (Observatoire de la Finance 2008).

## 1 The mounting tide of transactions in finance

According to the Bank of International Settlements (BIS 2010), between 1984 and 2009 the share of the financial sector in GDP almost doubled in the United States and in the United Kingdom (from 5 per cent to more than 8 per cent of GDP) while in the European Union it grew slightly from 5 per cent to somewhat above 6 per cent. Even if the macro-economic mode of accounting for the financial sector value added is still in discussion (Sen and Stiglitz 2009) the figures reported above clearly suggest that a structural change has taken place in developed economies. Indeed, since the late 1970s, the financial sector has been one of the important drivers of macro-economic growth of the developed economies, especially those hosting a world-class financial centre.

This expansion is also visible through most of the statistical series describing financial activities. A closer examination of some of these series shows precisely what the main drivers behind the growth of financial services were in the three decades between 1975 and 2007:

- Capitalization of markets expressed in terms of nominal GDP more than doubled in all developed counties, while it has nearly quadrupled in the United States;
- The value of outstanding debt obligations (public and private) grew in similar proportions to the above in both internal and international markets;

- In 2007, the notional value of trades in derivatives amounted to 8 times the world GDP, while these instruments barely existed in the late 1970s;
- The value of foreign exchange transactions in 2005 amounted to more than 15 times the world GDP while it was insignificant in the mid-1970s.

The precise quantitative handling of statistics related to financial activities is difficult because of the lack of a comprehensive methodology and homogeneity in the way data is collected and presented. One main conceptual difference that has to be remembered is that some of the series relate to financial transactions and measure flows of trades in financial assets during a period, while others refer to the balance sheet values and measure values of these assets at a certain date. According to a rough estimate: in 2005 the value of world financial assets (stock data) amounted to about 12 times world GDP, while the value of annual financial transactions (flow data) amounted to 70 times the same GDP. To make the point even stronger: in the mid-1970s the turnover, that is, the total value of transactions, in the so-called "real economy" was about 10 times larger than the turnover in financial assets while in 2005, financial transactions amounted to 30(!) times the turnover of the "real economy." It appears that, in three decades, the ratio of financial transactions compared to the transactions in "real economy" has been multiplied by 300 (Farrell and Lund 2007; Dembinski 2009; McKinsey Global Institute 2010, see also www.beyondglobstat.org). Due to the still-lacking comprehensive and solid statistical methodology, these figures can serve to provide, at best, orders of magnitude. However, despite their weaknesses, they allow one to grasp the scope and speed of change in the role and way finance works in quantitative terms.

Beyond their statistical and technical aspects, these changes have far-reaching ethical consequences for the working of the economic and social fabric, which will be discussed at length in the next section. The long-term trend of expanding volumes and values of financial transactions sheds light on the products and markets that stand behind the expansion of the share of the financial sector referred to above. Clearly this expansion has been a transaction-driven one, leaving financial relations to play an important but less visible role. Three underlying processes have driven this expansion:

1. Financial innovation which, for at least three decades, has been continuously generating new forms of assets and financial products, which in turn breed ever more additional transactions;

2. Increased velocity of financial assets (i.e. steady acceleration in the speed of their circulation) which is tantamount to ever shorter average periods of holding a given asset. In this context, the so-called "nano-trading" pushes the holding period to its technical limits;
3. Long-term continuous increase in demand for holding financial assets, such as shares, has seen their valuations steadily rise.

The mounting tide of financial transactions sketched above provides ground for labeling the three decades between the mid-1970s (the collapse of the Bretton Woods systems and the first oil shock) and the beginning of the crisis in 2007, as the "three euphoric decades of finance." These decades were precede by three decades (between the end of WWII and the oil crisis) that Jean Fourastié has called "the glorious decades" (Fourastié 1979) because of high growth, low inflation, and low unemployment.

According to the standard view, the financial sector fulfils a set of basic functions in every modern economy: (a) facilitation of payments, (b) collection of savings, (c) financing of investments, and (d) management of risk through its pricing and trading (Crane et al. 1995). This being said, the relative importance of these functions may vary in time and space, as do technical tools, institutions, and techniques. These four key-functions perform two allocation processes vital to any developed economy: on the one hand the process of *allocation of capital* (to which the first three functions of the list contribute), and, on the other hand, the process of *allocation of risk*, which is carried out in the bouquet of activities associated with the fourth function. Although these processes are still today technically and institutionally interwoven, they are clearly distinct from the analytical point of view.

These two allocating processes are very different in nature. The process of *allocation of capital* is carried out through the establishment of medium- and long-term financing agreements or contracts between a party that has excessive cash and wants to exchange it – temporarily or permanently – for a future stream of revenues and a party that is willing to use this cash in a productive way (credit or investment) to generate the expected stream of revenue. These financial contracts, if properly and legally packed and priced may find their place on balance sheets of different institutions and become financial assets. Each of such contracts is associated with specific risks that relate to the conditions (micro- and macro-economic) of the successful completion of the project and the execution of the agreed payments. As a result of the matching needs, *medium- and long-term financing relationships* are established in the economy.

Things are different when it comes to the *allocation of risk*. The main reason for allocating risk is to provide to the various economic agents a financial protection (hedging) against future adverse events or misfortunes. As the spectrum of future adverse events or misfortunes and their possible or expected occurrences are permanently updated by new information, the allocation of risk is a never-ending, permanent process that ideally would require a continuous reallocation of all financial assets existing in an economy. The reallocation proceeds through exchanges among interested parties of already existing financial assets. In consequence, the allocation of risk is a *transaction-related process* where each party permanently adjusts the risk/return profile of his or her portfolio by changing its composition in response to the newest relevant information. He or she does this by exchanging, or committing to exchange as with derivatives in the future, existing assets.

Until the late 1970s, the two above-mentioned allocating processes were closely connected because most of the existing financial contracts were not transferable. In consequence, once an economic actor had entered a financial agreement or relation, he remained exposed to the risks associated with it until the natural termination of the contract. When assets are non-transferable, each actor can only marginally adjust his or her portfolio's risk/return profile by carefully selecting the characteristics of each new contract he or she decides to enter. Such was the traditional way banks used to manage risks by adjusting the structure of their balance sheets – assets' as well as liabilities' sides – through the prudent selection of their new counter-parties and clients. As long as non-transferable assets prevailed, allocation of risk was just another, technically non-autonomous, aspect of the capital allocation process (Albert, 1991).

Since the late 1970s, a profound transformation of world finance has taken place. An accelerating emancipation and growing autonomy of the risk management and allocation activities drive it. Today, capital allocation and risk allocation are distinct processes, connected through the financial markets where assets are traded. Three factors have mainly contributed to this general trend by which the two processes became institutionally distinct:

1. The radical growth in the volume of transferable financial assets, that is, contracts allowing for an almost costless substitution of parties during the duration of the financial relation. This long-term trend led to the relative strengthening of financial markets where

such assets are traded and the corresponding weakening of classical savings and credit banks;
2. The invention and expansion of a new class of financial assets: the derivatives. These contracts allow one to exchange today future commitments related to an underlying financial asset or index. The most widely-known and used type of derivative is options. An option is a contract whereby a party buys (or sells) today the possibility of buying or selling at a specified future moment, an underlying asset at a price agreed upon today;
3. The development of so-called structured finance and its synthetic products. These very sophisticated products combine other existing assets or contracts with conditional commitments such as insurance contracts or options. They are designed either to cover an ad hoc risk or to take advantage of pricing inefficiencies. Much, although not all, of these products are tradable like the infamous Collateralized Debt Obligations (CDOs) or Credit Default Swaps (CDSs).

The three evolutions, described above, contributed to making the transactions easier and less costly which, in turn, increased the traded volumes (depth and liquidity of markets), the number of transactions, and the price volatility. Progressively the risk-allocating function of financial sector acquired independence by developing its own instruments (derivatives), its own techniques (asset management), and professional skills. These grew in importance within the universe of finance in comparison with the more traditional activities related to the allocation of capital. It appears in consequence, that the expansion of transactions (see above, the statistical orders of magnitude) has been mainly driven by the needs of the risk-allocating function, which, in this way, thoroughly contributed to the expansion of the financial sector and to economic growth. This change has also been apparent in the revenue structures of main financial institutions. During the period under discussion, the share of fees and trading commissions increased steadily to represent today well above 50 per cent of the operating income of major banks, not to speak of non-bank financial institutions. During the same period, the capital allocating activities increased in line with, but not faster than, GDP.

The emphasis on financial activities, which during the "three euphoric decades" moved from classical relation-based finance to a much more transaction-soriented one, fundamentally affected the mutual relationship. Until quite recently, financial relations (either credits or investments) were created because parties to the contract were sensitive to the project's promise of generating medium- or long-term revenue streams.

Even if some of many of these contracts were technically transferable, it was above all a guarantee allowing – in case of necessity – the financing party to exit a relation before its natural termination (provided he or she was able to find a buyer willing to step in his or her place). In most cases, not the (transaction) selling price, but the initially expected revenue flows were the prime motives for initiating a financial relation. This suggests that, in those times, financial relations were mainly designed to meet the needs and requirements of the parties directly involved. Things have changed since.

The logic behind the development of the CDOs provides a good example of how the relationship between financial relations and transactions has changed. CDOs are modern, synthetic (complex) products designed by financial engineers. They combine in one single asset combined characteristics, and use for this a great number of "primary" financial relations or contracts. The combination is aimed at presenting a risk/return profile attractive to a potential buyer, that is, to a third party who is not one of the initial parties to any of the "primary" relations. In other words, CDOs are financial artifacts or packages that proved attractive to actors different from the original parties to the underlying "primary" financing relations. A fundamentally ethical question arises at this stage: in the last analysis, pro qui bono are the "primary" relations initiated and by whom? Does this relation stem from a matching of the needs of the parties, or does the prospect of a profitable sale of a CDO trigger the intermediary to actively (not to say aggressively) propose to a potential financed party with characteristics that are of interest to the final buyer of the CDO product, an attractive "primary" relation? To what extent do such "primary" financial relations serve the medium-and long-term needs of parties, and to what extent do they serve above all those that use them as "raw material" or "components" required for synthetic products? Do the initiators of financial relations, here specialized financial intermediaries, have in mind interests other than their own?

The well-documented recent tragedy of the American sub-primes provides an illustration of the true motives and behaviors behind the "originate and distribute" (O&D) strategy. The O&D strategy has been applied for years, above all but not exclusively, by investment banks that made fortunes by using their financial engineering skills to produce and market the corresponding CDOs. The crisis has shown that in many (but not all) cases the CDOs proved harmful to the two parties to the underlying financial relations: to the owners of homes unable to pay their debts, as well as to the ultimate holder of CDOs such as pension funds or households who understood only after the sub-prime collapse how risky their assets had been (BIS 2007, 2010).

What the O&D strategy clearly shows is that the hierarchy between relations and transaction has been inverted for the sake of the latter. The prospect of transaction became a strong driver for generating and calibrating new relations. It looks like, in the case of CDOs, long-term relations (mortgages, credit cards, or student credits) have become instrumental for the prospective transaction in which the intermediaries had a clear interest. The hierarchy between relations and transactions has been inverted when long-term constraints have been imposed on some for the sake of immediate gains by others. The following quotation from the encyclical seems to find in the case of CDOs, but more widely in the case of immoderate acceleration and multiplication of financial transactions, a very clear illustration. "Economy and finance," says the Pope, "as instruments, can be used badly when those at the helm are motivated by purely selfish ends. Instruments that are good in themselves can thereby be transformed into harmful ones" (CV 36). The Pope continues, "Financiers must rediscover the genuinely ethical foundation of their activity, so as not to abuse the sophisticated instruments which can serve to betray the interests of savers. Right intention, transparency, and the search for positive results are mutually compatible and must never be detached from one another" (CV 65).

## 2 Relation and transaction

The evolution of financial dealings shows that in real social and economic life, transactions and relations are not just abstract categories. They are two distinct but interrelated modes of social interactions that stay in complex and dynamic mutual relationship. The purpose of the present section is to investigate and compare these two categories so as to understand better their mutual influence and interaction.

Transactions are the key characteristic phenomena of a market economy. They are the locus where equivalence is assessed, where "equivalent exchange" takes place and where money operates and shows its power. According to Jacques Juilliard, equivalent exchange allows the "reduction ad pecuniam" to take place which he then compares to a pagan form of transubstantiation. As real and potential transactions are overwhelmingly present in modern societies, the transacted goods tend to lose their specificity and their natural in-commensurability (as well as exchange parties). As the perspective of monetary transaction becomes overwhelming, the world turns every day flatter and more clearly one-dimensional (Julliard 2008).

In fact, according to the still dominant "scientific" view, the market economy is about equivalent transactions, they are the self-contained basic units of any purely economic society. As quanta or atoms allow one to see the physical world as magma, transactions give the impression that they reach beyond the surface of social and economic realities: with the help of transactions anything can be fragmented at will. Once fragmented by transactions, the world seems easy to organize, manage, and govern. What matters in transactions are goods and services exchanged, and their value, not the persons who complete the exchange. Thus, impersonality and anonymity are main characteristics of transactions. In a perfect market transaction, price and quality do not depend on the identity of parties involved. Thus, almost by nature, perfect transactions – not only financial ones – are price-sensitive and party-neutral.

The transaction-based worldview has also permeated the managerial literature under to main code names "nexus of contracts theory of the firm" and "principal-agent paradigm." Both of them are widely accepted and supported by a shared anthropological position of pure utilitarianism where money is the sole argument of any utility function. For the proponents of these theoretical approaches, homo economicus is the truest expression of the human nature for which the only reality that matters is a transaction-related one (Jensen and Meckling 1976, 1994). In consequence, these essentially a-moral theories propose only one instrument – contractual payments as incentives – for influencing the behaviors of others, whether within or without an organization (Posner 2010 and below).

A second important characteristic of transactions is their instantaneity. A transaction is equilibrated at the moment its conditions are agreed between the parties. It is an instant, a quantum of economic time when, like in a flash illuminating darkness around for a fraction of a second, equivalence is brought into motion. Like in quantum physics, transaction time is discontinuous, made of separate and perfectly static and self-contained moments.

A third characteristic of perfect transactions is their economic completeness. By this is meant that all the relevant peculiarities of the goods exchanged are taken account of in the valuation process – that no characteristic is left outside the perspective in line with the "no free lunch" principle. Only seldom are real world transactions complete in this sense, but financial transactions are considered to be the closest to perfect completeness.

Another important characteristic of the transaction is its instrumental nature. The transaction is a means of exchanging something that has less subjective value to me for something that has more. Buying and selling are thus pure means serving each of the parties to reach their own goal, which, by definition, lies beyond the transaction itself. Transactions are like milestones on a road.

From a macro-economic perspective, perfect transactions are tantamount to perfectly functioning markets that, in turn, according to the prevailing knowledge, guarantee the most efficient use of available resources. Mainstream economic theory, as well as policy, values efficiency highly. This said, macro-efficiency is a by-product of smoothly functioning markets that require perfect transaction and make them happen. These markets, financial and otherwise, are in charge of the continuous process of allocating goods, services, and risks.

As a result of the above-mentioned characteristics, transactions appear as economic quanta, ephemeral units independent of each other, easy to assemble, to sort or to categorize and also easy to quantify. In a transaction-based worldview, everything seems easy to manage in the impersonal and highly technical procedures used today in major corporations and taught in "best" business schools (Mintzberg 2004; de Gaulejac 2005; Posner 2010 and discussion).

Although *Caritas in Veritate* does not address transactions as a category directly, it does so indirectly, by emphasizing the uniqueness of the other in human dealings and by stating that the "principle of gratuitousness as an expression of fraternity" (CV 34). In this crude light, transactions appear as deriving their strength, at least from a strictly economic point of view, from standing in open contradiction to papal recommendations: purely impersonal, they are unable to express fraternity, and being self-sufficient and complete, they do not allow for gratuity (Dembinski, 1998).

As *Caritas in Veritate* invites people of good will to rediscover the "category of relation," it provides an excellent opportunity to compare this with the "category of transaction." If a transaction is anonymous and impersonal, quite the opposite is true for relations. Only when parties know each other in their peculiarities, might they enter a relationship. This is for instance true in a credit and debt relation in which room is left for the mutual adaptation and recognition of peculiarities and singularities of each of the parties. If transactions are instantaneous, relations have by definition a duration: some are everlasting, others are short, but all extend beyond the instant. This means that most relations have a built-in dynamic, in contrast to the self-contained and static transactions. If transactions are, or at least aspire to be, complete because they build on equivalent exchange, relations, by definition, are a succession of imbalances. Like walking, a relation is a succession of disequilibria: the energy gathered in a step sets the ground and makes the next step possible. At any moment in time, a living relation is thus, by definition, unbalanced.

Another way of looking at the non-equivalence, in which any relation is rooted, is to see it as a locus of gratuitousness and, possibly of gift. On these bases, reciprocity, not equivalence may develop. In a recent book, Cardinal Tarcisio Bertone says that unlike equivalent exchange, reciprocity takes into account the actual possibilities (i.e. possibly changing in time) of each of the parties (Bertone 2008). In this sense reciprocity, rather than exchange, seems to be the true engine of any relation.

This said, why do impersonal, self-contained, instantaneous transactions happen? What makes potential parties enter into transactions with unknown, faceless parties? In the final analysis, any exchange requires a certain, if limited, level of trust among parties. Where does this trust come from when the party is anonymous and thus cannot be trusted as such? Impersonal transactions will only take place when the institutional environment provides the necessary level of trust. This means that trust is external to the transaction itself. Auditors, solicitors, lawyers, experts, insurers, brokers, and so on embody the rule of law, which ultimately provides the minimal necessary level of trust to allow faceless actors to engage in exchanges and trade on more or less organized markets (Gambetta 1988).

In July 2002, the then chairman of the US Federal Reserve, Alan Greenspan very convincingly stressed the balance, which has be maintained in any market economy between personal and institutional trust, between trust from within and trust from outside transactions. This balance is extremely vulnerable to any mounting wave of ethical miss-behaviors and moral hazard type abuses.

> Well-functioning markets require accurate information to allocate capital and other resources, and market participants must have confidence that our predominately voluntary system of exchange is transparent and fair. Although laws and contracts govern business transactions, if even a modest fraction of those transactions had to be adjudicated, our courts would be swamped into immobility. Thus,

> our market system depends critically on trust – trust in the word of our colleagues and trust in the word of those with whom we do business. Falsification and fraud are highly destructive to free-market capitalism and, more broadly, to the underpinnings of our society.[1]

The case of relations is different; trust is a dynamic component of relation. In relations, trust is interpersonal, internal to the relation. As such, trust is one of the most important gifts, which a party to a relation – any relation including a business one – can give to the other party. Once introduced into a relational framework, trust can grow (or disappear) like a seed of a fruit that will blossom and mature in the next stages of the relation. Unpredictable as to its future, a relation is the locus of fecundity. Many business examples show that joint projects and cooperation often produce totally unexpected fruits, which exceed even the highest expectations. These are the fruits, in the full sense of the word, of fecund relationships.

By contrasting relations with transactions, their potentials clearly appear. Transactions with their commitment to instantaneous efficiency, deliver immediately everything that can be harvested at once. In contrast, relations balance the fruits of past efforts with the seeds for future results. Henry Mintzberg uses a different vocabulary, he speaks of exploitation and exploration, and says the following: "Every economy needs both exploration and exploitation, one to create, the other to realize the benefits of creation...The danger lies in tilting too far in either direction. Economies and companies that favour calculating... tilt too far in the direction of exploitation – of the efficiency at the expense of discovery" (2004, p.121).

Implicitly Mintzberg poses the key question: the question of sane proportions between transactions and relations (exploration and exploitation in his terminology). These broad questions have been raised also by Ferdinand Tönnies' famous distinction between *Gemeinschaft* (community) and *Gesellschaft* (society). The Popperian distinction between the *Closed Society*, held together by sticky relations, and the liberal *Open Society* where transactions prevail, provides a different insight into the same problem of sane proportions between transactions and relations. Indeed Karl R. Popper wrote in the 1940s "We could conceive a society in which men practically never meet face to face – in which all business is conducted by individuals in isolation who communicate by typed letters or by telegrams, and go about in closed motor-cars. Such a fictious society might be called a "completely abstract or depersonalised society" (Popper 1991[1945], p 174). In the age of mobile phones, computer screens, and traffic congestion, these words clearly suggest that Popper does not describe a "fictitious" (or absurd) society, but our way of living. The question thus is; does our transaction-dependent way of life still deserve to be called "society"? According to *Caritas in Veritate* (CV 19) gratuity is an essential dimension of fraternity which, in turn is foundational to any true (Christian and thus human) society, whereas in a transaction-based environment, gratuity appears as an imperfection and an inefficiency that is bound to be eliminated by a properly-working market mechanism.

## 3 The crisis: when transactions endanger relations

The current crisis is not just economic or financial – it is system-wide. The remedy therefore is not simply a matter of the financial sector coming back into line with the "real" economy, with the risk allocation process losing its importance in relation to the capital allocation process. The crisis is the outcome of years of unremitting pressure in the search for efficiency, which harvested more than it created. In consequence of the decades-long transaction drive, material, social, intellectual, and ethical relational foundations of societies based on political and economic freedom have been dangerously weakened.

The pressure of transactions has been cascading from the purely financial world to the rest of the economy. The doctrine of "shareholder value" first put large listed transactional corporations under pressure by imposing a short-term horizon and sky-high return on investment requirements (Mintzberg 2004). These then passed the pressure on in three interconnected directions: to their staff around the world, under increasingly fierce managerial pressure to keep improving their performance; to consumers, under growing pressure to innovate as a result of ever more sophisticated marketing techniques; and to smaller businesses, suppliers, and distributors in both the North and the South, which also found themselves under often unbearable pressure to perform. This pressure – which at first only affected the financial sector – thus spread to the rest of the economy and from there to the whole of our society, our culture, and our everyday lives. Today, short-term results prevail in all aspects of economic and social life: relations are being replaced by transactions, exploitation replaces exploration, and creativity and fecundity are less and less cared for (Frankel 2006). At the same time, the patience, loyalty, sustainability, and trust on which relationships depend have been undermined, and distrust is becoming more widespread daily. In financial markets, this trend was concealed for a long time by the abundance of liquidity which allowed transactions to run smoothly and to accelerate, but in mid-2007 the less organized markets suddenly ran out of liquidity – this showed how deep the level of distrust in these anonymous markets, in fact, was.

The trend toward more transactions has been greatly facilitated by the political appeal of deregulation and by the "laws," "theorems," and so forth that Nobel prize winners have put forward in support of financial rationality. The steamroller of the "efficiency ethos," validated by supposedly scientific truths, has steadily crushed moral and ethical resistance (Marglin 2008). The transaction-based efficiency ethos has gradually worn down moral resistance and become the ultimate criterion of judgment. The extreme focus on efficiency has resulted in internal organizational procedures in which tasks and responsibilities are assigned so specifically that staff lose sight of what their work actually involves. This has led to widespread "ethical alienation": staff no longer wonder, or care, whether their work is meaningful or justified because only short-term results count.

When separated from moral considerations, the "efficiency ethos" has led to increasingly crude manifestations of greed. This has created more scope for the selfishness that is inherent in human nature. Relationships and related trust are betrayed and all too often result in one partner's wish to get out and cash out, leaving the other partner abandoned. Such barefaced acts of betrayal or disloyalty risk destroying what is the essential mechanism in any free society or market economy, namely trust between people. The free market, based on the players' sense of responsibility, is making way for a "greed market" which will in turn require escalating controls, rules, and procedures in both the public and the private sectors. This is not only very costly, but makes players even less willing to behave in a responsible manner (Lewitt 2002, Partnoy 2004). The documentary movie "Inside Job" (Ferguson 2010) provides a breath-taking illustration of this point for the financial industry.

This diagnosis suggests that the fundamental values of freedom of judgment, responsibility, and solidarity – on which the common good depends, and without which a free and humane society cannot exist – are now under threat. The "euphoric decades" resulted in an over-development of transactions in proportion to relations to the point that the very fabric of our societies is in danger. The broken balance has to be restored and the richness of the category of relation rediscovered. From a Christian perspective, two interdependent and complementary instruments are proposed: veritas and caritas.[2]

The search for truth implies a critique of the epistemic, anthropological, and ethical foundations of assessment of the prevalent economic, financial, and managerial worldview.[3] This may end up challenging the dogmatic focus on economic and financial efficiency and justifying renewed ethical and political concerns about the common good. Where appropriate, the results should quickly be made an integral part of economic, managerial, and financial training courses. At the same time, they should lead to a redistribution of research and educational resources that will encourage a fundamental reform of economic thinking.

## 4 Conclusion

The shifting of emphasis from efficiency to fecundity, from exploitation to explorations is a long-term and multi-layer endeavor. If successfully initiated, it might be further supported by a self-accelerating process which will start once the strength of reciprocity and gratuity is first identified, and then acknowledged. The shift envisaged here is not a mere adjustment but a systemic change. Efficiency is still today the powerful organizing principle overriding all its potential challengers. The crisis has opened a window of opportunity by making clear the limits this organizing principle has reached. As a consequence alternative modes of thinking and of acting gain some visibility, praise, and status of exemplarity: *Economy of Communion* is one but not the only example.[4] Many initiatives under the umbrella of "solidarity-based economy" attempt to develop business models that extend beyond the purely transactional framework.

This implies the new types of incentives – not only material or monetary but also moral –be developed, which encourage long-term commitments in all areas of the economic and financial sectors. If horizons become longer, fewer long-term relationships will be sacrificed or exploited by untimely transactions geared to short-term gain. A new balance must be struck – in both qualitative and quantitative terms – between relationships and transactions, both of which are essential to society.

However, experiments are not enough; they will spread only when emphasis on relations is translated in legal terms. In OECD countries, legal frameworks changed so as to provide more flexibility tantamount to increased efficiency. This approach allows for permanent re-allocation (not only of risks) but endangers commitment, which is essential to creativity. The crisis shows that the pendulum has to swing back: legal frameworks (in finance, labor markets, taxation, accounting) have to shift to reward medium- and long-term commitment of parties to a common project or cooperation. Making transactions more "sticky" (in terms of reduced flexibility) would encourage relationships and efficient production rather than efficient allocation. This could lead to a rediscovery of the benefits of "shortening transaction chains."

Smooth systemic changes (transitions) require a shared political will, only revolutions come by surprise. Rehabilitating relations and restoring a sane proportion between them and transactions is a wide undertaking on which *Caritas in Veritate* is clear: "(t)he great challenge before us... is to demonstrate, in thinking and behaviour, not only that traditional principles of social ethics like transparency, honesty and responsibility cannot be ignored or attenuated, but also that in commercial relationships the principle of gratuitousness and the logic of gift as an expression of fraternity can and must find their place within normal economic activity" (CV 36).

If successful, the systemic change advocated here will also profoundly affect the financial sector. It will be restructured so that it performs in a more balanced way than today with two main roles through which it should serve, and not drive, the economy and society, namely by allocating capital and by allocating risk. In this way the balance between relations and transaction could be restored in the financial sector as well.

## Executive summary

This chapter is a contribution, mainly from an economic perspective, to the endeavor of mapping this "new trajectory." It aims to compare and investigate two basic forms of social, financial and economic interaction: namely the category of "relation" on the one hand, and "transaction" on the other.

The long-term trend of expanding volumes and values of financial transactions sheds light on the products and markets that stand behind the three-decades-long expansion of the financial sector. Clearly this expansion has been transaction-driven leaving financial relations to play an important but less visible role.

In every modern economy the financial sector carries out two allocation processes: the process of *allocation of capital* which is relation-based and the process of *allocation of risk* which is transaction based. Since the late 1970s, a profound transformation has taken place driven by the accelerating emancipation of risk allocation activities. Progressively this function acquired independence by developing its own instruments (derivatives), its own techniques (asset management), and professional skills. This change, from classical relation-based finance to one much more transaction-oriented, fundamentally affected their mutual relationship.

The logic behind the development of the CDOs provides a good example of how the relationship between financial relations and transactions has changed. These synthetic products aim to present a risk/return profile attractive for a potential buyer, that is, a third party who is not one of the initial parties in a financing relation. The well-documented recent tragedy of the American sub-primes provides an illustration of the true motives and behaviors behind the CDO driven "originate and distribute" strategy.

As *Caritas in Veritate* invites us to rediscover the "category of relation," it provides an opportunity to compare it with transactions. If a transaction is anonymous and impersonal, quite the opposite is true for relations. Only when parties know each other in their peculiarities, might they enter a relationship. This means that most of relations have a built-in dynamic, as opposed to the self-contained and static transactions. If transactions are complete, it's because they are built on equivalent exchange, relations, by definition, are a successions of unbalances.

By contrasting relations with transactions, their potentials clearly appear. Transactions with their commitment to instantaneous efficiency, deliver immediately, everything that can be harvested at once. In contrast, relations balance the fruits of past efforts with the seeds for future results.

The shifting of emphasis from transactions and efficiency to relations and fecundity requires new types of incentives – not only material and monetary but also moral – to be developed which encourage long-term commitments in all areas of the economy and the financial sector. If horizons become longer, fewer long-term relationships will be sacrificed or exploited by untimely transactions geared to short-term gain. The real challenge for practitioners, public and private, that feel inspired by *Caritas in Veritate* is to clearly prefer relations – as opposed to transactions – in their everyday deeds. The world may change only because we change.

## Notes

1. Testimony of Chairman Alan Greenspan (2002).
2. "Through this close link with truth, charity can be recognized as an authentic expression of humanity and as an element of fundamental importance in human relations, including those of a public nature. Only in truth does charity shine forth, only in truth can charity be authentically lived. Truth is the light that gives meaning and value to charity. That light is both the light of reason and the light of faith, through which the intellect attains to the natural and supernatural truth of charity: it grasps its meaning as gift, acceptance, and communion" (CV 3).
3. See Observatoire de la Finance (2011).
4. "Economy of Communion" is a movement of entrepreneurs, workers, and their business associates inspired the culture of giving, as opposed to the "culture of having" prevalent today: www.edc-online.org (accessed March 10, 2012).

## References


Bank of International Settlements (BIS). *Annual Reports*. Basel, 2007. www.bis.org (accessed August 1, 2011).

Bank of International Settlements (BIS). *Annual Reports*. Basel, 2010. www.bis.org (accessed August 1, 2011).

Bertone, Tarcisio. *L'éthique du bien commun dans la doctrine sociale de l'Eglise*. Rome: Librairie Éditrice Vaticane, 2008.

Crane, D. B., Froot, K. A., Mason, S. C., Perold, A. F., Merton, R. C., Bodie, Z., Sirri, E. R., and Tufano, P. *The global financial system: A Functional Perspective*. Harvard Business School Press, 1995.

Dembinski, Paul H. *Finance: Servant or Deceiver ? Financialisation at the Crossroads*. London: Palgrave, 2009.

De Gaulejac, Vincent, *La société malade de la gestion*. Seuil: Paris, 2005.

Dembinski, Paul H. "Le piège de l'économisme: quand l'arithmétique remplace l'éthique." In Beat Sitter-Liver and Pio Caroni, eds. *Der Mensch – ein Egoist? Für und wider die Ausbreitung des methodischen Utilitarismus in der Kulturwissenschaften*. Fribourg: Swiss Academy of Humanities and Social Sciences, 1998.

Ferguson, Charles (director), *Inside Job*, a 2010 Academy Award winning documentary film about the late-2000s financial crisis.

Fourastié, Jean. *Les Trente Glorieuses, ou la révolution invisible de 1946 à 1975*. Paris: Fayard, 1979.

Frankel, Tamar. *Trust and Honesty – America's Business Culture at a Crossroad*. Oxford: Oxford University Press, 2006.

Gambetta, Diego, ed. *Trust: Making and Breaking Cooperative Relations*. Oxford: Blackwell, 1988.

Greenspan, Alan. *Federal Reserve Board's Semiannual Monetary Policy Report to the Congress before the Committee on Banking, Housing, and Urban Affairs, U.S.*

*Senate*. Washington DC, July 16, 2002. Available at: www.federalreserve.gov/boarddocs/hh/2002/july/testimony.htm (accessed July 1, 2011).

Jensen, Michael C, Wilhelm H Meckling. "Theory of the Firm: Managerial Behaviour, Agency Costs and Ownership Structure." *Journal of Financial Economics* 3 (1976): 305-60.

Julliard, Jacques. *L'argent, Dieu et le diable*. Paris: Flammarion, 2008.

Levitt, Arthur, *Take On the Street: What Wall Street and Corporate America Don't Want You to Know. What You Can Do to Fight Back*. Random House. 2002.

Lowell, Bryan and Farrell, Diana. *Market Unbound: unleashing global capitalism*, New York: John Wiley & Sons, 1996.

Marglin, Stephen. *The Dismal Science: How Thinking like an Economist Undermines Community*. Harvard: Harvard University Press, 2008.

Michael Jensen and William Meckling, 'The Nature of Man', *Journal of Applied Corporate Finance*, Vol. 7, No. 2, 1994, pp. 4–19.

Mintzberg, Herny. *Managers not MBAs*. London: Prentice Hall, 2004.

McKinsey Global Institute. Debt and deleveraging: Global debt bubble and its economic consequences, 2012. Available at http://www.mckinsey.com/Insights/MGI/Research/Financial_Markets/Debt_and_deleveraging_The_global_credit_bubble_Update (accessed March 10, 2012).

Observatoire de la Finance. *Finance that Serves the Common Good, Manifesto for the Observatoire de la Finance*, January, 2008, updated March 2009. Available at: www.obsfin.ch/manifeste.htm (accessed January 26, 2012).

Observatoire de la Finance. *Appeal of Teachers and Researchers: Renewing the Research and Teaching in Finance, Economics and Management to Better Serve the Common Good*. Geneva-Fribourg-Zürich, April, 2011. Available at: www.responsiblefinance.ch/appeal (accessed August 1, 2011).

Partnoy, Frank. *Infectious Greed: How Deceit and Risk Corrupted the Financial Markets*. London: Profile Books, 2004.

Popper, Karl. *The Open Society and its Enemies*. London: Routledge, 1991[1945].

Posner, Richard "From the new institutional economics to organization economics: with applications to corporate governance, government agencies, and legal institutions" *Journal of Institutional Economics* (2010), 6: 1, 1–37.

Sen, Amartya and Joseph Stiglitz. *Report by the Commission on the Measurement of Economic Performance and Social Progress*. Paris: Presidency of the French Republic, 2009.

# 6

# Corporate or Governmental Duties? CSR as Subsidiary Co-responsibility

*Michael Stefan Aßländer*

> ...the principle of subsidiarity is particularly well-suited to managing globalization and directing it towards authentic human development. In order not to produce a dangerous universal power of a tyrannical nature, *the governance of globalization must be marked by subsidiarity*, articulated into several layers and involving different levels that can work together. (CV 57; italics in original)

Since the publishing of the encyclical letter *Quadragesimo Anno* (QA) the principle of subsidiarity has reached the status of a fundamental pillar in Catholic thought. Together with the principle of solidarity both principles should shape a humane societal and economic order, foster human development, and contribute to emancipation and self-realization of all human beings. Thus, in an address to the members of the Papal Foundation "Centesimus Annus" in May 2008, Pope Benedict XVI pointed out:

> A harmonious development is possible if the economic and political choices take into account...those fundamental principles which make it accessible to all. I am referring, in particular, to the principles of subsidiarity and solidarity....Only a shared culture of responsible and active participation can enable each human being to feel not as a consumer or a passive bystander, but an active collaborator in the process of world development. (Benedict XVI 2009)

One year later, in his encyclical letter *Caritas in Veritate* (CV), Pope Benedict XVI explains how such a shared culture of responsibility could be integrated in society. He points out that subsidiarity could also function as a core principle for reaching a just global society. Although the encyclical letter provides insights about how a societal order in the age of globalization can be shaped by the guiding principles of solidarity and subsidiarity, it does not address the new role of corporate actors in globalizing economies. When talking about the corporate world, criticizing its primary orientation on capital and investors' expectations and demanding respect for all stakeholders' interests, the encyclical mainly focuses on management obligation and does not address corporate duties in a subsidiary organized societal order (CV 40). Nevertheless, the tenet of subsidiarity and its interpretation in the encyclical letter *Caritas in Veritate* provide an interesting perspective for re-discussing the conception of Corporate Social Responsibility (CSR) as it is used in contemporary business ethics theory. Especially in the context of the ongoing debate about a suitable definition of CSR, the tenet of subsidiarity can fruitfully serve to define corporate duties that go beyond good management practices in day-to-day business procedures. This is particularly so with those that are more concrete than a purely discretionary social engagement dependent solely on the favor of the company's leaders. From the perspective of a societal order, shaped by subsidiarity as one of their basic principles, corporations bear a subsidiary co-responsibility in society and can be described as intermediate instances that have to take on concrete duties in a system of subsidiary societal task-sharing.

The outline offered here of the idea of corporate subsidiary co-responsibility as a new perspective of CSR is structured as follows: Section 1 analyzes the specific understanding of subsidiarity and the role of corporations in society as portrayed in the encyclical letter *Caritas in Veritate*. Section 2 delineates the European understanding of CSR from two different perspectives: CSR as a demand for honest business practices and CSR as voluntary corporate societal engagement. Because a CSR understood as a discretionary engagement, as laid out in the CSR-definition of the European Commission, causes difficulties – mainly in those cases where corporate activities are used to compensate governmental tasks – in Section 3 the tenet of subsidiarity is reconsidered as a regulatory principle allowing for the distinguishing between corporate duties and voluntary activities. Section 4 restructures the principle of CSR as a three-tiered concept, one which includes corporate management practices, corporate societal subsidiary co-responsibilities, and corporate discretionary engagement. The contribution closes with a summary.

## 1 Corporate social responsibility understanding in the encyclical *Caritas in Veritate*

Especially in chapter III "Fraternity, Economic Development and Civil Society" and chapter IV "The Development of People, Rights and Duties, the Environment" the encyclical letter *Caritas in Veritate* explicitly addresses the importance of the economy for societal development. Based on the critique that markets reliant solely on the principle of commutative justice are unable to realize distributive and social justice (CV 35), Benedict XVI points out that the commercial logic of modern economy must be directed towards the common good by the political community. Because the economy must be seen entirely as means for other ends, it can be used badly if these means serve only the selfish interests of the economic actors. Thus, Benedict XVI concludes:

> The economic sphere is neither ethically neutral, nor inherently inhuman and opposed to society. It is part and parcel of human activity and precisely because it is human, it must be structured and governed in an ethical manner. (CV 36)

In this context Benedict XVI refers in particular to the motivation of business actors and calls on them to serve the common good with the expression of his hope that "hybrid forms" of economic corporations in the marketplace will help to shape a solid society. He reminds us that an exclusively shareholder-orientation of economic enterprises risks limiting their social value. Thus, corporate social responsibility becomes a topic of increasing importance (CV 38–40). In this context Pope Benedict XVI highlights the positive effects of various efforts in the field of "business ethics," like business ethics education, socially responsible investment opportunities, and micro-credits. Nevertheless, he recalls that ethics must shape the entirety of business life and that it would be a mistake to see ethics solely as a "label" for specific economic activities. Using the term as a kind of ideological distinction would give rise to the mistaken inference that every business not labeled as "ethical" is unethical (CV 45).

As Pope Benedict XVI had already pointed out in the introduction of his encyclical letter, the whole economy has to be directed toward the common good and thus economic activities are only justifiable if they are intended to serve this higher goal in the human community.

> Besides the good of the individual, there is a good that is linked to living in society: the common good. This is the good of "all of us" made up of individuals, families and intermediate groups who together constitute society. (CV 7)

All layers of society have to take subsidiary responsibilities to reach this common good. In the interpretation of the encyclical, subsidiarity is seen as "guiding criterion for fraternal cooperation between believers and non-believers" and "an expression of inalienable human freedom" (CV 57). However, Pope Benedict XVI remembers that the tenet of subsidiarity formulates a principle of assistance and is not meant to replace individual efforts:

> Subsidiarity is first and foremost a form of assistance to the human person via the autonomy of intermediate bodies. Such assistance is offered when individuals or groups are unable to accomplish something on their own, and it is always designed to achieve their emancipation, because it fosters freedom and participation through the assumption of responsibility. (CV 57)

Consequently, the principle of subsidiarity is strictly linked to the principle of solidarity: without solidarity, there is the risk that subsidiarity will degenerate into social privatism, and without subsidiarity, solidarity leads to social paternalism (CV 58). Notably, in the context of a globalizing world subsidiarity and solidarity must be seen as guiding principles which guarantee the autonomy and independence of all members of society, especially for those citizens living in less developed countries, and allow for the shaping and coordinating of the various activities of different groups in society, always with a view to the common good (CV 47). Although Benedict XVI believes that "the principle of subsidiarity is particularly well-suited to managing globalization and to directing it towards authentic human development" (CV 57) his explanations concerning the duties of the various layers in a globalizing society remain quite vague and unspecific. Particularly regarding the role of multinational corporations and their duties in a societal order organized around the principle of subsidiarity, the encyclical does not sufficiently address their duties or discuss possible fields where responsibilities have to be shared. However, although not discussed in the encyclical explicitly, the tenet of subsidiarity may also function as a guiding principle for delimiting and defining corporate duties and thus may contribute to the discussion about CSR. To indicate how the tenet of subsidiarity may possibly contribute to the current CSR-discussion the following chapter gives a short overview of the European understanding of CSR and outlines the difficulties arising if CSR is seen mainly as voluntary corporate contribution to societal and environmental development (cf. European Commission 2001, p. 8). To overcome this weakness of the European understanding of CSR the tenet of subsidiarity will be reconsidered as a principle shaping responsibilities of political, civil, and economic actors in the context of a globalizing society.

## 2 CSR as a "parallel universe" – different interpretations of CSR

In recent business research CSR has become one of the most prominent topics. Even though there are an increasing number of publications on this subject, a commonly accepted definition of CSR is still lacking (cf. Crane et al. 2009; Aßländer and Löhr 2010). The reasons for this shortcoming are manifold: from different understandings of CSR in Europe (cf. European Commission 2001) and the United States (e.g. Carroll 1979, 2004); different rationales for CSR (cf. Garriga and Melé 2004); to an insufficient delimitation of CSR from similar conceptions like corporate citizenship (e.g. Buchholtz and Carroll 2009) or sustainability (cf. Montiel 2006; Ebner and Baumgartner 2006). In contrast to the US interpretation, the European understanding of CSR is shaped by the idea of sustainable development. As Norman Bowie and Patricia Werhane point out, the orientation of the triple bottom-line (cf. Elkington 1999, 2004) and the obligation to discuss corporate policy with stakeholders is one of the basic differences between US and European concepts of CSR (cf. Bowie and Werhane 2005, p. 114). Furthermore, in most European countries with developed welfare systems, corporate philanthropy, one of the major fields of CSR-engagement in the United States, is seen as superfluous because such responsibilities are primarily interpreted as governmental tasks (Matten and Moon 2008; Carroll 2004).

In Europe, political bodies like the European Commission have become the main drivers for promoting the idea of corporate social responsibility whereby CSR is commonly seen as a voluntary contribution by corporations to sustainable economic, social, and ecological development (cf. European Commission 2001). In its well known

"Green Paper – Promoting a European Framework for Corporate Social Responsibility" the European Commission defines CSR as:

> a concept whereby companies integrate social and environmental concerns in their business operations and in their interaction with their stakeholders on a voluntary basis. (European Commission 2001, p. 8)

Thus, the Commission highlights two different aspects of such responsibility. From a management perspective CSR presents a demand for business entities to ensure that their business is conducted in accordance with fundamental ethical standards. From a political perspective, corporations are seen as quasi-governmental actors that should engage voluntarily for a better society.

### A CSR as a technical imperative: the management perspective of CSR

From a management perspective, CSR aims to improve governance principles of organizations. In this sense, ethical standards that function as minimum requirements for a company's day-to-day business practices have to be defined:

> As issues of corporate social responsibility become an integral part of corporate strategic planning and routine operational performance, managers and employees are required to make business decisions based on additional criteria to those they were traditionally trained to expect. (European Commission, 2001, p. 17)

As the Commission points out, such ethical principles should be the basis for human resource management, health and safety policy, environmental management, and shape the relation to customers, employees, and local communities (cf. European Commission 2001). Nevertheless, the Green Paper remains vague concerning concrete norms that should be binding for companies and how they are to be integrated into business procedures. Other documents are more precise. The International Standard Organization (ISO), for instance, offers concrete guidelines and guidance to organizations for implementing core principles of social responsibility in their business. In its "ISO 26000 – Guidance Document on Social Responsibility" the ISO 26000 working group defines their responsibility as the:

> responsibility of an organization for the impact of its decisions and activities on society and the environment through transparent

> and ethical behaviour that contributes to sustainable development, including health and welfare of society; takes into account the expectations of stakeholders; is in compliance with applicable law and consistent with international norms of behaviour; and is integrated throughout the organization and practised in its relationships. (ISO 26000 2009, pp. 3–4)

To this end the working group outlines seven basic principles of responsible organizational policy including: (1) Accountability which means that management is answerable to the controlling organs of an organization, to legal authorities and to society in general; (2) transparency which means that an organization should disclose its policies and activities and their likely impact on society in an accurate and readily available manner; (3) ethical behavior as the standard of corporate behavior and which should include, at least, honesty, equity, and integrity; (4) respect for stakeholder interests, that is respect for the rights and legitimate interests of all groups that affect or can be affected by corporate policy; (5) respect for the rule of law which constitutes a mandatory corporate obligation to obey national and international law; (6) respect for international norms of behavior which mainly refers to international standards concerning environmental protection, workers' rights, or fighting corruption, especially in those countries where such rights are not protected or enforced by governmental institutions; (7) respect for human rights, which is seen as a universal principle of corporate behavior and is not negotiable (cf. ISO 26000 2009, pp. 10–14).

It is obvious that ISO 26000 has a strict focus on the implementation of ethical standards in corporate policy and stresses a managerial obligation to adhere to internationally accepted ethical principles and to enforce them throughout the corporation.

## B CSR as governmental demand: the political perspective of CSR

Although the Green Paper is concerned with the business dimension of CSR, the European Commission mainly highlights the necessity of strengthening and supporting voluntary contributions of corporations to social welfare and environmental development. The commission explains: "By stating their social responsibility…companies endeavour to raise the standards of social development, environmental protection and respect of fundamental rights…" (European Commission 2001: 4) and sees CSR as "a concept whereby companies decide voluntarily to contribute to a better society and a cleaner environment" (European Commission 2001, p. 5).

In this sense, corporations, as good corporate citizens, have to contribute to their social and natural environment by providing additional services that go beyond their regular activities. This is because corporations profit from society in many respects (e.g. legal security, infrastructure, educated workforce) and therefore have to give something back to the communities in which they exist (cf. Crane and Matten 2007, pp. 71–73; Bowie 1999, pp. 94–95; Enquete-Kommission 2002, pp. 458–459).

Nevertheless, from a political perspective such a view of a voluntary engagement suffers from a fundamental shortcoming. On the one hand, governments and society expect an additional contribution from companies. On the other, it remains up to the companies whether, in which field, and to which extent they want to contribute to social welfare. Thus, the CSR-definition of the Commission as "a concept whereby companies decide voluntary to contribute to a better society" creates a kind of "parallel universe" where the idea of corporate responsibility is used in parallel to the idea of governmental regulation. As a consequence, social or environmental problems should be solved either by nation governments, voluntary engagement of corporations, or by collaboration of public and private actors.

However, it remains unclear how the tasks should be shared. Thus, three modes of corporate contributions could be distinguished. It must be discussed whether corporations have (1) to *substitute*, (2) to *supplement*, or (3) to *compensate* for unperformed governmental duties in the selected areas (cf. Aßländer 2011, 119–120).

1. Corporate engagement as a substitute for governmental activities would mean that corporations provide services that create a choice between governmental or private delivery. Such services provide alternatives to governmental delivery in a specific sector. So, for example, corporations may found private business schools or endow hospitals, orphanages or establish retirement programs or worker insurance additional to governmental services. In these cases governments set standards, for example, for educational programs or healthcare services, but accept corporate engagement in these areas if it meets the predefined standards.
2. Supplementing government by corporate activities means either that existing governmental services are extended by additional opportunities financed by corporate actors or that new services are provided in the form of public-private partnerships that would not have been executed by government alone due to restricted financial capacity

or limited appropriate management skills. Thus, for example, in the first case an endowed chair or privately-financed research project may extend the educational and research opportunities of state universities, and in the second example corporations might contribute to reaching the UN Millennium Goals by participating in the "Partnerships for Development" program of the United Nations.

3. Compensation for a lack of government services means that governments cut down their engagement and withdraw from classical fields of social and environmental politics. Services formerly provided by the government or the community no longer exist, and instead it is the private financer, namely corporate donors that covers the need. Note that the pressure for corporate engagement that compensates for withdrawn governmental activity is not limited to the financial aspect. Some scholars consider corporations to be quasi-governmental actors which engage to administer citizenship rights (a) in cases where governments fail to administer citizenship rights, (b) where governments have not as yet administered such rights or (c) the same where the administration of such rights is out of reach of nation-state regulation (cf. Matten and Crane 2005).

Although Matten and Crane point out that they just want to outline recent developments and to show how corporations have entered the political arena as administrators of citizenship rights, the question remains whether such failures of governmental regulations as have been seen inevitably creates a duty for corporations to assume these obligations, or whether communities should be concerned with improving governmental involvement and performance in this area. Moreover, in all cases where governments take this conception as a pretext to reduce their efforts around environmental and social issues it will lead to serious problems.

Whereas the first two cases seem to be less problematic, the latter causes difficulties. If corporations should compensate for a lack of state activities on a voluntary basis and without specified objectives or areas of engagement, it is doubtful that corporate activities can really compensate for a reduced engagement of nation states in all relevant areas, and on a sustained basis to boot. To clarify corporate duties and societal responsibilities a political conception is needed that allows for differentiation between corporate and governmental obligations. The thesis of this author is that the conception of subsidiarity as it is formulated in Catholic Social Teaching and set out in various encyclicals might provide a solution for the questions of when, in which spheres, and under which circumstances do corporations have to take on social responsibility.

## 3 Subsidiarity and CSR in the light of the Catholic social encyclicals

The tenet of subsidiarity, as referred to in *Caritas in Veritate* and other encyclicals, clarifies that, especially in the social context, nothing should be assigned to a larger community that can be accomplished by a smaller and subordinate entity (QA 79; CV 48; *Compendium* 2004 185–186). Thus, Pope Pius XI in his encyclical *Quadragesimo Anno* points out:

> Just as it is gravely wrong to take from individuals what they can accomplish by their own initiative and industry and give it to the community, so also it is an injustice and at the same time a grave evil and disturbance of right order to assign to a greater and higher association what lesser and subordinate organizations can do. For every social activity ought of its very nature to furnish help to the members of the body social, and never destroy and absorb them. ... The supreme authority of the State ought, therefore, to let subordinate groups handle matters and concerns of lesser importance. (QA 79–80)

The principle of subsidiarity serves as a norm for task-sharing among governmental and private actors as well as an organizational principle for corporations. Whereas, on the one hand, subsidiarity defends the subordinate entities against illegitimate overregulation of higher societal or political organs if the objectives in question can be achieved at the lower level, it constitutes, on the other, a right to assistance if the subordinate entities are unable to solve their problems themselves (cf. Nell-Breuning 1964, 1968). Referring to the problems of the "Social Assistance State" Pope John Paul II in his encyclical letter *Centesimus annus* mentions both impacts:

> Malfunctions and defects in the Social Assistance State are the result of an inadequate understanding of the tasks proper to the State. Here again the principle of subsidiarity must be respected: a community of a higher order should not interfere in the internal life of a community of a lower order, depriving the latter of its functions, but rather should support it in case of need and help to coordinate its activity

> with the activities of the rest of society, always with a view to the common good. (CA 48)

Similarly, in his new encyclical Pope Benedict XVI sees subsidiarity foremost as an evolutionary principle enabling personal self-realization and development aimed at affirming rights but also based on the idea of corresponding individual self-responsibilities (CV 47).

We have recently seen cases of scholars extending the principle of subsidiarity to the organizational context; thus, for example, Melé (2005) argues that organizations that follow the principle of subsidiarity guarantee a higher degree of worker autonomy and are therefore ethically preferable to organizations that violate it. In this sense, subsidiarity is seen as a principle respecting personal dignity and freedom and thus can function as an ethical norm shaping organizational structures. Furthermore, under the condition of global economy, subsidiarity is also discussed as an organizational principle for shaping responsibilities and interrelations of political, civil, and economic actors in a globalizing society. Thus, for example, John Kelly discusses subsidiarity as a principle for regulating business and political relations among nation states in a global society, and widens the scope of subsidiarity by integrating supranational institutions in his conception (Kelly 2004).

Pope Benedict XVI strengthens the importance of subsidiarity regarding globalization. In his encyclical *Caritas in Veritate*, he points out:

> the governance of globalization must be marked by subsidiarity, articulated into several layers and involving different levels that can work together. Globalization certainly requires authority, insofar as it poses the problem of a global common good that needs to be pursued. This authority, however, must be organized in a subsidiary and stratified way. (CV 57)

Although he is right in claiming that "integral development of peoples and international cooperation require the establishment of a greater degree of international ordering" and "the construction of a social order that at last conforms to the moral order" (CV 67), Pope Benedict XVI seems to be too optimistic when he describes the specifications of such an international authority. He points out that such an authority would need to be regulated by international law, would be obliged to follow the principles of subsidiarity and solidarity, and should be internationally recognized and vested with executive power to guarantee the observance of principles of social justice (CV 67).

Hence it is all the more important to focus on the role of corporations in a globalizing economy shaped by the principle of subsidiarity. Although not directly addressed in the encyclical, corporate actors have become important players in the field of civil-governmental task-sharing and must be accepted as a new group of intermediate actors in the sense of the tenet of subsidiarity. It is obvious that the extension of corporate responsibilities for social and environmental issues, as proposed, for example, by the European Commission, cannot mean that corporations have to compensate governmental responsibilities but that they bear a subsidiary co-responsibility for social and environmental issues in their communities. Therefore, in the context of globalization, CSR should not be seen as a voluntary contribution of corporations to social and economic sustainability but must be developed as a core element of subsidiary responsibilities.

## 4 CSR as subsidiary co-responsibility

In a "post-national" world the principle of subsidiarity seems to be at least redundant if not outdated. In recent academic discussion about CSR, corporations are often seen as new political actors in a globalizing world that can no longer be controlled by nation-state regulations or governmental law. In particular, multinational enterprises are able to bypass nation-state regulations by shifting their activities to countries with less restrictive regulations. However, corporations and corporate behavior are not without monitoring and regulation. The power of control is now with NGOs that are able to ensure the acceptable behavior of multinational corporations by threatening them with shaming campaigns or boycotts (e.g. Scherer and Palazzo 2007, 2008, 2009; Palazzo and Scherer, 2006; Matten and Crane 2005; Crane and Matten 2007).

On the other hand, nation states have not become powerless. As Anthony Giddens points out, governments faced a two-fold devolution of power that led to a decrease but also to an increase of power:

> Globalization creates a strong impetus and logic to the downward devolution of power, but also to upward devolution. Rather than merely weakening the authority of the nation-state, this double movement – a movement of double democratization – is the condition of reasserting that authority, since this movement can make the state more responsive to the influences that otherwise outflank it all round. (Giddens 1998, p. 72)

In this sense nation states are not outdated; nevertheless, they have to redefine their political authority. Governments increasingly have to play the role of mediators balancing the various interests and efforts of political, economic and civil actors (cf. Giddens 1998, p. 53).

This leads back to the discussion of corporate responsibilities. As far as the political aspect of CSR aims to include corporate actors into the process of generating social accomplishment governments need clear rules to define the specific areas where corporate efforts are necessary or desired. Whereas additional voluntary contributions of corporations can be considered to be less problematic in this context, the possible compensation of governmental by corporate activities has to be discussed in more detail.

The principle of subsidiarity describes mutual responsibilities of lower and higher order instances in society and defines in a clear manner how duties should be shared: (1) Issues of lesser importance should be handled by lower instances if these are able to do so; (2) in such cases the accomplishment by lower order instances is seen as an essential duty; (3) in areas of higher importance for society or in cases where subordinates are unable to solve their problems, governmental interventions are necessary.

Applied to the CSR-discussion this would mean that we have to conceptualize CSR as including a perspective that interprets CSR as corporate co-responsibility in accordance with the principle of subsidiarity. In this sense, corporations play the role of intermediate social actors like clerical, political, or economic associations and bear specific duties to enable and to foster civic rights. Whether such duties might be assigned as legal obligations by an international authority, as Pope Benedict would prefer, or whether such duties must be seen as a purely moral commitment of corporations is an important political question. Given the fact that such an international authority is not yet on the horizon, it seems to be more realistic to base the principle of subsidiary corporate co-responsibility on the idea of moral obligation and the self-understanding of corporations as part of society. Nevertheless, such duties do not derive from the factual engagement of corporations but result from political and moral obligations in a societal order shaped by the principle of subsidiarity. Especially in those fields where societal tasks can be carried out more efficiently by lower order organs and these organs have adequate competencies and experiences and sufficient means to accomplish these tasks in accordance with the principle of subsidiary task-sharing, the lower order organs have at least a moral obligation to do so. In this sense corporate subsidiary co-responsibility would mean that corporations bear specific duties in fields where social or environmental problems can be solved by them more easily due to their higher competencies (cf. Dunfee and Hess 2000). Thus, for example, corporations have to contribute to the ongoing education of their workforce, so as to maintain their long-term employability. Similarly, they have to collaborate in professional associations to develop industrial or professional standards, or to foster the reintegration of unemployed in the labor market.

Although it is debatable how far such corporate co-responsibility will reach and in which areas corporate contributions can be expected, corporate engagement in this field is not an option but an essential obligation. Even though regulatory standards are needed to steer corporate CSR activities in globalizing economies, democratic decisions have to be taken about which areas corporations are expected to engage in, and under which conditions, and which areas must remain "corporate-free."

As a concluding remark, we can add that further research might concern how distinct subsidiary co-responsibilities of corporations can be identified in detail; in "post-national" globalizing societies the assignment of distinct co-responsibilities will depend on deliberative democratic processes at a national and supranational level. Additional research in the fields of political and social sciences would help to clarify how the assignment of corporate co-responsibilities can be backed by legitimate democratic decision processes.

## Executive summary

CSR as defined by the European Commission focuses on two different aspects of CSR. One is the necessity of implementing CSR-relevant aspects in the governance structures of corporations to assure that policies and procedures adhere to minimal ethical requirements. The other is that corporations should contribute to a better society and a cleaner environment by additional voluntary activities. The latter aspect especially raises serious questions about the state of corporate activities in such a political view of CSR. First of all, it remains unclear whether and where corporations have to substitute, to supplement or to compensate for a lack of governmental efforts. In particular the "mode" of compensation poses serious problems because – given that such activities are considered to be voluntary contributions in discretionary fields – it cannot be taken for granted that corporate activities can compensate for unperformed governmental duties in all relevant areas on a sustained basis.

To solve this problem CSR should be completed by a third perspective that focuses on a subsidiary co-responsibility of corporations and allows for the defining of corporate duties that go beyond good management practices and are more concrete than voluntary engagement. In this sense corporations are seen as intermediate instances that have to bear concrete duties in a system of subsidiary societal task-sharing. Thus, three areas of CSR can be differentiated:

1. The technical aspect of CSR focuses on management procedures and governance structures in corporations and defines ethical standards that should become part of a company's day-to-day business practices.
2. CSR as subsidiary co-responsibility describes non-voluntary responsibilities of corporations that result from their role as intermediate social actors; such engagement is legitimated by democratic structures and the regulatory principle of subsidiarity and defines long-term corporate duties in society.
3. CSR as voluntary contribution refers to the occasionally philanthropic engagement of corporations that might assist governmental efforts in the fields of social development or environmental protection.

Thus, from the perspective of subsidiarity as outlined above, corporations have at least a moral obligation to accomplish "what can be accomplished by a lesser and subordinate entity" (QA 79).

## References

Aßländer, M.S. "Corporate social responsibility as subsidiary co-responsibility: A macroeconomic perspective." *Journal of Business Ethics,* Vol. 99, 1, 2011: 115–128.

Aßländer, M.S. and A. Löhr. "Zum Klärungsbedarf der Modevokabel 'Corporate Social Responsibility'." In M.S. Aßländer and A. Löhr, eds. *Corporate Social Responsibility in der Wirtschaftskrise.* München: Rainer Hampp, 2010.

Benedict XVI. "Address of his Holiness Benedict XVI to the "Centesimus annus –Pro pontifice" foundation." In A.Q. Curzio and G. Marseguerra, eds. *Social Capital and Human Development.* Milano: Libri Scheiwiller, 2009.

Bowie, N.E. *Business Ethics – A Kantian Perspective.* Malden, MA: Blackwell, 1999.

Bowie, N.E. and P.H. Werhane. *Management Ethics.* Malden, MA: Blackwell, 2005.

Buchholtz, A.K. and A.B. Carroll. *Business and Society.* Mason, OH: South-Western, 2009.

Carroll, A.B. "A three-dimensional conceptual model of corporate social performance." *Academy of Management Review,* Vol. 4, 4, 1979: 497–505.

Carroll, A.B. "Managing ethically with global stakeholders: A present and future challenge." *The Academy of Management Executive,* Vol. 18, 2, 2004: 114–120.

Crane, A. and D. Matten. *Business Ethics.* Oxford: Oxford University Press, 2007.

Crane, A., A. McWilliams, D. Matten, J. Moon and D. S. Siegel. "The corporate social responsibility agenda." In A. Crane, A. McWilliams, D. Matten, J. Moon and D. S. Siegel, eds. *The Oxford Handbook of Corporate Social Responsibility.* Oxford: Oxford University Press, 2009: 3–15.

Dunfee, T.W. and D. Hess. "The legitimacy of direct corporate humanitarian investment." *Business Ethics Quarterly,* Vol. 10, 1, 2000: 95–109.

Ebner, D. and R.J. Baumgartner. "The relationship between sustainable development and corporate social responsibility." *Corporate Responsibility Research Conference,* Dublin, September 2006.

Elkington, J. *Cannibals with Forks – The Triple Bottom Line of 21st Century Business.* Oxford: Capstone, 1999.

Elkington, J. "Enter the triple bottom line." In A. Henriques and J. Richardson, eds. *The Triple Bottom Line, Does it all Add up?* London: Earthscan, 2004.

Enquete-Kommission. *Zukunft des Bürgerschaftlichen Engagements. Deutscher Bundestag – Bericht: Bürgerschaftliches Engagement: auf dem Weg in eine zukunftsfähige Bürgergesellschaft.* Opladen: Verlag Leske und Budrich, 2002.

European Commission. *Green Paper Promoting a European Framework for Corporate Social Responsibility COM(2001) 366.* Brussels: Commission of the European Communities, 2001.

Garriga, E. and D. Melé. "Corporate social responsibility theories: Mapping the territory." *Journal of Business Ethics,* Vol. 53, 1–2, 2004.

Giddens, A. *The Third Way. The Renewal of Social Democracy.* Cambridge: Policy Press, 1998.

ISO 26000. *Draft International Standard ISO/DIS 26000 – Guidance on Social Responsibility* ICS 03.100.01. Genève: ISO Copyright Office, 2009.

Kelly, J.E. "Solidarity and subsidiarity: 'Organizing principles' for corporate moral leadership in the new global economy." *Journal of Business Ethics,* Vol. 52, 3, 2004: 283–295.

Matten, D. and A. Crane. "Corporate citizenship: Toward an extended theoretical conceptualization." *Academy of Management Review,* Vol. 30, 1, 2005: 166–179.

Matten, D. and J. Moon. "'Implicit' and 'Explicit' CSR: A conceptual framework for a comparative understanding of corporate social responsibility." *Academy of Management Review,* Vol. 33, 2, 2008: 404–424.

Melé, D. "Exploring the principle of subsidiarity in organizational forms." *Journal of Business Ethics,* Vol. 60, 3, 2005: 293–305.

Montiel, I. "Corporate social responsibility and corporate sustainability – separate pasts, common futures." *Organization & Environment,* Vol. 21, 3, 2006: 245–269.

Nell-Breuning, O. v. *Christliche Soziallehre.* Mannheim: Pesch-Haus, 1964.

Nell-Breuning, O. v. *Baugesetze der Gesellschaft.* Freiburg im Breisgau: Herder, 1968.

Palazzo, G. and A.G. Scherer. "Corporate legitimacy as deliberation. A communicative framework." *Journal of Business Ethics*, Vol. 66, 1, 2006: 71–88.

Scherer, A.G. and G. Palazzo. "Toward a political conception of corporate responsibility: Business and society seen from a Habermasian perspective." *Academy of Management Review, Vol.* 32, 4, 2007: 1096–1120.

Scherer, A.G. and G. Palazzo. "The future of global corporate citizenship: Toward a new theory of the firm as a political actor." In A.G. Scherer and G. Palazzo, eds. *Handbook of Research on Global Corporate Citizenship.* Cheltenham: Edward Elgar, 2008.

Scherer, A.G. and G. Palazzo. "Globalization and CSR", in A. Crane, A. McWilliams, D. Matten, J. Moon and D.S. Siegel, eds. *The Oxford Handbook of Corporate Social Responsibility.* Oxford: Oxford University Press, 2009.

# Part II

# Management and Human Development

# 7
# Human Development and Business Practice

*Robert G. Kennedy*

> Profit is useful if it serves as a means towards an end that provides a sense both of how to produce it and how to make good use of it. Once profit becomes the exclusive goal, if it is produced by improper means and without the common good as its ultimate end, it risks destroying wealth and creating poverty. (CV 21)

In recent years, the world has had a jarring set of lessons about economic fragility and interdependence. We have been reminded that a relatively small number of people in key positions can make decisions that have broad and sometimes very harmful consequences. This realization brings many people to wonder about the benefits of business and free markets.

More than any of his predecessors, Pope Benedict XVI has turned his attention, in the encyclical *Caritas in Veritate*, to the role that business plays in the contemporary global community. He reminds us that business, and economic systems generally, must have the well-being of human persons as their ultimate goal. To forget this, to substitute as goals what are merely instruments (e.g., profit, efficiency, market share) is to invite distortion and even disaster.

This chapter provides background and context for Pope Benedict's analysis of business and the contribution its activities may and ought to provide to the human community. Grounded in a conception of the human person that rejects the excesses of both liberal economic theory and socialism, his writing offers new possibilities for understanding the nature and function of business. In particular, this chapter explores the implications for business of his convictions about the nature of authentic human development and the importance of gratuity, or beneficence, for sound business practice.

## 1 The economists and the Popes

The early economists, to the degree that they considered themselves scientists of a sort, were inclined to model their discipline on the physical sciences, which is to say that they were engaged in investigating and discerning the order and regularity of the economy, which they understood to be a reality, like the natural world of the physicist and chemist, that human persons could observe but did not create.[1] Of course, even though economists generally agreed that this objective reality they called the "economy" was characterized by observable laws, they disagreed strongly about the content of those laws.

Whatever their particular disputes, economists tended to regard the economy as a reality not only governed by its own laws and logic but also as an arena that was inherently amoral. That is to say, since the economy was an objective reality, as distinct from a human artifact, its rules and regularities lay outside moral evaluation because they were, at root, outside human control. At least two important implications followed from all this.

One was that it made no more sense to think of the economy as something that ought to serve human well-being than it would to think that the weather ought to serve human interests. What was required was that persons adapt to economic regularities and not attempt to shape the economy to their ends. The second implication was that conflict was inevitable in the economic sphere. On the socialist analysis, those who possessed and controlled wealth would resist the historic inevitability of economic progress (e.g. from capitalism to socialism) and class conflict would be required to overcome this resistance. On the liberal analysis, attempts to manage the marketplace would be more or less marginal and ineffectual and the conflict of natural selection would continue apace.

*Rerum novarum* (1891), by Pope Leo XIII, was an initial effort to address some of the issues of the day.[2] Subsequent encyclicals affirmed, augmented, and refined the themes of *Rerum novarum* and often added further topics and insights. The fundamental source of disagreement between the popes and the economists has always been divergent conceptions of the nature of the human person. This divergence has many elements but we can focus on two.

One element concerns the relationship between the person and the community. Economists inclined to the socialist vision are likely to see the community as the prior reality and the individual as subordinate to the community, even to the point of being simply expendable for the sake of important community objectives. Alternately, liberal economists, influenced by such philosophers as Hobbes and Locke, are likely to understand individual persons as radically isolated by nature. That is, human persons are at their best (in principle, at least) when living in isolation. They are free of the burdens and obstacles constituted by other persons and (in principle, at least) entirely free to choose and pursue any objectives they wish to achieve their personal fulfillment.

A second element is in some ways more profound. Economists generally deny the transcendent destiny of the human person. Socialists tend to be materialists and so will deny that there is any immaterial or spiritual destiny to which human persons are drawn and ought to orient themselves. Liberals may agree with the materialist thesis or they may declare themselves agnostic about the possibility of immaterial ends of human life. In any event, whether transcendence is denied outright, marginalized as doubtful, or simply privatized,[3] the common view is that the idea has no relevance for the discipline of economics. An entailment of this is that transcendence has no place in deliberations about public policy or workplace practice.

These views, though they may now be associated with different schools of economic thought from those of the 19th century, are with us still today. Following Leo XIII, the popes have responded by trying to flesh out an alternative to the visions of the economists. In *Caritas in Veritate*, Pope Benedict XVI continues this project.

In the Catholic tradition, in contrast with the economists, the first thing we must say is that each human person is an image of God, which is to say that each person without exception possesses some characteristics that mirror (in some diminished way) several of the essential characteristics of God himself, namely, intelligence, freedom, and sociability (GS 12, CCC 311, 1879).

The last element, the claim that human persons are social by nature, stands in sharp contrast to the visions of the economists. For the socialists, community is important, so important that the identity of the individual is created by and even subsumed into the community. In its worst forms, the community becomes identified with the State[4] and the individual life is thought to be no more than an instrument of service to the State (as opposed to the claim that the State exists to promote the welfare of each individual). Individuals have at best a weak claim on the State for what they require for a decent human life, while the State has an absolute claim on what it may require from the individual.

## 2 The Catholic view of the community

For the classic liberal, communities of whatever sort, from families to societies, are merely instruments to promote the satisfaction of individuals. Communities are not natural but rather deliberate objects of choice. That is, human persons, who never cease to be essentially isolated individuals, only derive instrumental benefits from their participation in communities. The participation itself is not a benefit nor is it a natural component of human fulfillment. In fact, persons are by nature neutral with regard to achieving their goals alone or in collaboration with others.[5]

As a result, the normal state of life on the liberal view is competition wherever scarcity is involved. Competition for material goods, for education, for career, for power. The preferred state of affairs is a meritocracy (however "merit" might be defined) which permits talented individuals to acquire the rewards available to their ability, skill, and determination.

By contrast, the Catholic view holds that persons are made for, are hard-wired for, unity and community but not in such a way as to extinguish identity. It is natural for us to form communities in all sorts of ways and we have a preference for acting in common with others over acting alone. Our natural fear is not that we will be compelled to live out our lives surrounded by family and friends but that in the end we will be alone. In John Courtney Murray's lovely phrase, community "is a need of human nature before it becomes the object of human choice."[6] As a result, society is the natural environment for human persons. Participation in social life, with its rich fabric of specialized communities, is itself an element of human fulfillment. The State, which is only one aspect of civil society, is entirely ordered to sustain and protect that society.

The economy is another element of civil society, not independent of it but integrated within it and properly ordered to its well-being. This is a key point because the papal vision of the economy rejects the notion that it is an objective reality that cannot be ordered to serve human well-being. Quite to the contrary, the popes insist that the economy must serve man and that it is abusive to think that man must serve the economy (QA 119, 135). Entailed in this view is the conviction that the economy, here understood as a system of relationships and practices, is fundamentally shaped by an underlying (and perhaps unexamined) conception of the nature of the person. If this conception of the human person, this anthropology, is defective then the economic system built upon it will also be defective and toxic – even if it succeeds in delivering some benefits.

When the popes survey economic structures, they see a mixed package of harms and benefits. For example, in developed countries they see an unprecedented level of material prosperity but at the same time they call attention to assaults on marriage, family, and many other human goods. They see very high levels of consumption without a corresponding elevation in authentic human development; to borrow a phrase from *Gaudium et spes*, they see a great increase in "having" that does not produce an increase in "being" (SRS 28, GS 35). They see a less-developed world, a southern hemisphere, that envies the prosperity of the North but cannot participate in it.

This is not to say that they disparage modern economic development; far from it. They recognize the enormous benefits that modern industry and economic organization has produced but at the same time they see so much unrealized potential and so much waste, that is, energy and resources that are poured into the satisfaction of wants that do not lead to authentic human fulfillment.

What they would prefer to see is the establishment of a global common good. In the classic definition of Pope John XXIII, this common good would be "the sum total of those conditions of social living whereby men are enabled more fully and more readily to achieve their own perfection" (MM 65).

More concretely, these conditions follow from the nature of the human person. As intelligent and free, persons are also creative and responsible. They are "born to labor as the bird to fly" (QA 61) and so should have work that is ordered to genuine human goods, suitable for human persons, and that enables workers to support themselves and their families in reasonable comfort and security. They have a right to own property and conditions should permit them to acquire enough to provide for their immediate economic security, for their retirement, and for a modest legacy for their children (RN 10, 35).

This being said, let us now turn to *Caritas in Veritate*.

## 3 The message of *Caritas in Veritate*

One of the key economic insights of the modern age was the comprehension that wealth can be created through human effort and ingenuity, that it is not simply a fixed resource to be possessed by some and not by others. Throughout much of human history, while nations sometimes sought to increase their wealth through trade (which in principle could make all of the trading partners better off), far too often they chose to acquire wealth through conquest and colonization instead. By the beginning of the 20th century imperial ambitions were waning but the acquisition or creation of wealth was still largely considered a national affair. It was not until the middle of the century, following World War II, that we came to appreciate more fully the interdependence of peoples throughout the world (MM 59–67). It was not until then that we began to perceive a new challenge, which was the goal of creating and sustaining prosperity not merely for one nation but for the whole human community.

This goal, which we came to call development, changed the way we looked at the world. By the time that Pope John XXIII wrote his first social encyclical, *Mater et magistra*, in 1961, it was apparent (to him and his advisors at least) that the content of the social question had shifted and was now focused on the peaceful economic (and political) integration of humankind. Only six years later, Pope Paul VI expanded on this insight when he published *Populorum progressio* (PP), which explicitly focuses on the challenge of development. It was to commemorate and build upon this document that Pope Benedict XVI wrote *Caritas in Veritate*.

To some degree there was a convergence between the visions of Popes John and Paul and movements in the secular world. They agreed that the economic arena was now global and that where once the Economic Problem was how to *distribute* the world's resources, the question for the future was how to *develop* the world's people. But, as has always been the case, the popes saw the situation with different eyes from secular economists. The critical difference had to do with the nature of development itself.

The secular vision is essentially materialist. Development means an increase in the capacity to produce material goods and related services, leading to an increase in capital resources and general wealth.

It should surprise no one that the popes had something different in mind. They insisted that the fulfillment of human persons, as embodied spirits, involved much more than material prosperity alone could provide. To be sure, poverty was a great evil, and lifting populations from poverty was a very worthy goal but it was not enough nor could material prosperity be rightly achieved at the expense of other aspects of human fulfillment. This material prosperity might do a great deal to address the human person's bodily needs but it did not ensure, and might sometimes seriously conflict with, his higher, more fully human potential. To drive this point home, Pope Paul VI distinguished between "economic growth" and human development (PP 14). To be authentic, he insisted, economic growth "must foster the development of each man and of the whole man." In the papal tradition this has come to be called "integral human development."

This notion of integral human development is critical to our understanding of Pope Benedict's views about the proper objective of business operations and so deserves to be explored in greater detail.

Properly speaking, development has both personal and communal aspects. On the personal level, development is a synonym for the process that leads to a fully mature human being. It is, in the most fundamental sense, something persons do for themselves, not something that is done to persons.[7] A lack of material resources – food, shelter, clothing, medical care, and so on – can be a formidable obstacle to personal development but a sufficiency of these resources does not ensure development. As a practical matter, persons need to work at assembling these resources to support themselves and their families but they cannot stop there. Integral development consists in the formation of the intellect (knowledge and wisdom) and personal freedom (moral virtue and skills), in the actualization of the capacity to participate in society and culture, and in deepening one's relationship with God.

However, Benedict goes beyond the discussion of development begun by his predecessors to call our attention to something further, which is embraced by the logic of gift. Human persons are images of God not only insofar as they have intellect and will but also to the extent to which they are givers. God, as Creator, is the giver *par excellence*. Human persons are dependent beings. The world in which we live and even our very lives are gifts, not acts of justice. We have done nothing to deserve what we have received from the Creator.

While our posture with respect to God will always be that of receiver, or taker, we may grow in maturity, we may develop our capacity to be true images of God, by becoming givers with regard to other persons. To put it another way, integral human development involves gradually actualizing our potential to image God and, though it seems contrary to the logic of the world, we pursue this in part by giving of ourselves and not remaining takers only.

On the communal level, development is synonymous with establishing and sustaining the common good of the civil society, which in the modern era embraces the whole of the human community. Broadly speaking, this entails perfecting the three critical dimensions of society: politics, culture, and the economy. The political dimension focuses on the proper functioning of leadership and authority in the community and its exercise of power. The cultural dimension embraces the pursuit of truth and beauty and consists in the shared convictions, rituals, and structures which bind individuals into one people.[8] The economic dimension, of course, is oriented toward the creation, acquisition, and distribution of the material resources required for human life. The successful operation of each of these dimensions is not an end in itself but is, like the common good taken as a whole, instrumentally ordered to the good of each and every person in the community.

Building on this foundation, then, in the context of *Caritas in Veritate*, what does Pope Benedict see when he looks at the contemporary world?

He sees a world in which the economic aspect of human development remains unfulfilled, as it was in Paul VI's time, but not closed off (CV 21). That is, there is much that remains to be done, and the need to do it continues to be urgent, but there is real hope that it can be done. He sees a more complicated challenge to development, as the world has become more interdependent and as distinctions between rich and poor nations have become less clear (CV 22). The gap between the very poor and the very wealthy appears to be growing, especially as the phenomenon of "superdevelopment" noted by Pope John Paul II has not abated (SRS 28). And more acutely than any of his predecessors he notes threats to the natural environment, and correspondingly to future generations, arising from inadequate stewardship of the gift of the Earth (caused in part by our failure to craft supra-national means of exercising authority in response to challenges that span national boundaries) (CV 48–51).

More positively, he insists, with Paul VI, that the obstacles facing economic development are not principally material but more deeply a failure of thought (intellect), commitment (will) and fraternity (solidarity) (CV 19).[9] Without a transcendent vision of the person, "[the possibility of] development is either denied or entrusted exclusively to man, who falls into the trap of thinking he can bring about his own salvation and ends up promoting a dehumanized form of development" (CV 11).

## A Development as a vocation

As Pope Paul suggested, the remedy for this failure of vision is the idea of vocation. This begins with an acknowledgment that so sharply divides secular economic theories from the papal social tradition, the acknowledgment that man is a creature, dependent for his existence, his nature, his abilities, and his future upon a Creator, who lovingly sustains him in being and calls him to fulfillment and a transcendent destiny. This changes the nature of the Economic Problem entirely.

A provident Creator has provided for his creatures; the Christian God is not a God of scarcity but rather a God of abundance. To despair of the possibility of development in the fullest sense is to lack trust in both God and man (CV 14). It is to doubt God's loving providence on the one hand and to underestimate the capacity of human beings to shape their social environment, which includes its economic structures and processes.

But we are called to development; progress is a vocation (CV 16).[10] This is not to be understood as an intimidating challenge but as a gift, an invitation offered to free persons and accepted as the most fundamental exercise of responsible freedom. The recognition of vocation begins in the acknowledgment of dependency and the admission that, absent the invitation from the Creator, the human person is incapable of supplying the ultimate meaning of his own life (CV 16).

The critical importance of transcendence to a proper understanding of human life is why Benedict insists on the necessity of religious freedom for development:

> ...the deliberate promotion of religious indifference or practical atheism on the part of many countries obstructs the requirements for the development of peoples, depriving them of spiritual and human resources. God is the guarantor of man's true development...(CV 29)

Absent religious freedom, and especially when this freedom is discouraged or suppressed by the State, human persons lack not only the orientation to their proper end but also the practical freedom to pursue it.

Finally, the vocation to development has a social character, in keeping with human nature. Persons are not called to develop simply as individuals but rather to use their talents and skills (gifts, after all) to assist one another to progress. This is true at both the personal level and at the level of relations between nations. Recognizing this as a vocation gives us the courage to open ourselves to the needs of others.

### B The Principle of Gratuitousness

In *Caritas in Veritate*, Benedict introduces the concept of gift, which is not new in the social tradition, and also the Principle of Gratuitousness, which is new. Although the principle is never articulated in the document, perhaps we can tease out its meaning and situate it within the larger moral tradition.

Gratuity implies a unilateral act, something done not in response to the prior act of another but a free act not chosen in expectation of reciprocity. Gratuity differs essentially from exchange, in which a response is required to preserve the equality of the partners to the exchange. To be sure, gratuity calls for a response but it is a response of gratitude, not an action on the part of the recipient that seeks to restore equality with the giver. For Christians, this is more than anything else a description of their posture before God, whose gifts to human persons are wholly gratuitous, are acts of love for human creatures and never acts of justice (CV 34).

As we consider our status as creatures, nothing can be more fundamental than the recognition of our dependency and God's gratuity. This must be the model for our relationship to and interaction with one another. As beneficiaries of God's merciful love, we should also love one another and will for each person we encounter the genuine good for that person just as far as it is in our power to support it. Such support entails not merely a passive inclination to rejoice in the good that comes to others but also a willingness to seize opportunities to act to ensure that good. I submit that this can be taken as an articulation of the Principle of Gratuitousness and further, that this is consistent with the classic moral virtue of beneficence.

According to St Thomas, the virtue of beneficence is related to the virtue of charity.[11] It is the virtue by which we are habitually moved to seek the good of those we love, and since in charity the love we have for God spills over into love for all of his human creatures, beneficence moves us to seek the good of all. And our confidence in God's providence, rooted in the experience we already have of His gifts, assures us that in actively seeking the good of others we are not compromising or surrendering our own good. Gratuitousness and beneficence, then, properly orient and make possible genuine human cooperation in the economic arena and suppress destructive forms of competition.

## C Creating "space" for the logic of gift

Benedict speaks in *Caritas in Veritate* of the need to create space in the economic sphere for the creation and operation of businesses that will be animated by the logic of gift (CV 20, 37). We might understand this to mean that there is a need for changes in attitude in several different areas that will open the way for new possibilities in organizing and managing businesses. Let me suggest only a few arenas in which these changes may be necessary and appropriate.

First, the way in which we conceive of the proper role and objectives of management will need to be adjusted. We have come to think of management as a technical exercise. The objective is given – make the maximum profit possible – and the manager is conceived as a technician who will bring certain skills to this task. To create room for new forms of business, management must come to understand that its goals are really aspects of human well-being and that it serves these goals *professionally*, just as physicians, lawyers, engineers, and other professionals serve human well-being in their proper arenas.

Second, investors ought to reconsider what their proper objectives ought to be in investing their resources (which are gifts, after all) in enterprises. It is certainly reasonable to seek an adequate return on investment but the percentage return cannot be the only factor employed in judging adequacy. We create room for the logic of gift and for new forms of business when we acknowledge that serving (or at least not harming) the well-being of employees and customers is an important consideration in making investment decisions. Managers who are punished by financial markets for serving a wider range of goals than profit alone are denied the space that Benedict says they require. Indeed, though he does not suggest this, one could imagine the possibility of creating special investment vehicles (or even special capital markets) that would embrace a broader range of goals and insulate managers from the destructive pressures of present financial systems.

Third, in some nations it may be appropriate to provide space by changing laws concerning publicly-held corporations. In some jurisdictions, the prevailing law tends to assume that the over-riding duty of management is to maximize returns to shareholders. Managers who might embrace the logic of gift risk provoking litigation from shareholders whose only interest is in higher profitability.[12] In some instances (for example, to discourage hostile takeovers), legislatures in various parts of the United States have changed laws permitting managers to consider harms and benefits to various stakeholder groups and indemnifying them against shareholder litigation if their good business judgment on behalf of these stakeholders results in a marginally smaller return to shareholders.

Benedict also alludes to new forms of business associations, which might include a blending of for-profit and not-for-profit elements in ways that do not fit neatly into existing categories. Changes in law and practice may be necessary to make these experiments possible as well.

## 4 Some implications of *Caritas in Veritate* for business

By introducing the logic of gift and the idea of gratuity, Benedict invites us to reconsider the dominant model we employ to think about business. This dominant model is shaped by the logic of exchange, which tends to present business as a network of transactions between employers and employees, vendors and customers, and companies and investors. The parties to these transactions give only in expectation of return, which creates a sharp focus on a narrow range of results, notably profits, wages, and return on investment. The highest value in this system is justice, which is surely not unimportant, but this also closes off other possibilities. Furthermore, the logic of exchange inclines participants to treat one another impersonally, as neighbors, perhaps, but not as brothers (CV 19).

By contrast, the logic of gift opens up new possibilities, leading in the direction of charity, beneficence, fraternity, and solidarity. The logic of gift as applied to business begins with the assumption that giving, not taking, is not only the starting point for human development but is also the model for development in the economic order. To be sure, just as not all individuals mature from being receivers and takers to being givers, so also much of the economic sphere will not move beyond the logic of exchange. Nevertheless, it may be possible for some businesses to do so. Benedict wishes to outline the practical form this development might take and to encourage the creation of "space" for enterprises to explore it.

The logic of gift and the idea of gratuity challenge the conventional notion of what business is about. A business animated by the logic of gift will still engage in transactions and still be bound by the requirements of justice. The logic of gift is not a substitute for the logic of exchange; it embraces that logic and completes it, opening up new possibilities for serving human welfare through the economic order. It does this by reconceiving the purposes of business and the measures of success.

For example, the logic of gift suggests a different view of the role of profit in a business. The new objective of a business is to serve in some concrete way the well-being of each of the individuals associated with it: managers and employees, customers and investors. The particular well-being of these persons, considered in the context of what the business is able to provide (good employment, useful products and services, sound investment) is the real measure of success of the business. On this account, profit is not evil but it must be understood as a means and never an end. That is to say, profit is like nourishment to an organism;

without food the organism dies and without profit (or more broadly, a surplus of revenues over expenses) no organization can continue to operate. Every responsible manager, no matter what the nature of the organization (and this includes the Church), should aim at operating "profitably," or at least in such a way as to avoid waste and loss. A serious problem arises when profit comes to be regarded not as a necessary condition that permits the organization to continue its operations but as the end of the operations after all (CV 21). This is especially serious when the pursuit of profit dominates and distorts the arena of finance.[13]

The logic of gift also provokes us to think differently about other aspects of business. For example, the conventional view tends to assume a condition of scarcity, such that competition becomes destructive rather than a common pursuit of excellence. In its worst forms, this destructive competition focuses a company's efforts on defeating or eliminating its competitors, not on improving its products and services or the well-being of its stakeholders. The logic of gift, by contrast, acknowledges that the Creator is a God of abundance, not scarcity, and therefore people in business may use their gifts and talents in full pursuit of excellence, confident that they do not do so in vain. This does not imply a sort of altruism or self-sacrifice but rather a complete rejection of destructive competition. Businesses that embrace the logic of gift can be fierce competitors. This ferocity, however, is not hostility toward others but an intense focus using the Creator's gifts as effectively as possible strengthened by a confidence that this pursuit will be rewarded. (Needless to say, the rewards are not merely profits but other aspects of genuine human fulfillment as well.)

Entrepreneurship and business development can also take on a different character. Where the conventional view searches for opportunities for profit, the logic of gift provokes business to assess the gifts it possesses and to search for genuine needs that can be served by these gifts.[14] Profit, once again, becomes a means, not an end. It enables a company to employ its gifts and to continue serving genuine needs, both of which are real human goods that are part of the broader purposes of business. Conceiving of development this way also awakens a business to the needs of the poor, the satisfaction of which needs is a genuine and important contribution to the common good.

The logic of gift is rooted in charity, not justice. The receiver of a gift has, by definition, no right to what he receives. When this logic is brought to the world of business, it focuses the attention of management on the well-being of customers, employees and investors (to name three key stakeholders).[15] In others words, it encourages beneficence, which, for example, moves us to consider not merely what customers want to buy but what in fact are their real needs (CA 36). This, I think should be understood in two ways, one negative and one positive. On the negative side managers should firmly reject the production of goods and services that undermine human well-being – even if there may be a profitable market for such goods and services and even if others will provide them if we do not. I have in mind such obvious things as pornography and non-therapeutic drugs but the list might be expanded to include products that do little more than pander to consumer impulses or encourage waste. To be sure, the freedom of customers must be respected and people will find value and derive pleasure from a wide variety of things and experiences.[16] I am not suggesting that business people priggishly censor their customers' choices but rather that we all give thought to whether what we produce really addresses reasonable human needs.[17]

The more positive aspect of this invites us aggressively to identify needs that we might address that may otherwise be neglected, especially the needs of the poor. The natural tendency, at least from a secular perspective, is not so much to identify needs as to identify opportunities for profit. Beneficence moves us instead to look for the needs and to use our ingenuity to devise ways to make the satisfaction of those needs profitable. So, for example, we might think creatively about the needs of the poor in less-developed countries and try to craft appropriate solutions for those problems, rather than selling them solutions created first for markets in developed countries.

A second group of people to be served is employees. The papal tradition strongly urges that, in addition to respecting the fundamental obligation to pay a fair and living wage, managers should set in place structures that allow workers to earn an ownership interest in the companies to which they contribute their labor (QA 61–62). Pope John Paul spoke of the aspiration that companies be true communities, dedicated to serving human needs and providing a livelihood for all members of the working community (CA 43). But this is only one aspect of seeking the well-being of employees. An organization should seek to provide stable employment and never to treat employees as expendable factors of production. Work should be meaningful (which is to say that it should be oriented to producing goods and services of quality that address genuine human needs) and designed to be fully respectful of human dignity and human limitations. Most generally, managers should seek, as far as possible, to draw employees into a genuine community of work, to draw on their intelligence and give scope to their capacity for responsible freedom, and share with them the rewards (and perhaps the risks) of the operation.

Finally, a business should seek to create (not only take or appropriate) value for owners and investors. One of the principal contributions that a business makes to a community is the creation, and not merely the transfer, of wealth. Businesses should indeed aim at the creation of wealth to the extent that it is consistent with its other legitimate goals and obligations. (At the same time, goals related to customers and employees are properly balanced with the reasonable creation of wealth for owners and investors.) Benedict acknowledges that capital markets often impose unreasonable constraints on managers, sometimes severely restricting their ability to address the other proper goals of a business. In this context, it is important to give some attention to the duty of investors, who fail in solidarity when they demand returns that retard a business's capacity to satisfy real human needs.

In *Caritas in Veritate,* Pope Benedict has built upon the foundation he laid in his first encyclical, *Deus caritas est,* as well as the tradition of his predecessors. The encyclical must be read in light of the papal social tradition and the larger Catholic moral tradition. In many ways the message of *Caritas in Veritate* is not new, nor is it intended to be new. At the same time, the Holy Father has urged us to think about developments of this tradition, particularly as we appropriate more deeply the implications of the primacy of charity and gratuity, and he has sharpened our understanding of the relationship of charity and truth, augmented our vision of human development, and given us a new tool to discern the proper objectives of business and the economic arena in the Principle of Gratuitousness.

## Executive summary

Papal thinking about business and the economy, as it has developed over more than 120 years, differs in important respects from the dominant theories in the discipline of economics, liberalism, and socialism. The difference stems from conflicting visions of the nature of human persons and the relationship of the individual to society. Where economists tend to be materialist and to limit human fulfillment to its material components, the popes insist that human well-being involves far more than this. Authentic human development certainly includes material elements but it also entails personal and spiritual growth. Pope

Benedict XVI draws on this tradition for his recent encyclical, *Caritas in Veritate*, in which he focuses far more than his predecessors on the contribution that business can make to human well-being. For Benedict, one key to understanding business correctly and to appreciating the powerful and positive role it can play in social life is the logic of gift. Genuine human fulfillment, on his view, is only found in the gift of self, that is, in serving the needs of others. As a consequence, a successful business must orient itself to gratuitousness, or beneficence, which is a deep commitment to address the needs of potential customers (especially the poor) through products and services, the needs of workers by organizing good and fruitful work, and the creation of wealth for investors and the community.

## Notes

The author wants to acknowledge with gratitude the contribution of his colleagues at the University of St. Thomas, especially Professors Michael Naughton and Jeanne Buckeye, to my understanding of *Caritas in Veritate*. Some of the useful insights are really theirs, even while the errors are my own.

1. Hayek 1974.
2. See the Introduction of this book, pp. 1–18.
3. A variation on this theme suggests that transcendent goals might exist but they are entirely arbitrary, chosen by individuals for reasons that need satisfy no one else. But to affirm this is to say no more than that, while some individuals choose to pursue non-material ends, these ends are not ends for human persons as such but merely the non-rational choices of some persons. Thus, there are still no transcendent ends natural to human persons.
4. A common characteristic of totalitarian systems, whether or not they share the socialist rejection of private property. Note the famous comment of Benito Mussolini (1927) "Everything in the State, nothing outside the State, nothing against the State."
5. See a charming discussion of this notion in Friedman 1996, pp. 317–332, where he summarizes the work of Nobelist Gary Becker.
6. Murray 1960, p. 7.
7. "Endowed with intellect and free will, each man is responsible for his self-fulfillment even as he is for his salvation... He is the chief architect of his own success or failure." (PP 15)
8. The discussion of charity and truth in the introduction to *Caritas in Veritate* is perhaps the most innovative contribution of the encyclical to the social tradition. Its implications pertain first of all to the cultural dimension of society, since it is the shared understanding of the truth about the human person and the common commitment to charity and justice that give effective direction to the political and economic dimensions. To the degree that a society is unclear or in conflict about the truth, and to the

degree that it is confused about or lacks commitment to charity and justice, to that degree the political and economic dimensions will be misdirected and perhaps toxic to human well-being. To put it another way, neither the political dimension nor the economic dimension (including the marketplace) possess internal principles of direction that move them reliably to serve integral human fulfillment. For good or ill, they derive their directive principles from the culture and so reflect and perhaps magnify any distortions in that culture's understanding of the person.

9. Note the lapidary phrase: "As society becomes ever more globalized, it makes us neighbors but it does not make us brothers."
10. Quoting Paul VI here, "every man is called upon to develop and fulfill himself, for every life is a vocation."
11. Aquinas, S Th IIaIIae, q. 31, on beneficence.
12. It must be noted that maximizing profitability is, in fact, an impossible goal to pursue. No one can know what the maximum profit might be for any company in any particular time period. It is always possible to imagine, after the fact, that something might have been done differently to produce a slightly higher profit. This goal becomes mischievous, however, when a manager attends to something like the well-being of employees and opens himself to the charge that, say, protecting jobs deprives the shareholders to the maximum profit to which they have a "legal" right.
13. Prof Paul Dembinski, of the University of Fribourg and the Observatoire de la Finance in Geneva, has recently published a splendid book on the problem in finance. See Dembinski 2008.
14. For a secular affirmation of this view, see Drucker 1994, pp. 95–104. Drucker also famously rejected the notion that profit is the objective of a business, saying that the real objective of a business is to create a customer. In this article, he argues that an enduring business needs periodically to survey its environment to determine how potential customers can be served by the capacities it possesses.
15. Of course, what I say here about customers is equally true in an analogous way of clients, students, patients, citizens, or any category of person served by any organization.
16. Consider the values that collectors may attach to items that non-collectors would willingly discard.
17. Keep in mind that a human need is not only, as some are inclined to think, something without which one dies. A human need is an aspect of human fulfillment and anything that genuinely contributes to authentic human fulfillment satisfies a need.

## References

Dembinski, Paul. *Finance: Servant or Deceiver? Financialization at the Crossroads.* New York: Palgrave, 2008.

Drucker, Peter. "The theory of the business." *Harvard Business Review,* Sept-Oct 1994: 95–104.

Friedman, David. *Hidden Order: The Economics of Everyday Life.* New York: HarperCollins, 1996: 317–332.

Hayek, Friedrich. "The pretense of knowledge." *Nobel Prize Lecture*, December 1974.
Murray, John Courtney. "The civilization of the pluralist society." In J.C. Murray ed. *We Hold These Truths*. New York: Sheed and Ward, 1960: 7.
Mussolini, Benito. Speech given before the Italian Chamber of Deputies, May 1927.

# 8

# The Profile of the Manager in *Caritas in Veritate*

*Gregory R. Beabout*

> [F]rom the perspective of the Church's social doctrine, there is a growing conviction that *business management cannot concern itself only with the interests of the proprietors, but must also assume responsibility for all the other stakeholders who contribute to the life of the business*: the workers, the clients, the suppliers of various elements of production, the community of reference. (CV 40; italics in original)

*Caritas in Veritate* [*Charity in truth*], the 2009 encyclical that treats social development in the context of contemporary globalization and the financial crisis, "requires a *profoundly new way of understanding business enterprise*" (CV 40, italics in original). My goal in this chapter is to draw out of the encyclical a profile of the type of manager endorsed by Pope Benedict XVI and to indicate several points of contact with ongoing discussions in the contemporary literature. Borrowing phrases from the encyclical, a distinction is drawn between two kinds of managers: the *short-term cosmopolitan capitalist* and the *far-sighted steward*. As distinct character-types, these two models of management involve contrasting self-understandings of the role of the manager. I show that Pope Benedict XVI criticizes several qualities of the *short-term cosmopolitan capitalist* (CV 40) while praising the holistic, humanistic approach of the *far-sighted steward* (CV 40). The proposed model sounds suggestive and attractive in certain ways, but it also raises a series of questions. What is the role of the manager? How should managers conceive their activities? What dispositions are required of this type of manager? How might one acquire the outlook needed to excel as a *far-sighted steward*? In order to bring into focus the proposed conception of the manager found in *Caritas in Veritate*, I place themes from the encyclical in dialogue with several strands in the contemporary literature. I focus especially on: (1) the recent increased interest among business ethicists in practical wisdom; (2) leadership literature that focuses on stewardship, servant-leadership, and transformational-leadership; and (3) recent efforts to rethink business education by emphasizing the integrative role of the liberal arts. I conclude by showing that the encyclical's call to understand economic development in light of a "new humanistic synthesis" (CV 21) points to a need to develop a "business humanities" approach as a part of management education, analogous to the development over the past several decades of the field of "medical humanities."

## 1 The context of *Caritas in Veritate*[1]

*Caritas in Veritate* aims "to pay tribute and to honour the memory of the great Pope Paul VI, revisiting his teachings on integral human development" and then "to apply them to the present moment" (CV 8).[2] If the encyclical were a symphony, the topic of management and the proposal to re-envision the manager as a *far-sighted steward* would be one among many other melodic motifs, perhaps an evocative counterpoint that arises and repeats itself several times amid a larger, many-hued composition that is rich and textured. The encyclical is a text that is in conversation with both the rich tradition of Catholic social teaching and the contemporary context of a global economic recession. The unifying theme of the encyclical is "the development of peoples with the splendour of truth and the gentle light of Christ's charity" (CV 8). As indicated by the opening words of the text from which the title is drawn, the central argument is that an appropriate response to the challenges of global development and progress toward the common good requires both love and the truth.

As with previous social encyclicals from the Vatican, *Caritas in Veritate* is addressed both to Catholics and "to all people of good will." Specific sections seem aimed at distinct audiences: political leaders, religious leaders, aid agencies, those responsible for the structure of global institutions, and business leaders. The focus of the text moves back and forth, ranging from theological and philosophical questions to matters of global economic and political development. In addition, the level of analysis ranges from individual human persons to large-scale institutions and social structures. The encyclical applies the theme of love in truth to (1) "individuals, their moral conscience and their personal and social responsibility" (CV 36), (2) "micro-relationships (with friends, with family members or within small groups)", and (3) "macro-relationships (social, economic and political ones)" (CV 2). The text invites all people of good will to take up a common inquiry seeking new ways to realize authentic human development. "Remarkable convergences and possible solutions will then come to light, without any fundamental component of human life being obscured" (CV 32). This shared quest, it is suggested, should be undertaken in a manner that respects the order "proper to each element and in the light of an integral vision of man, reflecting the different aspects of the human person" (CV 32). Focusing on the encyclical's proposed new conception of the manager does not rule out an emphasis on individual moral reform or the need for structural transformation at the levels of the business enterprise or the global economic system; to the contrary, multiple approaches can be complementary.

## 2 Two character-types in *Caritas in Veritate*

The encyclical includes repeated calls for new and creative solutions. "The current crisis obliges us to re-plan our journey, to set ourselves new rules and to discover new forms of commitment, to build on positive experiences and to reject negative ones" (CV 21). The pope writes, "Old models are disappearing, but promising new ones are taking shape on the horizon" (CV 40). One aspect of this is the distinction drawn in the encyclical between two different types of managers, each with a distinctive self-understanding.

In describing these two, I find it helpful to recall Alasdair MacIntyre's description of the manager as a *character* (1981, pp. 25–35). MacIntyre develops the notion of the manager as a *character* by drawing both from literature and from Max Weber's account of "ideal types." Weber developed an "ideal-type" theory in his classic book, *The Theory of Social and Economic Organization*. According to Weber, an "ideal type" is a "synthesis of a great many diffuse, discrete, more or less present and occasionally absent concrete individual phenomena, which are arranged…into a unified analytical construct" (Weber 1947, p. 88). I am using the term "type" in this sense. MacIntyre describes the modern manager (as office executive who devises policies to organize social groups to efficiently and effectively accomplish a given end) as a central character "in the social drama of the present age" (1981, p. 27). MacIntyre uses the notion of *character* "because of the way it links dramatic and moral associations" (1981, p. 27). For the one who inhabits a given role, a particular character-type acts to guide, structure, and constrain action. For others who come upon this character, it is crucial to be able to recognize and interpret the intentions of such characters because, whether encountered on the stage or in the drama of life, characters "partially define the possibilities of plot and action" (1981, p. 27). So, blending MacIntyre's notion of a *character* with Weber's notion of a "type," we can investigate the two sorts of managers described in *Caritas in Veritate*.

Drawing from terms used in the encyclical, I name these two character-types the *short-term cosmopolitan capitalist* and the *far-sighted steward*.[3] Distinctive dispositions shape the thoughts, desires, feelings, self-understandings, and actions of each. From the encyclical, we can draw out a fuller description of these two types of managers.

## A The manager as short-term cosmopolitan capitalist

Pope Benedict XVI offers both a description of a well-known managerial type and stinging criticisms of this character. It should be clarified that the pope is not critical of all managers who work in the capitalist system, nor is he specifically critical of those who might consider themselves cosmopolitan. The encyclical tradition contains a subtle treatment of capitalism. Pope John Paul II, in his 1991 encyclical, *Centesimus annus* (CA), distinguished between various forms of capitalism; he praised "the fundamental and positive role of business, the market, private property and the resulting responsibility for the means of production, as well as free human creativity in the economic sector" (CA 42) while criticizing forms of capitalism that fail to see that economic freedom needs to be circumscribed "within a strong juridical framework which places it at the service of human freedom in its totality, and which sees it as a particular aspect of that freedom, the core of which is ethical and religious" (CA 42). In a similar way, *Caritas in Veritate* is not critical of capitalism *per se* or of all mangers who work in a capitalist system with short-term responsibilities; nor is it opposed to a cosmopolitan setting. The pope is awakening us in particular to certain dispositional tendencies, especially insofar as they are shallow and short-sighted.[4] In section 40, the following characteristics of one type of manager are identified:

1. They work in large firms.
2. They find themselves expected to produce quantifiable short-term results.
3. They are employed as replaceable units.

4. They work in many cases without a stable director, that is, without a person or family who feels responsible in the long term for the life and results of the company.
5. They often rely on outsourcing because they are encouraged to pursue efficiency by taking advantage of economies of scale.
6. Perhaps because of recurrent outsourcing, they have cultivated in others, and may themselves feel, a diminished sense of responsibility regarding the impact of their firm's activities on various stakeholders: the workers, the suppliers, the consumers, the natural environment, and the broader society.
7. Their remuneration is performance-based as measured in terms of profits and as a result they frequently find themselves answerable only to the shareholders of anonymous funds.
8. Like the shareholders of such funds, they frequently feel a sense of mobility and hence do not consider themselves to have any responsibilities to a specific geographical area (CV 40).

Why does the pope draw attention to this sort of manager? It seems clear that the pope aims to criticize this character, but it is not a wholesale criticism; the pope is not criticizing those who are cosmopolitan, nor is he criticizing every form of capitalism. What are the precise shortcomings of this character-type?

This character, as described in the encyclical, seems disinclined to engage in serious reflection on the tension between perceived self-interests (or shareholder interests) and questions about what makes for a good human life. In some cases, policies, laws, or institutional constraints may make it difficult for such a manager to deliberate with others about broader moral and social questions. Such a character tends to become blind to several crucial truths. The dispositional leaning of this character is to neglect the long-term impact of decisions, to treat human persons as replaceable objects, and to ignore the impact of managerial decisions on the local community, the natural environment, and the broader society. The pope suggests that such managers act in a fragmented and alienated manner, acting as if the professional and business significance of managerial decisions are entirely separable from all human significance (CV 41). Such a character tends to disregard the truth that every human action is a "personal action" (CV 41), as if one could be relieved of all responsibility for one's business decisions by saying, "It is nothing personal." In focusing one's concerns on increasing shareholder value without regard for others who are impacted by the decision, the *short-term cosmopolitan capitalist* acts without regard for truth or charity.

### B The manager as "far-sighted steward"

Within the encyclical, Pope Benedict suggests an alternative type of manager who operates according to a quite different paradigm. The pope does not provide concrete examples of such managers; nor does he offer a single, orderly description. However, it is possible to draw from various parts of the encyclical to piece together a number of characteristics of the type of manager that the pope prefers. *Caritas in Veritate* lists the following ten qualities of the manager as *far-sighted steward*:

1. While there may be contemporary examples of *far-sighted stewards*, this sort of manager exists outside mainstream contemporary business models; this type of manager is described as a promising new one that is "taking shape on the horizon" (CV 40).
2. They are "far-sighted," concerned with the responsible use of financial resources, focusing on long-term sustainability more than short-term profits (CV 40).
3. They may exist in various types of enterprises, (not simply public v. private or for-profit v. not-for-profit), and they favor "cross-fertilization between different types of business activity, with shifting of competences from the 'non-profit' world to the 'profit' world and vice versa, from the public world to that of civil society, from advanced economies to developing countries" (CV 41).
4. They operate according to "traditional principles of social ethics like transparency, honesty and responsibility" (CV 36).
5. They attend to the concrete particularities of their social context by remaining "aware of the profound links between their enterprise and the territory or territories in which it operates" (CV 40).
6. They recognize that business activities are first and foremost the activities of human persons; hence, they treat workers as persons, recognizing the dignity of each worker by providing opportunities for everyone to make a personal contribution that develops his or her capacities as a person (CV 41).
7. They operate with "person-based" and "community-oriented" concerns for common goods, global integration, and openness to transcendence (CV 36, 42).
8. They operate with an ethic of stewardship, that is, they are attentive to the environment, recognizing that the "environment is God's gift to everyone, and in our use of it we have a responsibility towards the

poor, towards future generations, and towards humanity as a whole" (CV 48).

9. They operate according to the "logic of gift" and the "principle of gratuitousness" (CV 35–36).
10. They reason together with others about the ends being pursued by their enterprise; the good of financial success is balanced with a range of other goods, including the well-being of "the workers, the clients, the suppliers of various elements of production, the community of reference" and the natural environment (CV 40).

We are now in a better position to answer some of the questions raised at the beginning of this chapter. What does it mean to manage as a *far-sighted steward*? What dispositions and self-understanding characterize the *far-sighted steward*?

## 3 The dispositions and self-understanding of the far-sighted steward

This proposed alternative type of manager, the *far-sighted steward*, might strike some as perhaps initially counterintuitive in certain ways. However, it actually shares a great deal with other recent proposals for management reform: (1) the recent increased focus on the need for business leaders to cultivate the virtue of practical wisdom, and (2) the stewardship literature, especially the leadership literature.

### A The far-sighted steward and the retrieval of practical wisdom

In his recent presidential address to the Society for Business Ethics, Dennis Moberg focused his remarks on the need for business leaders to retrieve the ancient virtue of practical wisdom. Moberg noted, "Practical wisdom has received scant attention in business ethics" (2007, p. 535), although the publication of his remarks went a long way to redress this shortcoming. Of course, practical wisdom has an ancient pedigree as one of the four cardinal virtues. This intellectual excellence goes by many names: prudence, foresight, sagacity, and practical reasoning. Aristotle used the ancient Greek term *phronesis* to distinguish knowing how to act from knowing how to make things (*techne*) and knowing eternal truths (*sophia*) (Aristotle, 2002 (*NE*) 1140a1–1141b23). In medieval Latin, the term *prudentia* was formed from a contraction of the ancient term *providentia*, that is, divine foresight. The prudent person could see clearly well into the future. The virtue tradition praises *prudentia* as *auriga virtutum*, the herding charioteer that gathers all the other virtues and guides each judgment of conscience.[5] As a disposition, it is an acquired trait, an enduring personal quality, a state that allows one to discern the true good in every circumstance and to choose the right means of achieving it.

The recent interest among business ethicists in retrieving the ancient virtue of practical wisdom has forerunners; Robert C. Solomon, writing in the early 1990s, developed an Aristotelian approach to business ethics in which he treated *phronesis* under the name "good judgment" (1992, pp. 328–9, 1993, pp. 174–9).

Moberg begins his account of practical wisdom with a dictionary definition: "the ability to judge rightly in matters relating to life and conduct" (2007, p. 536). He immediately refines that definition, defining practical wisdom as "a disposition toward cleverness in crafting morally excellent responses to, or in anticipation of challenging particularities" (2007, p. 536), and he goes on to provide a range of common business situations that call for practical wisdom (ambiguous situations, binds, dilemmas, and leadership predicaments) followed by an incisive account of the virtue.

In a similar way, Gary Weaver has written that among those concerned with business ethics and organizations, more attention "needs to be paid to the notion of practical wisdom" (2006, p. 358). A number of writers have done so recently (for examples, see Sison 2009, Clarke 2010, Melé 2010, Maines 2010). Barry Schwartz and Kenneth Sharpe (2010), in their recent book, *Practical Wisdom*, bring into focus many instances in which contemporary social institutions encourage short-sighted decisions that are unwise, selfish, and foolish; the aim of their book is to retrieve Aristotle's emphasis on *phronesis* in order make this virtue relevant to our contemporary context, especially in the context of business, law, education, and medicine.

As Moberg notes, the disposition of practical wisdom is developed through experience, reflection, and inspiration (2007, p. 547). The person with limited experience, or the person who is disposed to experience the world only through a narrow, limited perspective, is prone to aim at goals that are obvious or readily quantifiable in the short-term. The person of practical wisdom has a well-developed moral imagination that allows one to empathize with alternative points of view and anticipate how others might feel about a particular situation (2007, p. 549). The person of practical wisdom is excellent at "a creative mode of inquiry that pulls together different views and abstract ideas into a unified whole" (2007, p. 550).

In *Caritas in Veritate*, when Pope Benedict calls for managers who are far-sighted, he points especially to the importance of recognizing "the profound links between their enterprise and the territory or territories in which it operates" (CV 40). "Paul VI invited people to give serious attention to the damage that can be caused to one's home country by the transfer abroad of capital purely for personal advantage" (CV 40). So, when *Caritas in Veritate* praises the quality of being far-sighted, the disposition being suggested is the traditional cardinal virtue of prudence or practical wisdom that has been the subject of increased attention in contemporary business ethics literature.

### B The stewardship literature: servant-leaders and transformational-leadership

The notion of stewardship is an explicit and recurring theme in *Caritas in Veritate* (CV 27, 48–51, 67, 69). The text states, "Human beings legitimately exercise a responsible stewardship over nature, in order to protect it, to enjoy its fruits and to cultivate it in new ways, with the assistance of advanced technologies, so that it can worthily accommodate and feed the world's population" (CV 50). The pope speaks of stewardship primarily with ecological concerns in mind. "The environment is God's gift to everyone, and in our use of it we have a responsibility towards the poor, towards future generations and towards humanity as a whole" (CV 48). The pope clarified and expanded his teaching in his World Day of Peace message delivered on January 1, 2010 when he stated that the Church

> is concerned that the question be approached in a balanced way, with respect for the "grammar" which the Creator has inscribed in his handiwork by giving man the role of a steward and administrator with responsibility over creation (Pope Benedict XVI 2010, 13).

As a result of Pope Benedict's emphasis on stewardship and environmental responsibility, *Newsweek* dubbed him the "Green Pope" (Stone 2008). In addition to Pope Benedict's concerns for environmental responsibility, he also uses the notion of stewardship in a broader sense to include care for all of the gifts that we have been given and charged with preserving and passing on to others. As stewards, we have been put in charge of a multiple gifts: "ecological, juridical, economic, political and cultural" (CV 48). In this way, Pope Benedict uses the notion of stewardship broadly, referring to a wide range of projects that will impact coming generations and which "need to be marked by solidarity and inter-generational justice" (CV 48).

The leadership literature in business frequently uses the notion of stewardship in this broader sense, referring not simply to the responsibility to care for the natural environment, but to "the attitudes and behaviors that place the long-term best interests of a group ahead of personal goals that serve an individual's self-interests" (Hernandez 2008, p. 122). Stewardship is not primarily the result of formal rules; rather, it "is facilitated through organizational structures that help leaders to generate interpersonal and institutional trust, clarity regarding organizational strategy, and intrinsic motivation in followers" (Hernandez 2008, p. 122).

Peter Block, in his book, *Stewardship: Choosing Service over Self-Interest* (1993) extends and expands ideas that he had earlier developed in *The Empowered Manager* (1987). Block writes, "Stewardship is to hold something in trust for another. Historically, stewardship was a means to protect a kingdom while those rightfully in charge were away, or, more often, to govern for the sake of an underage king" (Block 1993, p. xx). Block is writing for managers and leaders of organizations, challenging them to change their orientation by encouraging them to "choose service over self-interest" and to "reside over the orderly distribution of power" (Block 1993, p. xx). The task of the manager-as-steward, according to Block, is "to systematically move choice and resources closer to the bottom and edges of the organization" (Block 1993, p. 18). His book is filled with examples of how the manager-as-steward can empower members of the organization to become active participants in decision making. Block provides suggestions for redesigning management practices, flattening the organizational structure, rethinking staff functions, and redesigning reward systems. Block seems to be unaware of the deep similarities between the form of management that he is proposing and the notion of subsidiarity, a central principle in the social encyclicals of Catholic thought – that decisions should be made at the level appropriate to each issue.[6] Despite Block's seeming lack of awareness concerning subsidiarity, he makes explicit reference to the original religious context of the notion of stewardship "to care for the earth" (1993, p. 41). On the whole, Block situates stewardship in the context of managerial leadership: "Corporate stewardship has come to mean financial responsibility for both the institution and the community it lives in" (1993, p. 41). Understood this way, according to Block, stewardship is "the willingness to be accountable to the well-being of the organization by operating in service, rather than in control, of those around us" (1993, p. xx).

Block's notion of the manager-as-steward is influenced in part by Robert Greenleaf's idea of the servant-leader. In his seminal and now classic book, *Servant Leadership: A Journey in the Nature of Legitimate Power and Greatness* (1977), Greenleaf proposed a model of organizational leaders as servants. Servant-leaders give priority to others, aiming to build up others and help them flourish by empathically listening to others and helping them draw out their deepest aspirations and purposes. Larry Spears, the longtime successor, President, and CEO of the Robert K. Greenleaf Center for Servant-Leadership (1990–2007) identified 10 characteristics of servant-leaders: listening, empathy, healing, awareness, persuasion, conceptualization, foresight, stewardship, commitment to growth, and building community (Spears 1997, pp. 4–6). As understood by Greenleaf and Spears, stewardship is the recognition that leaders have the task to hold their institution in trust to serve the good of society; in that way, "stewardship and servant-leadership are closely aligned ideas" (Spears 1997, p. 85).

The notion of servant-leadership is also quite similar to the managerial model found in the literature of transformational-leadership, an approach that has been developed by James MacGregor Burns and Bernard M. Bass. MacGregor Burns, in his seminal 1978 book, *Leadership*, and then Bass, in his 1985 book, *Leadership and Performance beyond Expectations* (1985), drew a distinction that is now well-known in leadership literature: they distinguish between transactional and transformational leaders. Transactional leaders motivate workplace performance through a system of rewards and punishments, while transformational leaders provide an inspiring mission, inviting others "to transcend their own self-interests for the good of the group, organization or society; to consider their long-term need for self-development rather than their need of the moment; and to become more aware of what is really important" (Bass 2008, p. 50).

While both servant-leadership and transformational-leadership might be viewed as alternatives that are somewhat out-of-the-mainstream compared with older command-and-control models that are bureaucratic and more rigidly hierarchical, each have been extensively studied, empirically evaluated, and applied in a range of organizations (Bass 2008).

Pope Benedict's proposed managerial model, the character-type that I have called the *far-sighted steward*, is similar to these; the points of contact merit further investigation. In particular, in these approaches, the self-understanding on the part of the manager toward one's task involves preserving something in trust for the well-being of others by operating in service to the well-being of others and the good of society, including future generations; this is carried out by encouraging initiative, participation, and decision making by those impacted, and by encouraging responsible reflection and deliberation about what is really important beyond the immediate needs of the moment. In these and similar ways, the managerial character-type proposed in *Caritas in Veritate*, the *far-sighted steward*, shares a great deal in common with several strands of contemporary leadership literature.

With regard to the pope's praise for the *far-sighted steward*, an objector might protest that choosing service over power and self-interest runs counter to the logic of the marketplace. Such an objector might point to a rationality of economic utility that is entirely separate from humanistic concerns. Aren't economic activities to be judged solely according to a quantifiable logic of cost/benefit analysis that focuses on measurable outcomes? How would Pope Benedict respond to this sort of objection?

## 4 A holistic, humanistic approach to business management

One of the central points of *Caritas in Veritate* is to provide a response to the objection that economic concerns are entirely distinct from human concerns. Pope Benedict proposes that the economic crisis, while complex, points to the need for a deeper and increasingly interconnected understanding of economic development. Indeed, the text calls for "new efforts of holistic understanding and a *new humanistic synthesis*" (CV 21; italics in original). According to this proposed mode of thinking, technical concerns need to be integrated with "the fully human meaning of human activities, within the context of the holistic meaning of the individual's being" (CV 70).

The direction of this response moves beyond a call for "business ethics," especially if business ethics is understood merely in terms of a "code of ethics" or set of principles intended to place limits on an otherwise unbridled pursuit of profits. Prior to the onset of the economic crisis, the concern with business ethics was already on the rise in university settings, in centers of business ethics, and among many practitioners in various business contexts. Further, in recent decades, there has been an increased interest in ethical banking, ethical investing, and so forth, both in the area of micro-finance and in the growing area of socially responsible investing.[7] The adjective "ethical" can be abused, "even to the point where it includes decisions and choices contrary to justice and authentic human welfare" (CV 45), especially in instances that lack a clear emphasis on authentic personal development and a sound moral criterion. In a manner parallel to the way that some foods have been labeled "natural" or "organic" without any clear indication of what those terms mean, the term "ethical" is subject to similar abuse. With this in mind, the Pope calls for a holistic, humanistic approach.

This raises another question. How might the humanistic concerns of the *far-sighted steward* be cultivated? How might business schools cultivate in future managers the characteristics and traits that accord with a holistic, humanistic approach?

## A A lesson from medical humanities

One way to understand the encyclical's call for a "new humanistic synthesis" is to point to the development of the field of "medical humanities" while noting the relative lack of a corresponding field of "business humanities." Medical humanities developed as a response to shortcomings that were felt as medical culture became increasingly "dominated by scientific, technical and managerial approaches" (Greaves and Evans 2000, p. 1). As a pedagogical movement, medical humanities has a complicated history (Cook, 2010, pp. 3–4). The term "medical humanities" can be traced to the 1960s, but the medical humanities movement has expanded significantly in recent decades (Evans and Greaves 2010, p. 66). As physicians and healthcare professionals have increasingly found themselves buffeted by social and economic pressures, narrowed in their expertise by increased specialization, and feeling at times dehumanized by conceptions of medicine that emphasize analytical detachment, there was a felt need for a more humanistic approach to medicine.

Medical humanities developed as an effort to cultivate insight into the human condition among both medical students and healthcare practitioners. Drawing from the habits of mind and heart that characterize the humanistic disciplines, medical humanities aims to increase an awareness of human and social concerns, attentiveness to narrative and history, sensitivity toward suffering and the perspectives of those who might sometimes be forgotten, appreciation of creativity, alertness to distinct perspectives, reflection with others on questions of deep purpose, and a commitment to human well-being. As these concerns are widely recognized as essential for humane medical care, many medical schools now offer courses and programs in medical humanities. Students now pursue various degrees in the field of medical humanities, ranging from an undergraduate interdisciplinary minor to graduate studies culminating in the doctoral degree. Indeed, programs in medical humanities have become widespread at colleges and universities educating undergraduate students in nursing, pre-medicine, and other healthcare fields.[8]

The field of medical humanities is interdisciplinary in character. It includes professional associations in North America and Europe with multiple scholarly journals and a growing literature of book-length works. The field is characterized by an ongoing debate as to whether it is a new subdiscipline or a "novel interdisciplinary perspective which sought to reunify the arts and sciences in medicine as a whole and so provide a more rounded and humanitarian approach that rejected the notion of a subdiscipline altogether" (Evans and Greaves 2010, p. 66).

The concerns of literary critics, especially those who focus on narrative, have emerged as central in the developing conversation of medical humanities. By cultivating an attentiveness to the rich complexity of setting, character, and plot, a medical humanities approach encourages medical professionals to use humanistic and integrative approaches. In doing so, the hope is that medical professionals might bring together scientific and technical knowledge appropriate to the medical field with an increased awareness of each patient as a human person.[9]

## B Rethinking business: toward a business humanities approach

In contrast with the field of medicine, in the business sector, the notion of "business humanities" is comparatively underdeveloped. A number of recent books suggest that contemporary business education, especially as it is practiced in the United States, is seriously flawed. In *Academically Adrift: Limited Learning on College Campuses*, Richard Arum and Josipa Roksa offer a devastating assessment of higher education generally, and especially business education. They cite evidence that students concentrating in business coursework report lower levels of time spent reading and writing than students in the liberal arts (Arum and Roksa 2011, p. 81). Compared with business students, those majoring in liberal arts "demonstrated significantly higher gains in critical thinking, complex reasoning and writing skills over time than students in other fields of study. Students majoring in business, education, social work, and communications had the lowest measurable gains" (Arum and Roksa 2011, p. 121–122).

Of course, it is always in season to criticize higher education; jeremiads lamenting the sorry state of universities are nothing new. In the past, law schools, journalism schools, engineering schools, and the entire university system have all been subjected to severe criticisms, so it may be unsurprising that there is currently an appetite for authors criticizing business education. With that said, it is curious that two of the most prominent such recent works call for similar remedies.

In *Rethinking the MBA*, Srikant Datar and his co-authors situate their argument within the 100-year history of the MBA at Harvard Business School. On their telling, business schools such as Harvard were primarily vocational in character in the early years, with professors drawn from industry. In many cases, early B-school teachers were experienced practitioners. From the podium, seasoned veterans dispensed wisdom to the young primarily by telling stories of "what it's like out there." A watershed occurred in 1959 when, in the United States, Carnegie and the Ford Foundation issued reports with deep criticisms of business school research and theory. The proposed solution, which was significantly incentivized by grant money, was to gain academic respectability by conducting empirically-based scientific research supported with rigorous statistical analysis. In response to the Carnegie and Ford reports, business education "wisely and appropriately began to introduce greater rigor and disciplinary knowledge into their programs" (Datar et al. 2010, p. 322).

As business researchers began to focus their studies more narrowly while aiming for greater and greater precision, MBA faculty and the MBA degree increased in stature. However, Datar and his colleagues suggest that the pendulum has swung too far in the direction of the scientific research model. The risk is that business schools might institutionalize their own irrelevance, producing managers unable to see beyond narrow, quantitative studies. *Rethinking the MBA* proposes that it is time to rebalance the educational priorities of the business school. While emphasizing quantifiable analyses and methods, managers found themselves deficient in certain ways. In the MBA curriculum, less time was spent cultivating holistic thinkers capable of creatively reframing contexts nimbly across multiple frameworks, disciplines, and cultural perspectives. Executives found themselves highly proficient in technical analysis, but with few resources for engaging with others in dialogue and discourse about a sense of purpose or identity. *Rethinking the MBA* proposes "the center of gravity of MBA education shifted strongly toward 'knowing' and away from 'doing' and 'being'" (Datar 2010, p. 322). For that reason, the authors propose that it is time to "rebalance the scales" by "focusing more attention on issues of accountability, ethics, and social responsibility" (Datar 2010, p. 323). Without providing concrete specifics, Datar and his co-authors call for pedagogical and curricular innovations that teach managerial skills while instilling a sense of purpose and identity.

The call for reform is equally pronounced in a new Carnegie study. *Rethinking Undergraduate Business Education* notes many of the same problems. In the recent Carnegie study, the authors visited a range of business schools in the United States. "We were struck by the degree to which undergraduate business students take what they and others call an *instrumental approach* to their studies" (Colby 2011, p. 51). Many of the undergraduate business students interviewed in the recent Carnegie study consider required courses in the liberal arts as "requirements to get out of the way" rather than as exciting opportunities for intellectual exploration. In part, these attitudes have been institutionalized; they are "built into the curriculum and the advising system," so that connections between the humanistic concerns of the liberal arts, the personal traits cultivated in such courses, and the importance of those traits as crucially needed to excel in business, are rarely drawn (Colby 2011, p. 51).

The authors of *Rethinking Undergraduate Business Education* propose a remedy that shares a great deal with the recommendations of *Rethinking the MBA*. In particular, the recent Carnegie study proposes an integrative vision of liberal learning for business education. As they put it, "The purpose of liberal learning is to enable students to make sense of the world and their place in it, preparing them to use knowledge and skills as a means to engage responsibly with the life of their times" (Colby 2011, p. 60). They articulate this goal in four parts. (1) Analytical thinking: the ability to abstract from particular contexts to produce formal knowledge that is general in nature and subject to methodical investigation. (2) Multiple framing: the awareness that any particular scheme of analytical thinking frames experience in particular ways, and is subject to challenge from different perspectives or points of view that frame the same experience in quite different, apparently incompatible ways. (3) The reflective exploration of meaning: As the traditional heart of liberal education and humanistic learning, it raises questions about "who I am, how I engage the world, and what is reasonable for me to imagine and hope" (Colby 2011, p. 60) 4). Practical reasoning: the ability to deliberate and decide on the best course of action in a particular situation. The authors of the recent Carnegie study propose that, "Such thinking is characteristic of professional judgment, including that of business leaders, as well as being a key capacity of citizens and statesmen" (Colby 2011, p. 60).

To summarize, the recent books both criticizing business education and calling for rethinking business education propose an approach that parallels, in certain ways, the development of medical humanities. For that reason, it might be appropriate to call this a "business humanities" approach, recognizing that the proposed habits of mind and heart are cultivated in the liberal arts generally, including not only the disciplines traditionally associated with the humanities, but all of those disciplines and practices that together make up an integrated, humanistic approach. When we read in *Caritas in Veritate* a call for "new efforts of holistic understanding and a *new humanistic synthesis*," (CV 21) the encyclical is expressing something quite similar to that which we find expressed in contemporary calls to rethink business management.

## 5 Conclusion

*Caritas in Veritate* includes, as one of its motifs, a criticism of a managerial character-type, the *short-term cosmopolitan capitalist*, while endorsing a profile of the manager as *far-sighted steward*. By putting the *far-sighted steward* into conversation with the contemporary literature in three areas (practical wisdom literature in business ethics; leadership literature; and the literature pointing to the need to rethink business education by emphasizing more deeply the humanities and liberal arts), I have shown that Pope Benedict's proposal shares a great deal with ongoing conversations.

At the same time, it should be noted that, in certain ways, Pope Benedict's proposal goes beyond the points of contact with the contemporary literature that I have highlighted. In particular, the pope's emphasis on charity in truth, the central theme of the encyclical, merits deeper reflection. The same is the case with regard to what Pope Benedict calls the "logic of gift" (CV 34, 36). The humanistic synthesis proposed in *Caritas in Veritate* is ultimately theological in character; the points of contact that I have indicated are not intended to mean that the encyclical's proposal is reducible to the wisdom found in a humanistic approach to economics and business. The fullness of love is, in a sense, "already but not yet" fully present. "The human community that we build by ourselves can never, purely by its own strength, be a fully fraternal community, nor can it overcome every division and become a truly universal community" (CV 34). With realism, the encyclical invites "deeper reflection on the meaning of the economy and its goals, as well as a profound and far-sighted revision of the current model" (CV 32).

The *far-sighted steward* proposed in *Caritas in Veritate* offers a holistic, humanistic approach to management.

## Executive summary

This chapter draws from *Caritas in Veritate* a profile of the sort of manager endorsed by Pope Benedict XVI and indicates several points of contact with ongoing discussions in the contemporary literature. Borrowing phrases from the encyclical, a distinction between two kinds of managers is identified: the *short-term cosmopolitan capitalist* and the *far-sighted steward.* As distinct character-types, these two models of management involve contrasting self-understandings of the role of the manager. I show that Pope Benedict XVI criticizes several qualities of the *short-term cosmopolitan capitalist* while praising the holistic, humanistic approach of the *far-sighted steward.* The proposed model sounds suggestive and attractive in certain ways, but it also raises a series of questions. What is the role of the manager? How should managers conceive their activities? What dispositions are required of this sort of manager? How might one acquire the outlook needed to excel as a *far-sighted steward*? In order to bring into focus the proposed conception of the manager found in *Caritas in Veritate,* I place themes from the encyclical in dialogue with several strands in the contemporary literature. I focus especially on (1) the recent increased interest among business ethicists in practical wisdom, (2) leadership literature that focuses on stewardship, servant-leadership, and transformational-leadership, and (3) recent efforts to rethink business education by emphasizing the integrative role of the liberal arts. I conclude by showing that the encyclical's call to understand economic development in light of a "new humanistic synthesis" points to a need to develop a "business humanities" approach as a part of management education, analogous to the development over the last several decades of the field of "medical humanities."

## Notes

1. For a more detailed overview of *Caritas in veritate,* see the introductory chapter. For a helpful account of the encyclical in relation to the economic crisis, see Breen (2010, pp. 987–993).
2. He refers to the encyclical letter *Populorum progression* (PP; 1967) by Pope Paul VI.
3. While these precise names are not used in *Caritas in veritate,* I have drawn these phrases from the language of the encyclical. In naming the first type of manager the *short-term cosmopolitan capitalist,* I am drawing especially from these three sentences in the encyclical: "Moreover, the human consequences of current tendencies towards a short-term economy – sometimes very short-term – need to be carefully evaluated" (CV 32); "In recent years a new cosmopolitan class of managers has emerged" (CV 40); "The continuing hegemony

of the binary model of market-plus-State has accustomed us to think only in terms of the private business leader of a capitalistic bent on the one hand, and the State director on the other" (CV 41). In naming the second type of manager the *far-sighted steward*, I am drawing especially from these two sentences in the encyclical: "By contrast, though, many far-sighted managers today are becoming increasingly aware of the profound links between their enterprise and the territory or territories in which it operates" (CV 40); "Human beings legitimately exercise *a responsible stewardship over nature*, in order to protect it, to enjoy its fruits and to cultivate it in new ways, with the assistance of advanced technologies, so that it can worthily accommodate and feed the world's population" (CV 50, italics in original).

4. This type of manager, the *short-term cosmopolitan capitalist*, seems most associated with certain forms of shareholder capitalism.
5. For example, Eschmann notes that Thomas Aquinas describes the virtue of prudence in these terms; see Eschmann (1997, p. 197).
6. The notion of subsidiarity is referenced in *Caritas in veritate* in several places, including 47, 57–60, 68. The classic formulation of the principle of subsidiarity is found in the encyclical *Quadragesimo Anno*: "Just as it is gravely wrong to take from individuals what they can accomplish by their own initiative and industry and give it to the community, so also it is an injustice and at the same time a grave evil and disturbance of right order to assign to a greater and higher association what lesser and subordinate organizations can do. For every social activity ought of its very nature to furnish help to the members of the body social, and never destroy and absorb them" (QA 79). For a more detailed account, see Beabout (2008) and Beabout and Hodes (2007).
7. For discussion of ethical banking and socially responsible investing, see Harvey (1995), Fung (2010), and Beabout and Schmiesing (2003).
8. For a list of people and programs in medical humanities, see http://medhum.med.nyu.edu/directory.html.
9. As an example, see Charon and Montello (2002). For an example of a humanistic approach drawing from literature as applied to executive leadership, see Badarocco (2006).

## References

Aristotle. *Nicomachean Ethics*. Translated by C. Rowe. Oxford: Oxford University Press, 2002.

Arum, R. and J. Roksa. *Academically Adrift: Limited Learning on College Campuses*. Chicago: University of Chicago Press, 2011.

Badarocco, J. *Questions of Character: Illuminating the Heart of Leadership through Literature*. Boston: Harvard Business Press, 2006.

Bass, B. *Leadership and Performance Beyond Expectations*. New York: The Free Press, 1985.

Bass, B. *The Bass Handbook of Leadership: Theory, Research, and Managerial Applications*, 4th edn. New York: The Free Press, 2008.

Beabout, G. "Challenges to using the principle of subsidiarity for environmental policy." *University of St. Thomas Law Journal*, Vol. 5, 1, 2008: 210–231.

Beabout, G. and M. Hodes. "John Paul II on the relationship between civil law and the moral law: Understanding *Evangelium Vitae* in light of the principle of subsidiarity and the moral grammar of John Paul II." *Notre Dame Journal of Law, Ethics and Public Policy*, Vol. 21, 1, 2007: 71–109.

Beabout, G. and K. Schmiesing. "Socially responsible investing: An application of Catholic social thought." *Logos*, Vol. 6, 1, 2003: 63–99.

Block, P. *The Empowered Manager*. San Francisco: Jossey-Bass, 1987.

Block, P. *Stewardship*. San Francisco: Berrett-Koehler, 1993.

Breen, J. "Love, truth, and the economy: A reflection on Benedict XVI's *Caritas in veritate*." *Harvard Journal of Law & Public* Policy, Vol. 33, 3, 2010: 987–1029.

Burns, J.M. *Leadership*. New York: Harper & Row, 1978.

Charron, R. and M. Montello, *Stories Matter: The Role of Narrative in Medical Ethics*. New York: Routledge, 2002.

Clarke, C. "Practical wisdom and understanding the economy." *Journal of Management Development*, Vol. 29, 2010: 678–685.

Colby, A., T. Ehrlich, W.M. Sullivan, J.R. Dolle and L.S. Shulman. *Rethinking Undergraduate Business Education*. New Jersey: Jossey-Bass, 2011.

Cook, H. "Borderlands: A historian's perspective on medical humanities in the US and the UK." *Medical Humanities*, Vol. 26, 2010: 3–4.

Datar, S., D. Garvin, and P. Cullen. *Rethinking the MBA*. Boston: Harvard Business Press, 2010.

Eschmann, I. *The Ethics of Saint Thomas Aquinas*. Toronto: Pontifical Institute of Medieval Studies, 1997.

Evans, M. and D. Greaves. "Ten years of medical humanities: A decade in the life of a journal and a discipline." *Medical Humanities*, Vol. 36, 2010: 66–68.

Fung, H., S.A. Law and J. Yau. *Socially Responsible Investment in a Global Environment*. Northampton, MA: Edward Elgar, 2010.

Greaves, D. and M. Evans. "Medical humanities." *Medical Humanities*, Vol. 26, 2000: 1–2.

Greenleaf, R. *Servant Leadership*. Mahwah, NJ: Paulist Press, 1977.

Harvey, B. "Ethical banking: The case of the Co-operative Bank." *Journal of Business Ethics*, Vol. 14, 1995: 1005–1013.

Hernandez, M. "Promoting stewardship behavior in organizations: A leadership model." *Journal of Business Ethics*, Vol. 80, 2008: 121–128.

MacIntyre, A. *After Virtue*. London: Duckworth, 1981.

Maines, T. and M. Naughton. "Middle level thinking: The cultural mission of business schools." *Journal of Management Development*, Vol. 29, 2010: 669–677.

Melé, D. "Practical wisdom in managerial decision making." *Journal of Management Development*, Vol. 29, 2010: 637–45.

Moberg, D. "Practical wisdom and business ethics." *Business Ethics Quarterly*, Vol. 17, 2007: 535–561.

Pope Benedict XVI. *Message for the Celebration of the World Day of Peace*, January 1, 2010. Available at: www.vatican.va/holy_father/benedict_xvi/messages/peace/documents/hf_ben-xvi_mes_20061208_xl-world-day-peace_en.html (accessed February 3, 2012).

Schwartz, B. and K. Sharpe. *Practical Wisdom*. New York: Riverhead Books, 2010.

Sison, A. "Practical wisdom and the practice of business." *International Conference on the Business of Practical Wisdom*, Eichstätt-Ingolstadt, Germany,

September 2009. Available at: www.stthomas.edu/cathstudies/cst/conferences/PracticalWisdom (accessed July 20, 2011).

Solomon, R. "Corporate roles, personal virtues: An Aristotelean approach to business ethics." *Business Ethics Quarterly*, Vol. 2, 1992: 317–339.

Solomon, R. *Ethics and Excellence: Cooperation and Integrity in Business*. Oxford: Oxford University Press, 1993.

Spears, L. *Insights on Leadership: Service, Stewardship, Spirit, and Servant-Leadership*. New Jersey: Wiley, 1997.

Stone, D. "The Green Pope." *Newsweek*, April 16, 2008, www.newsweek.com/2008/04/16/the-green-pope, July 20, 2011.

Weaver, G. "Virtue in organizations: Moral identity as a foundation for moral agency." *Organization Studies*, Vol. 27, 2006: 341–368.

Weber, M. *The Theory of Social and Economic Organization*. Translated by AM. Henderson and T. Parsons. New York: The Free Press, 1947.

# 9
# Christian Humanism in Business

*Álvaro Pezoa*

> [Paul VI] grasped the interconnection between the impetus towards the unification of humanity and the Christian ideal of a single family of peoples in solidarity and fraternity. *In the notion of development, understood in human and Christian terms, he identified the heart of the Christian social message*, and he proposed Christian charity as the principal force at the service of development. (CV 13; italics in original)

*Caritas in Veritate* (CV) emphasizes the values of the Gospel, particularly love and truth (CV 1, and in many other passages), and stresses the importance of the Gospel for building a society according to freedom and justice (CV 13), and the greatest service that Christian humanism can provide to development (CV 78). In line with these statements, the aim of this chapter is to shed some light on Christian humanism and how this can contribute to human development through business. This requires taking into consideration some concepts related to Christian humanism as they are presented by Catholic Social Teaching[1] (CST), which offers the principles for reflection, the criteria for judgment, and the directives for action which are the starting point for the promotion of an integral and solidary humanism (*Compendium* 7).[2] These foundations do not replace, however, the personal effort necessary to interpret reality and seek appropriate ways of action.

CST aims to help clarify the question about the place that mankind has in the world. The orientation regarding existence, social cohabitation, and history largely depends on the answers given to the questions concerning the place of mankind in nature and society. The radical questions that have accompanied mankind from the beginning gain greater importance in the present day due to the ample challenges abounding, the novelty of scenarios, and the decisions that current generations are called upon to make. The first of these great challenges is that of *the truth about being-human*. The limit and relationship between nature, technology, and the moral are issues that strongly question personal and collective responsibility in relation to behaviors that ought to be adopted in relation to what mankind is, what it can do, and what it should be. The second challenge is that of *the understanding and management of pluralism and of difference* in all areas of: thinking, moral option, culture, religious adherence, philosophy of human, and social development. The third challenge is *globalization*, which concerns the destiny of mankind, and has a broader and deeper meaning than the purely economical one in this new historical era (*Compendium* 13–17).

## 1 Christian humanism

Mankind seems to increasingly and more clearly understand that it is linked by a single destiny that demands undertaking common responsibility, inspired by due humanism. Mankind is able to see that this unified destiny is often conditioned and sometimes imposed by technology or the economy and is able to perceive the need for greater moral conscience that guides the common path. This is why CST seeks to propose to all mankind an *integral and solidary humanism* that is able to encourage a new social, economic, and politic order based on dignity and freedom for all humans, acting in peace, justice, and solidarity (*Compendium, 6*).

### A Features of Christian humanism

The features that define the humanism proposed by the social teachings of the Church can be summarized as follows:[3]

1. It must encourage mankind to realize themselves in all the spheres of their being and reach all human purposes (PP 19).
2. In this sense, the said humanism cannot renounce its transcendent character: the measure of mankind is God and only under this supernatural aspiration can mankind realize themselves as humans in the light of the new Man, Jesus Christ.[4]
3. This new humanism cannot remain only in theoretical-doctrinal formulations or in mere statements; on the contrary, it must be able to find the ways and instruments that contemporary men require for their absolute realization. This humanism must not only analyze and describe the causes of dehumanization or the consequences of

unbelieving anthropocentrism, it must cast light on the guidelines for the changes that must be made and on the forces – especially the spiritual ones – that must be passed on to meet the demands imposed by this humanism itself.

4. Finally, the Christian humanism under consideration is expressed, from the point of view of truth, as humanism focused on charity, that is, love. It conveys the humanizing force of the divine love offered by Christ to mankind, so that they can build with Him a new civilization. "Only in *charity, illumined by the light of reason and faith*, is it possible to pursue development goals that possess a more humane and humanizing value" (CV 9; italics in original).

### B Christian humanism faced with non-transcendent humanisms

The Church has always taught that authentic humanism must be full, according to an adequate understanding of what mankind is, that is, a creature of God, made in His image and likeness, created by God for His glory and therefore, originated by Him and destined to come back to Him freely. Thus, in words of Paul VI, "There is no true humanism but that which is open to the Absolute and is conscious of a vocation which gives human life its true meaning" (PP 42).

This humanism differs deeply from those that have appeared over the course of time, particularly from those that have appeared in the contemporaneous age, such as: Marxism, the most radical secularist liberalism; and existentialism. These conceive mankind as beings liberated from God – and even from their own nature – either by means of the reductionist identification of mankind with a mechanism or piece of the big social machine and their concomitant depersonification, as in the case of Marxism,[5] or through the exaltation of the individual's subjectivity leading every person to become the only legislator of her/himself, as in individualistic liberalism or in atheistic existentialism.[6]

Considering that reality, the Vatican Council II expressly addressed humanisms' uncompromising connection with transcendence, highlighting the peculiar characteristics they currently entail: "unlike former days, the denial of God and religion, or the abandonment of them, are no longer unusual and individual occurrences. For today it is not rare for such things to be presented as requirements of scientific progress and of a certain new humanism. In numerous places these views are voiced not only in the teachings of philosophers, but on every side they influence literature, art, the interpretation of human sciences, history, and civil law itself. This explains the disturbance of many people" (GS 7) and the nonsense of the behaviors of many others.

In brief, the diffusion around the world of a certain "new humanism" obliges in these pages, at least, to give this very brief reference regarding this matter. The common denominator of the different lines of thought that support its existence, its common and unifying element resides in two basic aspects: its grounds, the denial of God; its objective, the annihilation of the person.[7] As you can see, the main proposals of the different lines of thought that must be grouped in this trend are radically opposed to the principles that make up the spirit of the humanism proposed by CST, particularly that proposed by *Caritas in Veritate*. For this reason, both insights on mankind and society differ and are different in their very essence and consequently, inevitably also in its practical consequences (CV 78).

## 2 Christian humanism in the light of contemporaneous challenges

### A What is the progress of current human development?

Since the appearance of encyclical *Populorum progressio* until the publication of *Caritas in Veritate*, important events have taken place. Where is human development today? The main novelty in the past forty years is "*the explosion of worldwide interdependence*, commonly known as globalization" (CV 33, italics in original). This makes mankind face risks, but also opens opportunities.

Benedict XVI, as well as Paul VI, has an articulated vision of human development, consistent with the being of man. Development cannot only be of a material nature and neither must it be exclusively understood or motivated in terms of benefits, because that would mean focusing on one part of human development, and would not be consistent with what man really is. To look at development from this point of view would be looking at it from a reductionist perspective.

The encyclical does not have a negative tone; it knows how to harmonize, specifying the difficulties and additional risks, and highlighting the opportunities. It highlights that economical development has generated great assets but, simultaneously, reveals that it has been and continues to be "weighed down by malfunctions and dramatic problems" (CV 21), the latter including a variety of contemporaneous social phenomena, either of economical[8] nature or not directly linked with economy.[9]

### B The great challenge for the economy and business world

Taking into account the scenario described above, it is quite evident that a new, deeper reflection on the meaning of human development, of the economy and its goals is required. In the words of Benedict XVI himself, "*broadening the scope of reason and making it capable of knowing and directing these powerful new forces*, encouraging them within the perspective of that 'civilization of love' whose seed God has planted in every people, in every culture" (CV 33; italics in original) is necessary.

Along this line of thinking, "Fraternity, Economical Development and Civil Society" is the title of the third chapter of the encyclical. Special attention must be paid to these pages, because they convey the core message of the document. Again, it elaborates the principle of gratuitousness, addressed in the preceding chapters. It reveals itself in life in society, preferably as fraternity (fellowship), and can and "must *find their place within normal economic activity*" (CV 36; italics in original).

## 3 Some essential elements of Christian humanism in business activity

*Caritas in Veritate* is based on a fine Christian anthropology, anchored in a solid starting point: mankind is a creature of God and was made in His image and likeness. Benedict XVI stated that the social question is today an "anthropological question" (CV 75). When we understand who the person is, all the features that her/his action should have are clearly revealed. As asserted in philosophy: "action follows being," that is, every being acts according to what she/he is. Indeed, this encyclical highlights that the real and effective human action should be consistent with what the person is and not with a fraction or only one dimension of her/him. For the same reason, from its viewpoint of the person – and, consequently, of human society – a set of essential elements can be gathered to mark the path toward a business activity more suited to mankind.

Freedom is undoubtedly one of the cornerstones of this letter. Moreover, in total it is an ode to freedom.[10] It permanently emphasizes the free dimension of the human being, calling on individuals to act in consistency with it, to be innovative in its use, and to rely on the free dimension of those who are to be helped.

Together with an emphasis on freedom, a parallel one on ethics is consequently made. All business and trade activities, as well as those related to investment and development, have a moral dimension

(CV 37); they do not only hold technological, economical, and financial dimensions. This means that they have an impact on human good. When we say morality, we refer to the exercise of freedom for good and, if we are talking about society, we are emphasizing the value of the exercise of freedom in relation to the common good (CV 17).[11]

In this, *Caritas in Veritate* follows the thread of the former encyclicals and of some concepts elaborated by Pope John Paul II, for instance, "the ethical character of every investment decision" (CA 36, CV 40). All in all, it is advised that the word "ethics" should not be abused. Frequently, voices are raised in the name of morality, but in the light of the authentic human plenitude, a "person-friendly" ethics is required (CV 45).

Consequently, even when our world, as it is currently, is one where human rights are much highlighted, and with good reason, *Caritas in Veritate* emphasizes that the same does not happen regarding obligations, to a point in which it warns: "individual rights, when detached from a framework of duties which grants them their full meaning, can run wild, leading to an escalation of demands which is effectively unlimited and indiscriminate. Overemphasis on rights leads to a disregard of duties. Duties set a limit on rights because they point to the anthropological and ethical framework of which rights are a part, in this way ensuring that they do not become license. Duties thereby reinforce rights and call for their defense and promotion as a task to be undertaken in the service of the common good" (CV 43). Acknowledging this reality, revaluation of responsibility is another idea that appears throughout the entire document. If the person, her/his freedom, and ethics are truly appreciated, then her/his responsibility becomes crucial, since ethics, in its core, entails the responsibility with which freedom is exercised.

In relation to freedom and responsibility, the principle of subsidiarity stands out. As mentioned, we have to help people to develop, but also to keep their freedom (CV 47, 57). Consequently, we have the duty to help them, to provide them with support, but allowing them to gain autonomy and grow, so that they gradually become conscious of and responsible for their obligations. In short, we must collaborate so that the peoples that are being helped become people in their fullest dimensions, because only in this way can cooperation to form better societies take place. It is clear that not only the generation of job opportunities and material conditions are questioned here as essential tasks of the company. A clear call to the formative task (CV 61) – not only to technical training – in and from the company can be inferred from this exhortation.

Consistently with the ideas mentioned above, the Pope neither proposes nor encourages welfarism, as it is usually understood. On the contrary, he encourages something far superior. If we refer to integral human development, we must appreciate the dignity of the person and, therefore, assume her/his freedom, because the said development would not exist if everyone else's freedom is not valued and enforced. The aforementioned subsidiarity principle, a permanent heritage of CST, emphasizes precisely this aspect when establishing that it is impossible to promote the person's dignity if family, groups, associations, local territorial realities – that is, those additional economic, social, cultural, recreational, professional, politic expressions that people give life to spontaneously and whose social growth they make possible – are not looked after. The network of these relationships makes up the social fabric and is the foundation of a true community of people (*Compendium* 185–187). The Church demands tutelage and promotion of the original expressions of sociability in its encyclical *Quadragesimo anno*, in which the subsidiarity principle is mentioned as a major principle of social philosophy (QA 48). According to this principle, all societies in a higher position must adopt a supportive (*subsidium*) attitude – of assistance, promotion, and development – toward the lower ones. Furthermore, the subsidiarity principle protects people and their free associations from the abuse of the upper social instances and encourages the latter to help individuals and intermediate bodies in developing their tasks. Every person, family, and intermediate body has something original to offer to the community. Therefore, getting people involved in their own development is a duty; they must be the authors of this development and, for the same reason, people have to be agents of their own growth.

Thus, the so-called corporate social responsibility (hereafter CSR) finds a natural space within the argumentation of the encyclical. Its essential aspects are analyzed, but it is also noticed that not all the theories or proposals about CSR are consistent with a true anthropological conception (CV 40). Concretely, the challenge consists in going beyond commutative justice, beyond exchanges, beyond profit-making, exceeding the exclusive market–State relationship, often seen as antagonists by contemporaneous society. Taking another step forward is imperative to see the economy from a solidary viewpoint. Then, it seems possible to make businesses with a vision of fraternity and gratuitousness (CV 38–39).

Likewise, the challenge for the company implies strengthening the social network and not waiting for everything to be resolved by the market – which finally is an abstraction – or by the provident State. All in all, breaking previously established models, leaving the known corporate patterns to forge a new modality of relationships, institutions and social organizations is required (CV 38).

*Caritas in Veritate* calls on business people to carry out all of this from within the company. Such a corporate initiative acquires a polyvalent meaning and is opposed to the way it has always been understood – possibly too linked to profit-making. Notwithstanding that profit making is not a problem per se – furthermore, it is legitimate – it is the definitive meaning of business activity. Neither can it be the final objective of companies, as in economic activity, because humans are the authors, the center, and the end (CV 25). The human is the one who carries out and gives meaning to the business activity; without it, the latter would not be understood or exist. Part of the capital can be subtracted from the business activity, but the person cannot be removed from it because the person is indispensable. The business activity exists because individual and concrete people give life to it. For this reason, as stated, the final objective of business activity is the person, the personal – and, viewed from a social point of view – human good. Following the cohesion of these arguments, Benedict XVI's call to procure meta-economic motivations in the realization of the trade activity can be understood better. "Business activity has a human significance, prior to its professional one" (CV 41).

He also invites us to become aware of the anthropological and ethical meaning associated with the globalization process. In this phenomenon, the Pope sees an opportunity to unite the human family, to understand and live humanity as a family, where all humans become brothers and are treated as such.

All in all, broadening and deepening its sharp analysis, the encyclical actually reveals the interrelation of the different aspects of human life in society. For instance, it addresses the demographic issue of birthrate and, by relating it to the economy, shows how demographic growth is finally the source of human development and even of economic development.

It also addresses the need to strengthen the family composed of a man and a woman, on a steady and permanent basis (CV 44), in evident contrast with certain proposed alternative family models that are currently being promoted and which are not consistent with the real human nature.[12]

## A Centrality of the person

From the core argument of *Caritas in Veritate* discussed in the previous pages, it can be clearly inferred that the main reality on which Christian humanism for business must be elaborated is the person (CV 47) with her/his inalienable *dignity*.

If companies reach deep awareness of the ontological value or *dignity* of the person and of the condition of equality of being between humans, they will find a solid ground to generate strong commitment with the integral development of its members. They are, nothing more and nothing less than unique and unrepeatable beings that, participating in the divine qualities, have a spiritual life of a rational, free, and transcendent nature. In addition, they are social beings by nature, called upon to achieve their human perfection – which leads them to the supernatural one – in the heart of community life. These characteristics of people, on one hand, make them an end per se and one which cannot be reduced to the status of mere means; and, on the other hand, they reveal that social life, and specifically the corporate one, has human good as a goal. In other words, business activity is performed by mankind for mankind. Its end cannot be other than human plenitude, to which it must contribute from its particular nature and situation. In this sense, companies must always be at the *service* of people.

Institutions that truly base their activities on a deep anthropological conception like the aforementioned, to be coherent at the moment of action, must also develop high esteem or valuation of human life. This conviction, if it is genuine, will have to be embodied in their entire activity, converting them into organizations that, in the day-to-day language, could be called "pro life"[13] and, therefore, they will defend and encourage the institution of family (CV 44), especially of those made up by each one of its members, never forgetting that family is the base of any corporate order.[14] Better families will tend to bring about better people and, consequently, will allow for a society with more plenitude in which there will always be the possibility of carrying out a business activity of greater quality, more sustainable, and even more profitable.

CST sees the company as an intermediate body between individuals and the State (*Compendium* 336–345). This means that the company must orientate all of its activities toward the common good of the society it is part of. This reality obliges companies to understand that their contribution to community does not end with the production and commercialization of certain economic assets, even when doing so is a duty for them, but that from their place in the social fabric, they must contribute to the full development of the community, which includes other aspects or dimensions associated with the business activity – apart from the family activity – such as the formational, psychological, moral, and spiritual ones, to quote only some of the most relevant.

Economic activity is carried out by human beings and, therefore, is not only related to things or material assets, but with people who have spirituality. Both the substratum itself and its purposes are aimed at the reality of the spirit in its broadest sense, that is, knowledge, moral habits, companionship, sense of body, and so forth. The professional work that supports it and makes it possible is, at the same time, a fruit of the spirit more than of the matter and corporealness, and the assets that the person obtains from her/his labor activity also largely exceed the realm of the strictly material and subsistence. Personal growth, acquired knowledge and practical wisdom, self-esteem, usefulness, willingness for service, and moral virtues are clear examples of these effects.

In the light of the concepts explained, the entire realm of business activity can be rethought and, consequently, re-orientated. As outlined above, business activity reaches full meaning if it is orientated toward human good, both in its personal and corporate dimensions. As a truly human reality, it must be orientated toward the good of humans themselves. This fact is even clearer if we remember that its aforementioned condition as an intermediate social organization means that in the community fabric, the company is between the family (basic cell of society) and the political society. A company that does not aim its activities at the family good and the greater society where it exists, strictly speaking, does not fully comply with its community function and, even worse, it may run the risk of deviating, making its particular interests the primary objective or replacing those corresponding to common good.

By only appealing to these principles, rooted in the anthropology and nature of social order, there could be reason enough to sustain the need of a business life more consistent with human good. In its analysis and proposals, *Caritas in Veritate* incorporates the said conceptual elements, which are deeply rooted in the best Christian theological and philosophic tradition.[15] However, notwithstanding the aforementioned, its most important contribution is having uplifted them to the level of faith and theology, to look at them and extract them based upon a consideration of God, particularly of God the Father, and the subsequent understanding of mankind as His creatures.

Other religions or thought traditions recognize benevolence and solidarity as human virtues and consider others as beings that deserve respect and compassion in their needs. But Christianity, while seeing God as a Father, demands that we consider others as brothers. This demands radical fraternity compelling gratuitousness, gift and solidarity *of an individual nature*, both in personal, family, and social relationships and, among the latter, concretely in the sphere of the economical–corporate links under discussion.

## B Transcendent, integral, and solidary humanism

The marrow of *Caritas in Veritate*, in essence seems to consist of taking the human being seriously and also his/her *dignity*. This can only be done by considering a human from two complementary points of view: as a transcendent being and as a being tending to completeness.[16]

The former, referring to the transcendence inherent in the person, is necessarily related to God. Only if there is someone completely and eternally absolute, can it be understood that mankind, of His own making, can participate – even imperfectly – of that entitative characteristic and, consequently, due to the special ontological dignity entailed, they must be highly valued. In any case, humans should never be treated as simple means or instruments to achieve certain objectives, no matter what these are.

The fact that humans are transcendent means that they have a degree of absoluteness and, consequently, at the same time they are linked to and separated from the physical world. For that reason, they must be treated considering their real condition, that is, as a certain end per se. Therefore, to effectively grant them the *dignity* that they entitatively hold, we must also consider a human as absolute and as related to the other humans. If we think that humans are simply autonomous beings (independent, absolute) – as proposed by some individualisms-liberalisms – and act accordingly, humans would be isolated in themselves, as radically independent beings who do not need others. However, more importantly, an isolated being does not have a spirit, since interiority only exists when there is a relationship with another spirit. Human beings, understood as such and treated accordingly, would be practically de-spiritualized, that is, "reified."

To relate with humans, not as objects, but as beings who have a spirit, we must interact with them, moreover, we must serve them. Effectively wanting and procuring good for others as the objective of our action is the most excellent behavior that a person can display regarding other people. In that regard, being *worthy* means *serving*. She or he who does not look to relate with others as a servant in her/his acts does not honor her/his ontological dignity. For this reason, it can be asserted that individualistic absolutism is unworthy, because it is not consistent with the authentic human nature, at least with its plenitude.

Precisely due to the contrary, that is, because in considering mankind only as an earthly-material being (not absolute), collectivist relativism does not enforce the dignity of the person because it denatures her/him, effectively making her/him into a simple useful means related to social ends to which people must be subordinated. This has been the position largely put forward, defended and applied – but not exclusively – by Marxist socialism. It is quite clear that, from this viewpoint, the person is also reified, both theoretically and practically.

Humans are beings with a vocation of completeness or totality. This means that they have multiple and different dimensions and, consequently, several inclinations and many possibilities of plenitude.[17] In principle, they have the chance of achieving everything that their own nature allows them. However, they actually cannot achieve more than just a few of these perfections. Even when considered as species, humans have several alternatives for plenitude; however, individually, every person faces limitations – of natural inclinations or capacities, of time and space – that only allow them to develop a few of these aspects in their lives. Then, due to their tendency to totality, humans necessarily have to relate to the rest of mankind. The person is a relational and social being by nature, because (s)he can only realize her/his completeness with the help of the others, living in community. Therefore, the more human possibilities developed by a society, the more plenitude can those people obtain from the different assets they benefit from.

At this stage of the argument, it may seem that the aforementioned, though plausibly true, would be hardly applicable to the field of business activity. This is just because a company is what can be called, from a social point of view, an intermediate social entity. On one hand, we may say that these kinds of societies are relative, because they value the person in a conditional manner and under some of her/his dimensions – for instance, as a productive worker – and, therefore, they do not make room for the person as an absolute. On the other hand, they seem to be constitutively aimed at trying to cover only some human need(s) or wish(es) or, in other words, part of the human purposes and not all of them. The meaning of the company is, precisely, to develop an area of human possibilities to such a degree that what is characteristic of companies is "specialized" and, consequently, divided work.

Furthermore, seeing human life as a whole, it is in the family where each person is seen – or, at least, should be seen – as a somewhat absolute being, as someone unconditionally loved just for the sake of existing. In contrast, it would be in the State or political society where (s)he is considered – or should be considered – as having a total character, considering the completeness of her/his possible perfections. In fact, the State is obliged to provide for all the needs of society and, consequently, of each individual. It should organize things so that each of its members achieve as close as possible the "having everything" required in human terms. For this reason, even before Christ, Aristotle maintained that it is in the *Polis* (the State) where man is called upon to perfect himself, that is, to achieve some plenitude.[18] However, in the intermediate society, in socioeconomic life, more specifically in the company, other laws seem to rule. There, the absolute and total do not count, on the contrary, the relative and partial seem to have priority.

The problem is that the relative and partial are meaningless unless they regard the absolute and total. That is, when socioeconomic life is lived as not orientated to the family and society in general, in other words, when it is lived as not aimed at *human dignity*, then the socioeconomic sphere is actually being made absolute and total. To draw back from an absolute reality and from a total one, we fall into others that, not being either an absolute or total reality, replace them. And this is what usually happens. At present, this kind of social configuration is called the bourgeois, consumer, capitalist society and so on. It is the prevailing form – and tone – of community nowadays.

To convert this materialistic social reality into a human one it is necessary to channel socioeconomic activity and, more precisely, business activity, toward humans, toward their *dignity*. Humanism in business mainly consists of placing as the ultimate goal of the company the effective realization of the *dignity* of all of those relating to it and, finally, that of the entire society.

It is quite clear that neither a company, nor a family, nor a university, nor a club, nor the Church itself can work well if they do not have a sound economy; and the sounder the better. Nevertheless, that is a condition for life, not an ultimate goal. Therefore, the economy must be looked after, because it is needed. However, a condition can never be an ultimate goal. Converting the economy and the business activity that moves it into goals is materialism, that is, indignity: Reductionism of people and society.

If, on one hand, the aforementioned thoughts are correct, the work – the relative and partial – developed in the company to achieve certain intermediate goals to cover some needs and wishes, must be connected with the absolute: it must be *dignified*. On the other hand, the company should be interested that everyone interacting with it gets closer to their completeness, their integral plenitude. This means, among other aspects, that commercial activities leave enough time for its members to develop other activities and promote culture and, very specially, strengthen family life, which in time will give the benefit of a greater sociability and humanity.

All the aforementioned cannot be reached only with the aim of achieving maximum benefits or by enforcing contractual justice or even by exercising distributive justice but only by living an authentic solidarity based on fraternity and aimed at charity, always with plenty of gratuitousness, donation, and at the mutual service of people:

> The great challenge before us, accentuated by the problems of development in this global era and made even more urgent by the economic and financial crisis, is to demonstrate, in thinking and behavior, not only that traditional principles of social ethics like transparency, honesty and responsibility cannot be ignored or attenuated, but also that in *commercial relationships* the *principle of gratuitousness* and the logic of gift as expressions of fraternity can and must *find their place within normal economic activity.* This is a human demand at the present time, but it is also demanded by economic logic. It is a demand both of charity and of truth. (CV 36; italics in original)
>
> This means a corporate practice that honestly recognizes human nature in its entire natural and supernatural richness and embodies, in the action, everything of which the person – as made – is the origin, center and end of any economical activity. This humanism may be fulfilled if every man and women and their business communities know how to nurture the moral and social virtues within themselves and spread them in society, "so they really become new men and creator s of a new humanity." (GS 30)

## 4 Practical aspects for business

Proposing a Christian humanism in business – transcendent, integral and solidary – in the light of the contents of *Caritas in Veritate* entails several practical implications. Among them, as an example, are four implications of special relevance: (1) dignifying professional work, (2) strengthening family life, (3) giving reality and full meaning to social responsibility, and (4) developing humanist business leaders.

## A Dignify professional work

Granting dignity to professional work can involve very different aspects. However, it essentially lies on the possibilities for human plenitude that enables the one who carries it out and its receptors. From this starting point, a decent job must fulfill several requirements ranging from the most basic to the most complex:

a. That the work activity must be ethical per se and that, accordingly, it must not violate the fundamental human rights.
b. That it allows one to obtain enough economic resources to make decent human life possible, both for the one who works and for those who depend on her/him, usually her/his family. It is worth mentioning that a decent human life entails far more than just surviving, because surviving is only a condition of possibilities to subsequently achieve both material and spiritual (cultural, knowledge, moral virtues, artistic, social, affective, etc.) human perfections.
c. Consequently, that it makes rest, amusement, and "noble leisure" possible. Humans need time to cultivate other dimensions of life that are not covered by professional work.
d. That a contribution to social common good is made, both due to the material nature of the economic assets and services, realization of which is made through work, and due to the non-economic human assets that are similarly generated (virtues, cooperation with other people, spirit of service, learning, etc.).
e. That the subjective dimension of the tasks performed be a source for the inner growth for those who work. That is, that the immanent aspect of the work activity be enriching per se, giving the individual who is the author of the professional work personal assets such as, for instance, growth in: technical/operational habits, intellectual/theoretical habits, knowledge, moral virtues, recognition, satisfaction with a job well-done, and more. For a Christian this work is also and above all a means of sanctification and to practice fraternal love.[19]

## B Strengthening family life

In order to shape strong personalities, it is necessary to have true, well-constituted families.[20] Without well-formed people it is not possible to expect that society, made up of them, develops adequately. Therefore, asserting that companies are not interested in the good of the family reveals an important misunderstanding of the nature of companies, their place in social order, and their own future.

Companies, as with any other corporation or institution in society, must be, at least, interested in having people able to continue, strengthen, and improve what they are doing. Does this mean that business corporations must subsidize families? Certainly, this is not their main task. Families themselves must take care of their members. Nevertheless, companies, like the State, can make this task easy or difficult. Specifically, companies can contribute so that, in the social sphere, families are respected, that is, intervening – with their internal policies and actions, with their CSR plans and activities and by means of the media, which depend, in part, on companies – so that the social common sense assumes, as something evident, that the family is crucial. Maybe this is the most important corporate social responsibility of companies: promoting family, generating conscience about its importance and that of the social links, both for people and society and, consequently, for the company itself.

Just as an example, we will mention, as proof of the aforementioned, that it is in the family where trust – the foundation of the entire society – is acquired and developed. There is practically no substitution in the entire corporate life able to undertake this formational task. Something similar happens with the acquisition of virtues, the will to cooperate, the awakening of the spirit of service and learning how to do our tasks well.

### C Giving reality and full meaning to social responsibility

Human life is filled with a huge set of small details. Taking the great meaning of this set of intangible things seriously means realizing that, without humanism, CSR cannot exist. Being socially responsible means, first, living righteously, taking into account the transcendent and social, not just the mundane and individualistic, human nature, and being aware that any personal decision, within or outside the company, has an implication for everyone else. A socially responsible person is someone who is concerned about giving real meaning to intangible things like trust, freedom, responsibility, and common good, discovering their true meaning and duly valuing them.

The important thing is that all of those who are leading the main driving forces of society – among them, in a privileged position, businessmen – are aware that creating society is everybody's work and, consequently, no one can lock her/himself in the job (s)he is doing, but when performing her/his concrete task, with her/his mind focused on everything, and carrying it out in the best possible way, (s)he is fulfilling her/his first responsibility.

### D Developing humanistic business leaders

Humanism has always been knowledge of integration because humans have multiple dimensions. Therefore, a humanist is (s)he who is always conscious of the links between the particular and the multiple aspects inherent of society because only in this way can we contribute – individually and organizationally – to the social totality. In other words, to take society forward, everyone needs to incorporate a humanism that allows us to look beyond ourselves to get to know others and what is alien, to understand the keys of social life and correctly integrate economy, politics, ethics, law, aesthetic (styles), and so forth.

A leader, who has an insufficient understanding of what the different dimensions of the human person and the different edges of a real society mean, cannot be authentically responsible for what (s)he is doing. A conscious manager must be humanistic, that is, (s)he must be able to see the completeness of the person and society, and cannot ignore it. For instance, if we are have a society of uneducated people developing good companies is not possible. For this reason, having good schools and universities should be of great concern. Otherwise, the economic bill that will be paid in the future will be huge. Likewise, the fact that the family is indeed the basic structure of society – unlike what is said and happens today – should be of primordial concern because otherwise, we would not be able to form people, even less leaders, that are really responsible.

In short, for proper leadership of companies, their managers must be formed, aiming to help them in the task of becoming true humanists who, without ignoring technology, know how to arrange the activity of the organizations that lead to the permanent search for human and social good.

We can see, then, that by breaking down the message in *Caritas in Veritate* it is possible to find the basic elements to configure and develop a consistent humanism in business in which the elite managing companies know how to consider each person in full, realizing that humans are not only a labor force, less a resource, or else only an individual whose rights cannot be alienable, but basically a person, that is, an *alter ego*, a brother (*frater*).

## 5 Conclusion

Standing on the aforementioned pillars, we can understand more clearly why a cry for the establishment of a new humanism can be found in the encyclical marrow, this time for humanism in business. Materialized in a call to everyone, believers, and people of good will, to see, understand, and practice a business activity that is made-to-measure for mankind, based on a Christian humanism. This is, in turn, built on understanding in the light of the teaching of Christ about who the person is and what society is, and about what humans are called upon to become. This provides us with a society consistent with what humans are and must be and, consequently, make their perfection possible.

One way or another and with several expressions, the encyclical seems to encourage that particular humanism in business. That is, to understand business life and practice under a comprehensive vision of mankind and its development. What is carried out in the company must be linked to a full consideration of the person and her/his social character. For this, an idea of development that does not only focus on the material because the spirit must also, and primarily, be attended to and, consequently, God must be included and not excluded. If we remove God from the public sphere and from the different social expressions of human life, the latter will be made up by cropped humans, with all the painful individual and social consequences that come with it. On the contrary, more than ever, a development in which God is present as the cornerstone becomes indispensable because He wants his creatures, people, to walk toward the plenitude they are destined for. In an authentic anthropologic conception, development takes part of what the person is and, consequently, it is the necessary requirement to achieve a purposeful life. If we really wish that gratuitousness, gift, and fraternity are included in the social, economic, and business order, the evident conclusion is to place God again as the beginning and end of all human activities. Then, the challenge for everybody – and due to their central position in today's world order, especially for businessmen and senior executives – consists in knowing how to place God in an intelligent, voluntary, and solidary manner in the midst of the world, in the marrow of the world's corporate life, more concretely, in the midst of the professional work and of the entire economic-business activity.

## Executive summary

From the content of Encyclical *Caritas in Veritate*, this work aims to unravel the main teachings and challenges that *Caritas in Veritate* put forward for businessmen and the business community. Specifically, the main challenge is making room for gratuitousness and gift in economic activity, as these traces are present in the very being of the person, asserted by the Christian faith as a creature made in the image and likeness of God. In the economic sphere, the said features are evident through the incorporation and practical application of the principles of fraternity and solidarity. In light of the encyclical, it is necessary to go beyond the existing models and, consequently, re-think and re-direct business activity to make it more made-to-measure for man, both in its personal–individual and social dimensions. This chapter proposes an essential principle to channel that activity: the *dignity* of the person. This principle, duly realized within a humanistic conception of the business activity, would allow the noble objectives to be reached boosted by *Caritas in Veritate*. In brief, based on a firm anthropology and, consequently, on a deep understanding of the social order, the encyclical seems to encourage clearly the transition toward a new transcendent, integral, and solidary humanism that should be applied in business. This leads to a humanism in business that would demand, as a fundamental premise, full understanding of the person as a transcendent being who attends to achieving integral spiritual and material development.

## Notes

1. For an official synthesis of CST, see *Compendium*. As introductory text of the CST, see Melé (2012). A systematic treatise on CST can be found, for instance, in Colom (2006).
2. Cf. *Compendium*, Introduction, 10, 12 and 13. Also, see the opening words of *Caritas in Veritate* (CV 1).
3. This subsection is, in general terms, a tribute to the ideas put forward by Cortés (2010).
4. "Due to his insertion in living Christ, men have an open way to a new progress, to a transcendent humanism that gives him his greatest plenitude; such is the supreme goal of personal development" (PP 16).
5. That is how Pope Pius XI explained it when he referred to atheistic communism: "There is no recognition of any right of the individual in his relations to the collectivity; no natural right is accorded to human personality, which is a mere cog-wheel in the Communist system" (Pius XI. Encyclical letter *Divini Redemptoris*, 1937, n. 10).
6. Jean Paul Sartre, maximum exponent of 20th century subjectivist existentialism, expressly stated that "There is no other universe except the human universe, the universe of human subjectivity" (Sartre 2009, p. 85). Indeed, according to the ideas of the French Philosopher, it was possible to talk about an existentialist humanism "because we remind man that there is no legislator but himself; that he himself, thus abandoned, must decide for himself; also because we show that it is not by turning back upon himself, but always

by seeking, beyond himself, an aim which is one of liberation or of some particular realisation, that man can realize himself as truly human" (Sartre 2009, p. 85).

7. *Cfr.* Cortés (2010, p. 117, n. 9), who quotes the French Theologian Henri de Lubac, in his work *The Drama of Atheist Humanism* (first published in 1944). Even when he distinguished three humanisms (August Comte's positivism, Marxist, and Nietzschean), he shows, however, the common grounds and the main objective of these different antitheist anthropocentrisms: "positivist humanism, Marxist humanism, Nietzschean humanism are, more than just atheism as such, antitheism, more concretely, anti-Christianity, due to the denial rooted in their grounds. No matter how opposed they may be to each other, their mutual implications, hidden or patent, are huge and have a common foundation consisting in the denial of God; they also coincide in their main objective of annihilating the human person" (De Lubac 1990, p.10).
8. Such as, for instance: the detrimental effects on the real economy of misused and speculative financial activity; the provoked and then unmanaged migration fluxes; the unregulated exploitation of the earth's resources; the increase of inequality notwithstanding the increase of wealth: "The scandal of glaring inequalities" (PP 9, CV 22); the excessive labor mobility which, in many cases, is generating psychological instability; hunger.
9. Among them are: contraception, abortion and sterilization, hedonistic sexuality; genetic manipulation, cultural eclecticism; denial of the right to religious freedom; fundamentalist terrorism; religious indifference: the so-called practical atheism. An technocratic ideology where technology enslaves men; environmental development, ecology, and naturalism issues, with the risks that some radical naturalisms entail, in which God is confused with nature of men in a sort of pantheist magma.
10. *Caritas in Veritate* contains many explicit references to freedom in (9, 10, 11, 17, 29, 38, 56, 57, 68, 70). Thus, it is also explicitly present in several allusions in the text to matters associated with freedom, such as ethics, responsibility, duty, and subsidiarity.
11. Here Benedict XVI notes that Paul VI already "had a keen sense of the importance of economic structures and institutions, but he had an equally clear sense of their nature as instruments of human freedom. Only when it is free can development be integrally human; only in a climate of responsible freedom can it grow in a satisfactory manner."
12. The latter ideas come from a conceptual context deeply rooted in reality and from solid grounds to support, among other things, a correct action in the sphere of conciliation between family life and professional work and of the so-called Family-Responsible Companies (FRCs).
13. "Openness to life is at the centre of true development" (CV 28).
14. For that reason, it would be easy to determine that families are the primary source of the future members of business corporations and, simultaneously, are the privileged shaper of the characteristics that both the community life (where companies will be inserted) and the markets (where they will participate). The principles, virtues, vices, and deficiencies that the family institution may have will always be determinant in the constitution of social

reality as well as of the characteristics and inclinations of future citizens, professionals, and consumers. These are reason enough for business persons and senior executives to do their best to generate conditions to vivify and strengthen the family.

15. There is deep conceptual background in three encyclical letters on the economic and social order by the immediately preceding Pope, *Laborem excerens* (LE 1981), *Sollicitudo rei socialis* (SRS 1989), and *Centesimus annus* (CA 1991).
16. Regarding the concept and meaning of humanism in business, we recommend an early and enlightening work by Rafael Alvira (1992) in this field, whose suggestive Christian philosophic ideas have inspired the concept developed in this subsection.
17. Unlike animals, which are specialized *per natura,* humans are not specialized in life, and this is a necessary condition for a radical opening. Precisely because humans are not marked by an original specialization, they are open to infinity of different perfections.
18. *Cfr.* Aristotle. *Politics* I, 2 (1253 to 1–3, 30–33) and *Nicomachean Ethics* (1094 b1–11, 1095 to 14–18, 1181 to 10–12).
19. Regarding this latter, see Pope Paul VI, *Lumen Gentium* (LG nn. 31, 35–36 and 39–42) and the chapter 5th of the encyclical letter *Laborem exercens* (LE) by Pope John Paul II. St. Josemaria Escrivá contributed decisively to spread the practice of the sanctification of work (see Illanes 2003 and Rodriguez 1987).
20. The concepts developed in what follows are tributary of ideas proposed by Rafael Alvira (2011).

## References


Alvira, Rafael. "Qué es el humanismo empresarial." In A. Llano, R. Alvira, M. Bastons, T. Calleja, C. Martínez Esteruelas and I. Miralbell, eds. *El humanismo en la empresa.* Madrid: Rialp, 1992.

Alvira, Rafael. "Responsabilidad social y humanismo empresarial: libertad, bien común, familia y confianza." In R. Alvira Rafael. *Gobierno empresarial: la responsabilidad política del alto directivo en la sociedad.* Santiago de Chile: ESE – Business School, 2011.

Aristotle, *The Nicomachean Ethics* . Oxford/New York: Oxford University Press, 1925.

Aristotle, *Politics.* Oxford: Oxford University Press, 1948.

Colom, Enrique. *Curso de Doctrina Social de la Iglesia.* Madrid: Palabra, 2006.

Cortés, Carmen. "Humanismo cristiano para nuestra sociedad." In D. Melé and J.M. Castellà, eds. *El Desarrollo Humano Integral. Comentarios Interdisciplinares a la encíclica 'Caritas in veritate' de Benedicto XVI.* Barcelona: Iter, 2010.

De Lubac, Henri. *El drama del humanismo ateo.* Madrid: Encuentro, 1990.

Illanes, José Luis. *The Sanctification of Work.* New York: Scepter, 2003

Melé, Domènec. *Cristianos en la Sociedad*, 5th edn. Madrid: Rialp, 2012.

Paul VI. *Dogmatic Constitution on the Church: Lumen gentium*, 1964, available at: www.vatican.va/archive/hist_councils/ii_vatican_council/documents/vat-ii_const_19641121_lumen-gentium_en.html (accessed January 31, 2012).

Pius XI. Encyclical letter *Divini Redemptoris*, 1937. Available at: www.vatican.va/holy_father/pius_xi/encyclicals/documents/hf_p-xi_enc_19031937_divini-redemptoris_en.html (accessed January 31, 2012).

Rodriguez, Pedro. *Vocación, Trabajo, Contemplación*, 2nd edn. Pamplona: Eunsa, 1987.

Sartre, J. P., *Existentialism is a Humanism, Translated by Carol Macomber, introduction by Annie Cohen-Solal; notes and preface by Arlette Elkaïm-Sartre*. John Kulka, ed. New Haven: Yale University Press, 2007[1945].

# 10
# The "Logic of Gift" in the Business Enterprise

*Antonio Argandoña*

> The great challenge before us..., is to demonstrate, in thinking and behaviour...., that in commercial relationships the principle of gratuitousness and the logic of gift as an expression of fraternity can and must find their place within normal economic activity. (CV 36)

This proposal by Benedict XVI poses a tremendous challenge to economists, business owners, and economic policy makers. Can gratuitousness and gift play a significant role in the practical life of companies and countries, as a requirement not only of philosophy or ethics but "also demanded by economic logic" (CV 36)? The purpose of this chapter is to show that this role is possible: indeed, if economic organizations and national economies are to function properly, all human actions, including those having an economic content, must be open to gratuitousness and gift.

In the following chapter, we develop the concepts of love, gift, and gratuitousness, first in the encyclical letter *Caritas in Veritate* (CV) and then in the theory of the firm. We then explain the role of virtues, their relationship with the "logic of gift," and the fields to which this logic applies, closing with conclusions on the practical implementation of gift in the firm.

## 1 Love, gift, gratuitousness

One central point of the Christian message is that "God is love" (1Jn 4, 8). For a Christian, the deepest and most intimate truth is being in the very beginning a gift of God's love. A non-believer can perceive this experience through the love of his parents, relatives, and friends: the

Christian message is, then, not alien to the experience of other people. However, there is a definitive difference: the Christian doctrine is not built upon the experience of people giving and loving, but upon the very constitution of man.

The concept of love, which is vital for *Caritas in Veritate*, is closely related in the encyclical with that of gift. As previously noted, the very existence of the human person is the result of a free act of love of God. Love is a gift that "is given to us. It happens, it comes to me from the other, it enters me" (Ratzinger 2002, p. 172): "love is God's greatest gift to humanity" (CV 2). The gift "takes first place in our souls as a sign of God's presence in us" (CV 34); God's love "opens our lives to gift" (CV 8) and "places man before the astonishing experience of gift" (CV 34).

All men and women are worthy of love because God gives all of them the gift of his love. Being loved by God enables reciprocity: we are "God's friends" (Jn 15, 14). God not only creates the human person out of love, but also to love God and the other persons: we can and must give everyone the gift of our love as an expression of fraternity, communion, sociability, and solidarity (CV 34, 36, 38, 39). Loving and giving are not mandates imposed from outside but are necessary for man. There is reciprocity between the love with which God loves us and the love with which we love God and our fellow man.

Furthermore, "because it is a gift received by everyone, charity in truth is a force that builds community, it brings all people together without imposing barriers or limits. The human community that we build by ourselves can never, purely by its own strength, be a fully fraternal community, nor can it overcome every division and become a truly universal community" (CV 34).

Love is, originally, a gift that the human being receives and gives. In one sense, gift is broader than love: the individual gives many other things, in addition to love, and not all gifts are given out of love. In another sense, love is something more than a gift: it can be understood as the joy that a person brings us; or a feeling related with the affection we feel for a person, or with the wish to do good to that person or enjoy him or her;[1] or a virtue that drives us to seek the other person's good; or a decision, choice or voluntary action that is undertaken and learnt (Fromm 1956).[2]

Gift is free and it is voluntary; it is not the outcome of a legal or social obligation, although it may be part of a moral duty. This is what separates it from abiding by a legal obligation (to pay a tax, for example) or contractual ones (e.g. to deliver a ware). In principle, it is unilateral, insofar as it does not create an obligation for the receiver (at least a direct or immediate obligation) to return the gift, unlike business exchanges. It can also be part of a framework of reciprocity, when it gives rise to a series of mutual gifts, each one of which continues to be free and voluntary, but which leave the door open for the other person to give or not, in accordance with his or her possibilities or wishes.

Gift enables the giver to receive, which in turn opens up new possibilities: giving becomes a gift for the giver, because it develops his or her virtues and introduces him or her to the logic of overabundance. Indeed, if "the human being is made for gift" (CV 34), giving is not an obligation, a cost, or a loss but an opportunity for improving oneself as a person, to develop one's humanity. "Giving is to give without losing, [it is] the activity that is higher than the balance of gains and losses, gaining without acquiring or acquiring by giving" (Polo 1996, pp. 130–131). From the point of view of the receiver, the gift respects his or her dignity: it can make equal, through solidarity, those who were unequal, and make equal in dignity and basic rights those who were diverse (Zamagni 2006). Therefore, it does not create a relationship of power or domination of one person over another.

Gift is also a dynamic phenomenon. Our first experience of love is our being the recipients of God's and other people's free gift of their love, and this experience continues in our voluntarily responding to other people's invitation to give to and to love others, that is, our learning to give, giving to others, and giving to ourselves.

Benedict XVI often uses the word "gratuitousness" alongside the word "gift" (CV 36), such that it seems that the two are equivalent. Gift is defined as "something given voluntarily without payment in return, as to show favor toward someone, honor an occasion, or make a gesture of assistance."[3] The concept may encompass very different things: material goods, services, work (and, therefore, effort, skills and knowledge), parts of our body (blood, organs), our time, and so forth. And gratuitous is "given, done, bestowed, or obtained without charge or payment." Gratuitousness is usually focused on sharing scarce resources, but gift does not necessarily have to be associated with scarcity (Khalil 2004).

In economic activity, when an agent delivers goods or services, (s)he can do this to receive something in return (exchange of equivalents on the market) or under obligation (a tax), but a gratuitousness can also be included in these actions (a present, a discount on the selling price, a salary that is higher than that stated in the contract). Thus, gratuitous means that there is a certain disproportion between the value that the agent attributes to what is given and the value (s)he attributes to what is received.

Benedict XVI often talks about the "logic of gift" (CV 34, 36) and the "principle of gratuitousness" (CV 34, 36). The word 'logic' refers here to the relationship between elements (people, principles, objects, events) of a whole. The 'logic of gift' hence refers to the relationships found in a system (society, market, company) when the starting point taken is the individual's givingness, insofar as he is empowered for gift and called to give. A "principle" becomes "an accepted or professed rule of action or conduct," or "a fundamental, primary, or general law or truth from which others are derived": the "principle of gratuitousness" would therefore be the maxim or idea that governs or should govern a matter; in our case, gratuitousness as the guiding principle of man's life in society.

## 2 Love, gift, and gratuitousness within the firm

What does Benedict XVI mean when, in the words with which we opened this chapter, he suggests that "in commercial relationships the principle of gratuitousness and the logic of gift...can and must find their place within normal economic activity" (CV 36)?

In conventional or mainstream economics, where resources are considered to be scarce and human needs are considered to be unlimited, the market is the best way to organize economic activity, because it enables the greatest possible number of needs to be satisfied with the least quantity of resources. In the market, rational agents, each pursuing their own interests, be these altruistic or self-centered, cooperate to satisfy everyone's interests, needs, or motivations. As Adam Smith said, "It is not from the benevolence of the butcher, the brewer, or the baker, that we expect our dinner, but from their regard to their own interest. We address ourselves, not to their humanity but to their self-love, and never talk to them of our own necessities but of their advantages" (1937[1776] I.2.2). Love may be present but it is not necessary.

However, a large part of economic activity takes place within firms, which do not follow the logic of free, voluntary exchange, characteristic of the market, but the logic of hierarchy and authority, attributed to the owner of capital and those who are his or her representatives, the managers (Coase 1937). Economists view the firm as a collection of physical and human resources or assets that cooperate to produce goods and services. Coordination of these activities is attributed to the owner of the production factor that is able to obtain the greatest contribution of all resources, in other words, the greatest efficiency, and that resource is capital.

Thus, the owners of capital hire a manager to act on their behalf and manage the firm in accordance with their interest. The manager hires material and human resources and pays them the agreed price, exercising his or her authority to direct their activity within the limits of what is allowed by law, what is agreed in the contracts, and what is established by social norms. Fairness problems are addressed in the contracts, which also provide incentives so that workers make the necessary effort to ensure efficient production.

In the theory of the firm, as previously in the theory of the market, there is no systemic place for love. Each individual must abide by the contracts in which (s)he is involved and there is apparently no conceptual need for other duties. It is not even necessary to appeal to ethical arguments to demand compliance with fairness in contracts: it seems sufficient for them to be bound by law and for judges to enforce their observance.[4]

However, there are many cases of gratuitous conduct (Meier 2006, Titmuss 1971), which may be inspired by love, both outside the market (donations, private contributions to funding public goods, cooperation) and within the market (not-for-profit firms, free services, or reduced prices for certain beneficiaries).

The distinction between exchange and gift is not clear in economics. Theoretically, exchange occurs in the market, and gift outside the market, but we find a broad range of behaviors between the two extremes, and there can be many forms of gift included within commercial relations. The great variety of explanations that have been given to the components of gift and gratuitousness in human behaviors can be grouped as follows:

1) The act of giving entails the expectation of receiving something in return in the present or future (reciprocity, impure altruism) (Axelrod 1984), that may be tangible (tax advantages tied to donations, for example) (Okten and Weisbrod 1999) or intangible (reputation, willingness to cooperate, etc.) (Glazer and Konrad 1996, Harbaugh 1998), positive or negative (social approval or censure) (Godbout 2005), and affecting the agent himself or others, but always hoping for a benefit for himself (favoring the group or class to which the agent belongs, aversion to inequality) (Becker 1976, Fehr and Schmidt 1999).
2) The act of giving is performed because it gives a psychological or emotional benefit to the agent, either because his preferences function includes being useful to others or because of the self-satisfaction (*warm glow*) that the act of giving produces (Andreoni 1990).

3) The agent seeks the good of the individual he gives to (strong altruism) (Piliavin and Charng 1990).

The third type of explanation seems to be directly related to the love of benevolence (Argandoña 2010, 2011a), but this motivation cannot be ruled out in the other cases, not even in the exchange of goods on the market: the seller, for example, may seek the buyer's good, even when (s)he demands payment of the fair price. Other forms of love may also be applicable, both in commercial relations and outside the market (when we act moved by a desire to be friendly, comradeship, etc., or when we appreciate that which we like or favors us: love of concupiscence) (Argandoña 2010).

In any case, although the explanations given by economics may be correct, they usually follow the paradigm of self-interest (Monroe 1994) and do not pay sufficient attention to the agent's motivation or intention, because they assume that the agent's actions are motivated by only one thing, or that the various motivations form part of the same preference function, enabling a trade-off among them,[5] which leads them, for example, to exclude love in relations where there is a personal interest.

## 3 Virtues in the firm

In this section, we will show how the virtues and, specifically love, can and should be lived within the firm.[6] The current prevailing theories of the firm usually assume that the manager seeks to maximize the value of the capital for the owners: this is the only important goal, at least in the neoclassic and neoinstitutionalist models. Under certain conditions, this allows maximum economic efficiency to be achieved. Of course, there are other lower-level goals, but these are subordinated to the first goal: for example, employees will have their own preferences about their work conditions but the firm has the necessary instruments to optimize each employee's contribution.[7] However, if we start from a broader theory of human action within organizations, these assumptions need to be revised.

Any human action gives rise to three types of effects or results:[8]

1. Extrinsic effects received from outside, which are the environment's (positive or negative) response to the agent's decision. They may be tangible (goods and services that the environment, usually other people, provide to the agent in response to his or her action) or intangible (reputation, recognition, prestige, social relations, etc.,

or loss of prestige, damage to reputation, etc., also originating from other people).

2. Intrinsic effects which come from and end at the agent him or herself as a result of the action, and which may, in turn, be of three types: (a) satisfaction or dissatisfaction with the action performed; (b) the positive or negative "operational" learning of knowledge, skills, and abilities that the agent may obtain as a consequence of the interaction; and (c) another type of learning, which we can call "evaluative," because it influences, positively or negatively, the agent's ability to evaluate the consequences of his or her actions on him or herself and on others (for example, the ability to realize whether his or her action will make it easier or more difficult for other agents to cooperate in his future interactions), which will enable him or her to develop his or her ability to make good decisions in the future.
3. Effects that the agent does not receive or produce in him or herself, but which take place in other people, also as a consequence of the action. The most important point about these effects is that, as we have just pointed out, they cause certain types of evaluative learning in the agent, who learns to take or not take into account the effects of his or her actions on others.

In any action involving interaction between people, these three effects always occur to a greater or lesser extent, even if the agents ignore them or do not wish them. Therefore, these people may be moved to act by different motivations, seeking one or more of the results we have mentioned: extrinsic motivation (extrinsic results); intrinsic motivation (intrinsic results); and transcendent motivation (aiming for results in other persons).[9]

If these agents relate to each other within an organization, it is assumed that they seek to achieve a common purpose or goal which is to the interest of them all, albeit for different reasons, depending on the results pursued by each and, therefore, on the motivations driving them. Therefore, the action can be evaluated in accordance with three criteria (Pérez López 1991, 1993):

1. Its ability to achieve the organization's extrinsic results, which in turn are necessary to enable the extrinsic results pursued by the various agents. In the case of a firm, this ability is the generation of value in order to meet the expectations of financial reward of the company's stakeholders, such as owners, managers, employees, and so

forth. We will call this dimension "efficiency" and it can be identified approximately with the organization's financial performance.
2. Its ability to meet the agents' intrinsic results: their satisfaction (for example, through the work atmosphere that the organization provides to employees) and their "operational" learning (the development of their knowledge, abilities, and attitudes, insofar as they enable development of the firm's distinctive competences). This dimension would be the "attractiveness" of the action and, by extension, of the organization.
3. Its ability to develop "evaluative" learning, so that both the agent making the decision and the other people with whom s/he interacts develop their ability to make better decisions in the future, so that they are able to consider whether these decisions facilitate or hamper everyone's ability to develop the organization's common goals and, primarily, their ability to work in cooperation with each other – which Pérez López (1993) calls the "consistency" or "unity" of the action and of the organization.

It is not possible to condense these three dimensions into just one. The firm needs a minimum level of efficiency and attractiveness to function (to put it simply, it must offer its staff a salary that is sufficient, a minimally satisfactory workplace, and the ability to acquire the knowledge and operating skills that the firm needs for its growth). Up to a point, there is a limited trade-off between these two dimensions. However, what distinguishes this analysis from that of the theory of the firm mentioned above is the introduction of the third dimension, consistency, and with it, evaluative learning.

This learning happens when: (1) the agent strives to identify all the consequences of his or her actions on him or herself and on others in order to understand how they affect his or her decision making. Because, whether or not s/he knows or wishes it, with each action (s)he is re-learning to decide in accordance with certain criteria and not others, considering certain effects and not others, and assessing them in accordance with the three criteria mentioned above, efficiency, attractiveness and consistency, or omitting one or more of them. (2) Also when (s)he seeks to understand how the other agents learn to consider certain effects and not others, and to act in accordance with certain motivations and not others, in other words, how they change their decision criteria. We could call all this the "rational" component of evaluative learning. (3) The agent must also develop his or her ability not only to know, but to act virtuously, overcoming the temptation to act moved solely by a particular type of results, the extrinsic results (for example, out of convenience or laziness). In short, the agent must develop his or her moral virtues (Argandoña 2011c).

We can therefore say that in the firm, as in any human activity, the individual must live by the virtues that enable him or her to continue making ever better decisions in the future and which develop a framework in which organizations can maintain and improve their consistency, that is, the unity of action and their members' capacity for personal and social development. In other words, it must live by love, which is the virtue that furthers other people and brings order and unity among them. As St. Augustine says, "it seems to me that the brief definition of true virtue is 'order in love'" (Augustine of Hippo 2009 XV, 22, quoted in Lorda 2009, p. 508).[10]

In short, in the firm, the agent lives by virtues and seeks that others should live by them too. This, (s)he does as something that forms part of the action, which is necessary for satisfactory completion of the action (which is then morally correct) and for the quality of the human relationship in which (s)he is immersed (which improves ethically the person performing the action) and, therefore, of the organization too (because it also enables the improvement of the other people with whom it is related).

## 4 From virtue to the "logic of gift"

In the theory of action we have outlined, we see that, in any interpersonal action, the agent delivers and receives tangible and intangible goods and services; (s)he gives to him or herself or receives from others satisfaction and operational learning; (s)he does something because of them (to favor them or harm them) and learns to do something (good or bad) for them.

The recognition of the role of virtues in action forces us to consider the agent's motivation. When performing a commercial operation within the "market logic," agents may act out of extrinsic (profit, salary, reputation), intrinsic (satisfaction), or transcendent (service) motivation because all three motivations may be present in all decisions. This can also happen when the firm acts within the "logic of State": it may pay tax for fear of punishment, for the satisfaction gained from doing one's duty, or as a way of contributing towards society's common good. In the same way, when it carries out an action that we can describe as "charity" or social (for example, giving a discount to needy people), it may act to produce an extrinsic (reputation), intrinsic (its employees' satisfaction), or transcendent result (something that it considers good for its consumers or employees).

In any case, the presence of any given motivation is independent of the action's gratuitousness. A firm that performs the action of charity mentioned above with the sole purpose of achieving greater profit is not necessarily acting immorally but it is not improving its members' virtues either. On the other hand, a firm that pays its employees the salary strictly stipulated in their contract because it is its duty is acting in accordance with the moral virtue of justice, is learning to take into account its employees' needs and improving its moral quality.[11]

When an agent acts out of transcendent motivation, (s)he makes a "donation" which may be a free delivery of tangible or intangible goods and services, beyond what is gratuitous. Insofar as they give rise to a donation, virtues come within the "logic of gift," whose natural quality is "to give" in a very broad sense: give things and, above all, "give oneself," moved by love. Therefore, when a person acts within the logic of gift, (s) he also "donates" new virtues and abilities to him or herself. In the process, the logic of gift becomes two-way: (s)he gives and receives, but what (s)he receives are not other real or potential, present or future goods but, above all, moral improvement, and greater fulfillment as a person.[12]

All of this is understood more easily when one considers what the encyclical letter CV says about the logic of gift and justice. Charity does not oppose justice, which "prompts us to give the other what is 'his', what is due to him by reason of his being or his acting. I cannot 'give' what is mine to the other, without first giving him what pertains to him in justice" (CV 6). "Not only is it [justice] not an alternative or parallel path to charity: justice is inseparable from charity" (CV 6), so that "the logic of gift does not exclude justice, nor does it merely sit alongside it as a second element added from without" (CV 34). "Charity goes beyond justice, because to love is to give, to offer what is 'mine' to the other ... charity transcends justice and completes it" (CV 6). *Caritas in Veritate* points out that "in the past it was possible to argue that justice had to come first and gratuitousness could follow afterwards, as a complement" (CV 38), because the liberal philosophy put emphasis on justice as the main social virtue, minimizing the role of charity and love, but "today it is clear that without gratuitousness, there can be no justice in the first place" (CV 38). To treat men with justice, they must be treated with love.

## 5 The scope of the "logic of gift"

"The Church's social doctrine holds that authentically human social relationships of friendship, solidarity and reciprocity can also be conducted within economic activity, and not only outside it or 'after' it" (CV 36). The theory of action that we have presented helps us understand that the "logic of gift" and of virtue can and must be present in all human actions, both in the market and the firm and in relations between citizens and the State or in what we usually call civil society, and, of course, in private or family life.

In the exchange of equivalents, the agent gives a good and receives its price. If the exchange is voluntary, it cannot be said that something has been "donated" because the agent values what (s)he has received at least as much as what was given: "giving in order to acquire" (CV 39). The exchange of equivalents takes place mainly in the market, "the economic institution that permits encounter between persons... as they exchange goods and services of equivalent value between them, in order to satisfy their needs and desires" (CV 35), by means of the contract; it operates under the efficiency principle (obtainment of the best possible result with the resources available), and "is subject to the principles of so-called commutative justice, which regulates the relations of giving and receiving between parties to a transaction" (CV 35).

Gift can also be "through duty" (CV 39): for example, that is how the State collects taxes. In a broad sense, it can also be considered a form of "donation," because nothing is immediately given in return: the person who pays a tax receives public goods and services but not in accordance with commutative justice but with distributive (the value of what is received does not necessarily need to be proportional to what is given) and legal justice (which regulates citizens' relations with society) (Pieper 1965).

It is also possible to give without coercion and without expecting anything in return. This is what happens in civil society, which seems to be "the most natural setting" for this to happen in "an economy of gratuitousness and fraternity" (CV 38), represented by nonprofit institutions, non-governmental organizations, foundations, cooperatives, employee-owned companies, and so on, which must abide by the strict duty of justice and truth to prevent basic human needs from remaining unsatisfied and the men oppressed by such needs from perishing.[13]

The encyclical letter also explains that "both the market and politics need individuals who are open to reciprocal gift" (CV 39): all three areas of human relations, market, State, and civil society, must be open to the logic of gift (Zamagni 2006, 2007). Particularly in economic activities, "authentically human social relationships of friendship, solidarity and reciprocity can [and must] also be conducted within economic activity, and not only outside it or 'after' it" (CV 36).

## 6 Gift in the firm

All of the above leads to the core subject of this chapter: how can the logic of gift be lived in the firm? The encyclical letter points out the need for "a profoundly new way of understanding business enterprise" (CV 40), because "the great challenge before us ... is to demonstrate, in thinking and behaviour ... that in commercial relationships the principle of gratuitousness and the logic of gift as an expression of fraternity can and must find their place within normal economic activity" (CV 36).

We have already presented a conceptual framework for developing Benedict XVI's proposal from the viewpoint of the theory of the firm. Organizations, including those that pursue profit, must take into account the variety of motivations of those who work in them or relate to them; therefore, any action must be assessed from three viewpoints, which include the possibility of achieving the material results that the organization and its stakeholders seek (which we have called efficiency), and attaining an environment that is sufficiently attractive for people and for the development of their operational learning (attractiveness), but also where people can work for their own good and that of others (consistency). This means that people must live by virtues, including in the firm and in the market, and this involves entering a relationship of giving between people, a "logic of gift," which includes the provision of resources having an economic value (which would be part of gratuitousness in an economic sense, if what is given has a higher value than what is received) but also goes much further, encompassing feelings and affections, the moral improvement of others, the creation of a humane environment in the firm, the exercise of solidarity, the pursuit of the common good and many other "goods."

Benedict XVI goes, however, a step further, and not only asks for a new theory but also a new reality: "space also needs to be created within the market for economic activity carried out by subjects who freely choose to act according to principles other than those of pure profit, without sacrificing the production of economic value in the processes" (CV 37).

In economic life, we already find a range of organizations with different legal and ownership structures, different goals (obtaining profit, providing public goods or social services to their members, to needy population groups, or to the general public), different financial management criteria (maximizing profit or simply covering costs), different uses for its surpluses (for the benefit of their owners or other stakeholders), and so forth. We also find a very varied range of behaviors, often within the same industry. In any case, economics has also paid attention to forms of organization that are different from the for-profit firm.

However, the *Caritas in Veritate* goes beyond the mere coexistence of for-profit organizations with publicly-owned companies or administrations and with nonprofit organizations pursuing social goals when it proposes the creation of organizations that, while having structures and strategies that are similar to those of for-profit companies, voluntarily choose not to pursue profit as their primary or dominant goal, either because they plan to share all or part of the profits earned among stakeholders other than their traditional owners or because they waive a priori such profits, whether this be by incurring expenses that are not "necessary" for the business activity (paying above-market prices for their raw materials, for example), by obtaining revenues below those that would be allowed by the market (giving discounts to certain customers), and so on. "This is not merely a matter of a 'third sector', but of a broad new composite reality embracing the private and public spheres, one which does not exclude profit, but instead considers it a means for achieving human and social ends. Whether such companies distribute dividends or not, whether their juridical structure corresponds to one or other of the established forms, becomes secondary in relation to their willingness to view profit as a means of achieving the goal of a more humane market and society" (CV 46).

Is this possible? Viewed from self-interest-based anthropology, the answer is no: in a market subject to perfect competition, a firm that does not seek to maximize its value for its owners is doomed to disappear. This does not necessarily have to happen, if we relax the strict assumptions of the neoclassical model. For example, if resources are not homogeneous, nonprofit organizations may enjoy competitive advantages, like providers of capital that do not seek profit maximization, managers who are not interested in profiting personally at the cost of shareholders, customers who remain loyal for religious or social reasons, or employees who are willing to work for below-market salaries. Many companies enjoy some market power, that is, they earn "rents" that are usually shared among their owners or managers but which may also be distributed among other stakeholders.

These arguments show that, even in the profit-maximizing model, the principle of gratuitousness can be present – and it is, at least in certain fields and specific markets. In addition, Benedict XVI advocates the development of a legal, fiscal, institutional, social, and ethical framework that will not only enable third sector organizations to survive and flourish but also business companies that voluntarily pursue, without unnecessary discrimination or impediments, the achievement of non-economic goals in "a market that permits the free operation, in conditions of equal opportunity, of enterprises in pursuit of different institutional ends" (CV 38).

This adds two challenges to our analysis: (1) "shape and structure [must] be given to those types of economic initiative which, without rejecting profit, aim at a higher goal than the mere logic of the exchange of equivalents, of profit as an end in itself" (CV 38); and (2) it also necessary to foster the "shifting of competences from the 'non-profit' world to the 'profit' world and vice versa, from the public world to that of civil society" (CV 41), because "it is from their reciprocal encounter [between for-profit and non-profit organizations] in the marketplace that one may expect hybrid forms of commercial behaviour to emerge, and hence an attentiveness to ways of civilizing the economy" (CV 38). "Without prejudice to the importance and the economic and social benefits of the more traditional forms of business, they steer the system towards a clearer and more complete assumption of duties on the part of economic subjects" (CV 46). Benedict XVI even suggests that "the very plurality of institutional forms of business gives rise to a market which is not only more civilized but also more competitive" (CV 46). Or, to put it another way, the very existence of a variety of institutions, with different goals and motivations, may encourage new initiatives, probably as a result of cooperation, innovation, and imitation.

All this is nothing more than the practical translation of what we have said earlier about virtues and the "logic of gift": if the economic subjects are moved by a plurality of motivations, it is logical that they will create and develop initiatives that respond to those motivations, including economic organizations that seek to satisfy consumers' needs through the production of goods and services applying efficiency and innovation criteria and to earn profits (because this is required by the efficiency criterion and is necessary for the organization's survival and growth), but do not consider it to be the goal of their activity but "a means for achieving human and social ends" (CV 46). Thus, this challenge must ultimately be addressed on three levels:

1. Personal: how to persuade a larger number of entrepreneurs to start businesses that, without renouncing profit, go beyond it. *Caritas in Veritate* provides key points for addressing this challenge, from its first paragraph ("love – *caritas* – is an extraordinary force which leads people to opt for courageous and generous engagement in the field of justice and peace": CV 1) to its last pages ("the greatest service to development, then, is a Christian humanism that enkindles charity and takes its lead from truth" (CV 78).
2. Another level, that of the business organizations themselves, which must be conceived, organized, and managed to show that their economic and social success is compatible with the principle of gratuitousness and the logic of gift (CV 36). As is only logical, the encyclical letter does not offer any answers to this challenge, because that is a task that corresponds to business owners, managers, and academics.
3. Last, the national, international, and systemic levels, because, to quote John Paul II, "economic activity, especially the activity of a market economy, cannot be conducted in an institutional, juridical or political vacuum" (CA 48). That is the main task of nation states, even in a globalized world (cf. CV 42).

## 7 Conclusion

*Caritas in Veritate* is an original document, full of suggestions for experts and practitioners. The concept of gift occupies a central stage in it; a concept intended not just to inspire spiritual thoughts, but to guide the theoretical work of social scientists and the practice of entrepreneurs and politicians.

In this chapter we developed the concepts of love, gift, and gratuitousness from the Christian doctrine to the works of sociologists and economists. The neoclassical theories of the firm do not give space to love, but there are many contributions that explain the roles of love and gift in economic behavior. We propose a simple theory of human action that introduces moral virtues in the reasoning of economics and opens new possibilities to introduce love, gift, and gratuitousness in the theory and practice of the market, the State, and the firm. We conclude that entities organized according to the "logic of gift" and the "principle of gratuitousness" are not only possible, but necessary, and that a new paradigm that considers for-profit firms, State-owned companies, non-profit organizations, and any other intermediate institution is possible – and necessary.

## Executive summary

Managers try to attain the common goals of the firm by combining the actions of different people who share those goals in some way, but who also have different motivations. Taking good decisions means a variety of results, including profitability, but also making the collaboration of these people attractive for them, developing their abilities to improve the performance of the firm and, last but not least, achieving long-term consistency. For all of these they need the development of their moral virtues.

Traditionally, the Social Doctrine of the Church was founded on principles, values, and virtues. Charity (love) and justice are central in this doctrine, but, connected with love, the encyclical letter *Caritas in Veritate* introduces the "logic of gift" and the "principle of gratuitousness" as essential ingredients of economic life. In contrast to this, the traditional theory of the firm, based on contracts, has no place for love; and the economics of altruism and gift is inspired also by the self-interest paradigm, alien to the behavior ruled by love.

This chapter intends to develop the relationship between Benedict XVI's proposal on love and gift and the "logic of virtues" that has already been incorporated into the theory of the firm. After an analysis of the concepts of love, gift, and gratuitousness and of the role of virtues in firms' management, a parallel is developed between acting in a virtuous way and "donating goods," either material or not, including developing virtues and "giving love." This is done in three ambits, market (exchange of equivalents), State (duty), and civil society (fraternity); the encyclical underlines that the "logic of gift" should be present in all of these, not only in the third.

## Acknowledgment

This chapter forms part of the activities of the "la Caixa" Chair of Corporate Social Responsibility and Corporate Governance at IESE. The author is grateful for the comments received from the editors and people who attended the 16th IESE International Symposium on Ethics, Business and Society, where this chapter was first presented.

## Notes

1. The definitions of the word "love" are very varied: an intense feeling felt by a human being who, from his own insufficiency, needs and seeks union with another being (love of need), a feeling towards another person who naturally attracts us and who, bringing reciprocity to the desire for union, gives us completeness, happiness and energy to share life together, communicate and create (love of benevolence), a feeling of affection, inclination, and giving of oneself to someone or something.
2. We will not explore here the distinctions between words which are, in many ways, synonyms and which represent attitudes or behaviors that may be driven by love, although not necessarily, or not always: charity, generosity, benevolence, compassion, warmth, service, altruism (Argandoña 2010).
3. http://dictionary.reference.com/browse/gift (accessed January 31, 2012).
4. The explanation that we have given matches quite closely the model of the capitalist firm in most modern theories. There are other models and theories which modify some of the assumptions and mechanisms explained (Argandoña 2011b), but, in any case, these models do not attribute any role to love.
5. However, this is not applicable to all theories: for example, those that focus on the other party's response (hostile or friendly) or behavior (also hostile or friendly) concede a significant role to the intentions attributed to the latter (Fehr and Schmidt 2005).
6. The following draws from Pérez López (1991, 1993); cf. also Argandoña (2008a, 2008b, 2008c).
7. This version of modern theories of the firm does not do justice to many of the complications that have been incorporated over time. Cf. Argandoña (2011a).
8. For what follows, cf. Argandoña (2008a, 2008b, 2008c), Pérez López (1991, 1993).
9. We maintain the terminology of Pérez López even if it is not followed by other authors, because this triple classification of motivation is more complete than the traditional distinction between extrinsic and intrinsic motivations, especially in the identification of the evaluative learning.
10. On the need for charity for the existence of virtues, cf. Aquinas (S Th II-II, q. 23, a. 7).
11. Because, in addition, all virtues grow together: an agent who seeks to live more by justice every day will be fostering all the virtues, starting with charity.
12. But the key to the logic of gift is not the "gratuitousness" of the external action or of the result (giving something in exchange for a price that is zero or less than what one could obtain on the market), but the exercise of virtues, presided by love. And this can happen in firms that, apparently, do not live by gratuitousness, in the sense of "giving" without requiring anything in return.
13. This is why it is necessary to acknowledge, protect and foster the role of civil society as a "provider" of solidarity, because "the exclusively binary

model of market-plus-State is corrosive of society, while economic forms based on solidarity, which find their natural home in civil society without being restricted to it, build up society" (CV 39).

## References


Andreoni, J. "Impure altruism and donations to public goods: A theory of warm-glow giving." *Economic Journal*, Vol. 100, 1990: 464–477.

Argandoña, A. "Integrating ethics into action theory and organizational theory." *Journal of Business Ethics*, Vol. 78, 2008a: 435–446.

Argandoña, A. "Anthropological and ethical foundations of organization theory." In S. Gregg and J.R. Stoner Jr., eds. *Rethinking Business Management. Examining the Foundations of Business Education*. Princeton, NJ: The Witherspoon Institute, 2008b.

Argandoña, A. "Consistency in decision making in companies." *Humanizing the firm and the management profession*, IESE Business School, June 2008c.

Argandoña, A. "Love in companies." *IESE Research paper* D-856-E. Barcelona: IESE Business School, 2010.

Argandoña, A. "Beyond contracts: Love in firms." *Journal of Business Ethics,* Vol. 99, 2011a: 77–85.

Argandoña, A. "From action theory to the theory of the firm." In J. Canals, ed. *The Future of Leadership Development*. Houndmills, UK: Palgrave Macmillan, 2011b.

Argandoña, A. "Las virtudes en una teoría de la acción humana." In P. Requena and M. Schlag, eds. *La persona al centro del Magistero sociales della Chiesa*. Rome: Edusc, 2011c.

Augustine of Hippo (St. Augustine). *The City of God*. New York: The Modern Library, 2009.

Axelrod, R. *The Evolution of Cooperation*. New York: Basic Books, 1984.

Becker, G.S. "Altruism, egoism, and genetic fitness: Economics and sociobiology." *Journal of Economic Literature*, Vol. 4, 1976: 817–826.

Coase, R. "The nature of the firm." *Economica* Vol. 4, 1937: 386–405.

Fehr, E. and K.M. Schmidt. "A theory of fairness, competition, and cooperation." *Quarterly Journal of Economics*, Vol. 114, 1999: 817–868.

Fehr, E. and K.M. Schmidt. "The economics of fairness, reciprocity and altruism. Experimental evidence and new theories." *University of Munich Discussion Paper 2005–20*, Munich: Department of Economics, 2005.

Fromm, E. *The Art of Loving*. New York: Harper, 1956.

Glazer, A. and K.A. Konrad. "A signaling explanation of charity." *American Economic Review*, Vol. 86, 1996: 1019–1028.

Godbout, J.T. "*Homo donator* versus *homo oeconomicus." Finance and the Common good*." Summer, 2005: 38–46.

Harbaugh, W.T. "The prestige motive for making charitable transfers." *American Economic Review*, Vol. 88, 1998: 277–282.

Kahlil, E.L. "What is altruism?" *Journal of Economic Psychology*, Vol. 25, 2004: 97–123.

Lorda, J.L. *Antropología teológica*. Pamplona: Eunsa, 2009.

Meier, S. "A survey of economic theories and field evidence on pro-social behavior." *Federal Reserve Bank of Boston Working Papers 06–6*. Boston, MA: Federal Reserve Bank, 2006.

Monroe, K.R. "A fat lady in a corset: Altruism and social theory." *American Journal of Political Science*, Vol. 38, 1994: 861–893.

Okten, C., and B.A. Weisbrod. "Determinants of donations in private nonprofit markets." *Journal of Public Economics*, Vol. 75, 1999: 255–272.

Pérez López, J.A. *Teoría de la acción humana en las organizaciones. La acción personal*. Madrid: Rialp, 1991.

Pérez López, J.A. *Fundamentos de la dirección de empresas*. Madrid: Rialp, 1993.

Pieper, J. *The Four Cardinal Virtues: Prudence, Justice, Fortitude, Temperance*. New York: Harcourt, Brace and World, 1965.

Piliavin, J.A. and H-W. Charng. "Altruism: A review of recent theory and research." *Annual Review of Sociology*, Vol. 16, 1990: 27–65.

Polo, L. *Ética. Hacia una versión moderna de los temas clásicos*. Madrid: Unión Editorial, 1996.

Ratzinger, J. *Dios y el mundo. Una conversación con Peter Seewald*. Barcelona: Galaxia Gutenberg – Círculo de Lectores, 2002.

Smith, A. *An Inquiry into the Nature and Causes of the Wealth of Nations*. New York: Random House, 1937[1776].

Titmuss, R.M. *The Gift Relationship: From Human Blood to Social Policy*. New York: Pantheon Books, 1971.

Zamagni, S. *Heterogeneidad motivacional y comportamiento económico. La perspectiva de la economía civil*. Madrid: Unión Editorial, 2006.

Zamagni, S. "El bien común en la sociedad posmoderna: propuestas para la acción político-económica." *Revista Cultura Económica*, Vol. 25, 2007: 23–43.

# 11
# Entrepreneurial Spirit and the Role of Gratuitousness for Innovation

*André Habisch and Cristian R. Loza Adaui*

> The *earthly city* is promoted not merely by relationships of rights and duties, but to an even greater and more fundamental extent by relationships of gratuitousness, mercy and communion. (CV 6; italics in original)

Only in the past few decades has entrepreneurship become a mainstream subject in economic and managerial sciences. Increasing empirical evidence underlines that different entrepreneurial resources are major drivers of economic growth in western societies (Audretsch and Keilbach 2004, Audretsch et al. 2006, Acs and Audretsch 2010). It was the Irish economist Richard Cantillon (2009[1734]), who first used the word "entrepreneur," but attention to the topic was triggered by Joseph Schumpeter (2006[1912]). Schumpeter identified innovation as a core driver for the development of business and markets. He distinguishes two types of managers in the market: the innovators and the imitators. Innovators are those who threaten the *status quo* equilibrium by introducing new products or processes into the market. Schumpeter framed this entrepreneurial innovation as "creative destruction" (*schöpferische Zerstörung*) because new and better-adapted solutions crowded out and destroyed older ones. As a fruit of their innovation entrepreneurs realize their temporal competitive advantage until other managers imitate them and a new *status quo* is established. This can then be challenged by another disruptive innovation (Schumpeter 2006[1912], 2009). With Schumpeter "entrepreneurial spirit" (*Unternehmergeist*) and innovation found their entry into mainstream management.

On this conceptual basis, entrepreneurship has lately experienced attempts of prolific categorization; since W.J. Baumol (1986) differentiated the "initiating entrepreneur" from the "imitating entrepreneur," more attention has been paid to distinguishing between various types of entrepreneurship. Recent typologies, which are based on the objective and/or the finality of the venture, enumerate political entrepreneurship (Holcombe 2007, p. 143), social entrepreneurship (Mair et al. 2006, Sommerrock 2010), sustainable entrepreneurship (Dean and McMullen 2007), knowledge entrepreneurship (Senges 2007), and institutional entrepreneurship (Pacheco et al. 2010).

Within this growing area of research, however, only limited attention has been paid to ethical aspects of entrepreneurial initiatives. Two main lines of thought can be differentiated. Some authors focus on ethical dilemmas faced by entrepreneurs and others inquire into the interdependency of entrepreneurial activity within their relevant social context (Freeman and Venkataraman 2002, Hannafey 2003, Fisscher et al. 2005, Harmeling et al. 2009, Harris et al. 2009, Gasparski et al. 2010). Some scholars have discussed the relationship between entrepreneurial activities and Catholic social tradition, either in an historical perspective (von Nell-Breuning 1969, Melé 2000, Hannafey 2006, Percy 2010) or with a special focus on the entrepreneur as a person (Felice 2002, Cornwall and Naughton 2003).

Management academics study entrepreneurship as "the examination of how, by whom and with what effects opportunities to create future goods and services are discovered, evaluated, and exploited" (Shane and Venkataraman 2000, p. 218). Critics argue that during the past few decades research has focused more on "the actions and behaviors of entrepreneurs, rather than any characteristics of them" (Cornwall and Naughton 2003, p. 62). The merely instrumentalist approach of mainstream management science towards entrepreneurship has definitely highlighted important aspects but cannot illuminate the internal dynamics and the driving forces of the entrepreneurial process. This neglect is reductionist not only from a philosophical point of view but also from a managerial point of view. In economic practice successful innovation is not just a result of an optimized recombination of productive resources. Rather, as recent literature on Corporate Identity (Peters and Waterman 1982, Schein 2005) has illustrated, innovation is a social process, which also comprises ethical aspects in the sense of a "value proposition" toward employees. It implies a common "vision of a better world." How could that important characteristic of the entrepreneurial process be elaborated conceptually?

Going back to Schumpeter's original notion, the German word *Unternehmergeist* (entrepreneurial spirit) certainly covers the external and technical aspects of entrepreneurship; however, it also includes the "spirituality" of an entrepreneurial person. The concept of "entrepreneurial spirit" invites us to pay more attention to the entrepreneurial agent, his/her original characteristics, his/her aims and ambitions, and the "vision" that drives them to pursue new paths. The polysemantic character of the German word *Geist* (spirit) must be considered. In general, in German Idealism, *Geist* refers to a form of rationality able to unlock the moral and political spirit of a given sociocultural context. *Unternehmergeist*, so understood, would indicate the ability of the entrepreneur to respond adequately to the societal demands of his time and place, thus anticipating later, stakeholder-oriented notions of corporate initiative and responsibility.

Even if Catholic Social Thought never explicitly used the term, it may, from its own anthropology, contribute to a fully-fledged concept of entrepreneurial spirit. By 1981 John Paul II had emphasized the contribution of the *subjective dimension of work* – including managerial work – (LE 9). Ten years later, he also stressed the value of creativity in managerial ventures:

> A person who produces something other than for his own use generally does so in order that others may use it after they have paid a just price, mutually agreed upon through free bargaining. It is precisely the ability to foresee both the needs of others and the combinations of productive factors most adapted to satisfying those needs that constitutes another important source of wealth in modern society.... In this way, the *role* of disciplined and creative *human work* and, as an essential part of that work, *initiative and entrepreneurial ability* becomes increasingly evident and decisive. (CA 32; italics in the original)

Catholic tradition emphasizes that every person is called to continue God's creation (PP 27). In that perspective creativity not only helps to achieve personal realization, but also (potentially) contributes to the common good. Therefore, it is important to search for those innovations that combine the realization of the individual person and the striving for the common good. Certainly, many ground-breaking social innovations have been brought forward without any direct moral intent of contributing to the common good (Novak 1989). However, explicitly channeling creativity and management towards moral causes is definitely a more important driver in history (Alford and Naughton 2001, Melé 2009).

Entrepreneurship has always been implicitly present in the anthropological and social writings of the Catholic Tradition. An explicit reflection, however, can only be found in very recent Catholic Social Thought. For the first time in Papal documents John Paul II's encyclical letter *Centesimus annus* (CA 32) appreciates the fundamental role of entrepreneurship, creativity, and innovation in serving the common good. Benedict XVI's recent encyclical letter *Caritas in Veritate* followed on by highlighting business topics and economic reasoning in an unprecedented way (Grassl and Habisch 2011). As far as substantial argumentation is concerned we see two fundamentally new contributions of *Caritas in Veritate* in that respect: the Pontiff calls for a more detailed understanding of (different types of) enterprises and then introduces "gratuitousness" as a category of social action.

Benedict XVI addressed this topic stressing the meaning of entrepreneurial work for a person:

> Business has to be understood in an articulated way. There are a number of reasons, of a meta-economic kind, for saying that. Business activity has a human significance, prior to its professional one. It is present in all work, understood as a personal action, an *"actus personae"*, which is why every worker should have the chance to make his contribution knowing that in some "way he is working for himself." (CV 41; italics in original)

And stressing the power of creativity for the common good:

> Charity and truth confront us with an altogether new and creative challenge, one that is certainly vast and complex. It is about *broadening the scope of reason and making it capable of knowing and directing these powerful new forces*, animating them within the perspective of that "civilization of love" whose seed God has planted in every people, in every culture. (CV 33; italics in original)

Benedict clearly expresses an integral vision of the entrepreneurial process, which cannot be exhaustingly described with instrumentalist aspects only (Habisch and Loza Adaui 2010). Rather it also holds co-present a basic ethical ambition of the entrepreneurial process, a desire to "make the world a better place." Without taking this spiritual and "visionary" dimension of the innovation process properly into consideration, even the description of its instrumental aspects is incomplete or even wrong. Only when the "spiritual" program of this process is acknowledged can its "code" (in the sense of a series of externally perceptible re-combinations of tools, resources or instruments) be properly deciphered and interpreted.

In the following we take three historical examples for that endeavor. They are inspired by the Christian tradition and produced managerial, economic, and institutional innovations. We will analyze the entrepreneurial ventures for the common good in three different historical periods: (1) in pre-modern times, we focus on St. Benedict of Norcia and St. Francis of Assisi; (2) during industrialization we present the German textile entrepreneur Franz Brandts; and (3) finally in current times of globalization we analyze some experiences of modern social entrepreneurs.

At the end of this chapter we will argue that *gratuitousness*, as explained in *Caritas in Veritate*, should be one of the drivers of entrepreneurial innovation for the common good and that it is an important ingredient of the "entrepreneurial spirit" in the entrepreneurial ventures considered here.

## 1 Entrepreneurial spirit in medieval monasteries

A mostly implicit orientation of the creativity towards the common good has always been a driver of innovation. In order to prove this, it is important to remember some innovations of pre-modern times – supported in particular by religious orders and movements – that paved the way for socioeconomic change. These innovations have influenced not only economic relations, but have also enabled the creation of new social institutions and cultural developments in general.

In pre-modern times, the economy was not yet a separate sphere but was embedded in social and religious life. Therefore, it can be argued that the effect of institutional innovations had an immediate impact on the economic life of people as well (Bruni and Smerilli 2008, p. 26). In that sense, an entrepreneurial spirit can be identified in the ventures of spiritual (or charismatic) leaders. They were able to generate institutional innovations that included an immediate economic impact (Bruni and Smerilli 2008). It is therefore possible to consider them as innovators in the fields of economics and management.

Following that idea, we will briefly present the contributions of Benedict of Norcia and Francis of Assisi, and how they achieved remarkable intended and unintended impacts in the fields of economics and management.

Pope Benedict XVI recognizes the importance of Benedict of Norcia and his monastic movement referring to him as someone who "with his life and works, had a fundamental influence on the development of European civilization and culture" (Benedict XVI 2008). In fact, in recent years there has been a renewed interest in the monastic movements even in economics and management. The Benedictine movement has been a particular object of managerial studies (Inauen et al. 2010). The special character of a Benedictine governance structure is rooted in the Rule of Benedict, a compendium that structured monastic life for more than 15 centuries and focuses, in particular, on leadership styles (Galbraith and Galbraith 2004, Chan et al. 2011).

The biggest contribution of Benedict and the Benedictine founding fathers was the "monastic way of life," which can be characterized through prayer and labor (*ora et labora*). This did not relate exclusively to individual activity; rather it has a social meaning and covers many different activities: group prayer (*opus Dei*), manual work (*labor*), the use of talent and capacities (*artes*), intellectual work (*opus, lectio divina*), good practice according to the Gospel's call for loving thy neighbor (*bonum*), and as interior work or return to God (*conversatio morum*) (Tredget 2006).

For our purposes it is important to acknowledge that the communitarian monastic way of life, which is deeply ingrained by the practice of gratuitousness, became the social substrata of the first economic and commercial concepts. It was the sociologist of religion Max Weber who interpreted monastic life as the first form of "rationality," and this laid the grounds for the later emergence of economic and managerial rationality (Weber 2001). Examples include:

a. Management techniques of "communitarian administration" as the forerunner of a modern concept of accountability (Bruni and Zamagni 2007, ch. 2).
b. The division of labor within the monastery between the abbot, the prior, the dean, the cellerarius, the management of human talent and so forth (Wolf 2010).
c. Special forms of leadership with intrinsic motivation and the design of specific governance structures (Rost et al. 2010).
d. Democratic elements in the election of the abbot and the "visitation" to informally control the government of monasteries (Inauen et al. 2010, Rost et al. 2010).
e. Modern concepts of profit and prices resulting from practical necessities (Bruni and Smerilli 2008, p. 62).

Monasteries were not isolated organizations; they interacted closely with their social environment and deeply influenced the life of villagers and citizens. Their attempts to manage their day-to-day economic challenges in the spirit of the Gospel resulted in a form of practical wisdom, which found a place in monastery schools as well as in the education of economic elites.

During the late Middle Ages Franciscan economic thought paved the way for the first experiences of micro-credit within the *Monti di pietà* and the *Monti frumetari* in Italy: those institutional innovations addressed social and economic needs without welfarism (Bruni and Smerilli 2008, p. 72). With their "eschatological" intellectual approach the Franciscan school clearly anticipated modern economic and financial theory. Their "distance" from the world – prepared by a lifestyle of poverty – became a driver of a deeper understanding of value and utility in economic life (Bazzichi 2003, 2008).

In the field of management the practical wisdom of St. Francis and the *Franciscan fratres minores* has proposed concepts of "management by example" orientated towards the idea of *"exempla trahunt."* They advanced a concept of leading people by personal example instead of relying primarily on extrinsic motivations like payment of bonus, commanding, or regulating (Arens 2010).

Considering these examples of early European history the concept of "entrepreneurial spirit" is illustrated from a complementary perspective. From its very origins important conceptual, institutional, and economic innovations cannot be understood without taking their underlying spirituality into account. As the historical importance of medieval religious orders and monasteries illustrates, gratuitousness played an important catalytic role in the emergence of modern economic institutions. With the emergence of entrepreneurship in the specific modern form this becomes clear.

## 2 Entrepreneurial spirit during industrialization

With industrialization in the 16th century the dire situation of laborers became an important issue of Christian social engagement ("the social question"). The first reflection of this in contemporary moral thinking was just a prolongation of medieval forms: a call for charity and sympathy for the poor. Soon however, important social innovations took place; these were no longer introduced by monks and clergy alone but also by (lay) entrepreneurial business leaders, who voluntarily provided elementary goods for their workers. In the second half of the

19th century, they started with a patriarchal attitude, which was still orientated towards feudalist predecessors. Step-by-step it transformed into a different approach: workers were perceived as having personal dignity which came with the legitimate claim to organize themselves and to lobby for their interests. The regulatory idea of a partnership between labor and capital, which might overcome the destructive class conflicts, was in gestation (Stegmann and Langhorst 2005). Only as a consequence of entrepreneurial farsightedness did legal frameworks and social institutions emerge on a political level, which civilized the new labor environment and stabilized the modern industrialized society. Christian entrepreneurs triggered that collective learning process and contributed to the emergence of a western cultural alternative, to revolutionary socialism, with gratuitous entrepreneurial practices.

One of the Christian social entrepreneurs of these times was Franz Brandts (1834 – 1914). Born in Gladbach (Germany) in a family of textile entrepreneurs he travelled to England in 1863 to learn more about production techniques there. After his return to Gladbach in 1865 he convinced his father to give up the handweaving mill and to set up mechanical looms in the factory (Löhr 1979). Brandts always felt a broad responsibility; he made an active choice to become engaged in local politics in Gladbach. He became a member of the city council from 1871 until 1904. However, "neither his pioneer work as manufacturer or his local political activity would have made him famous beyond his native city if he had not already started at a young age to care about the situation of the workers" (Löhr 1979, p. 92). By 1867 he was one of the six entrepreneurial members of Gladbach's Chamber of Commerce who wanted to reduce the working day to just 12 hours. In 1872 Brandts started his own business and from the outset he introduced a series of social innovations on the governance as well as operational level of the firm.

### A Social benefits for the workers

The social benefits for the workers inside Brandts' factory were diverse. As documented in the "*Fabrikordnung*" – a document that will be explained in detail later – Brandts' factory had a health insurance fund, a family health insurance fund, an employee pension fund, a savings bank, a savings club, a kindergarten, a sewing school, baths, a library, and a music club with choir and orchestra (Löhr 1974). The employees could have lunch in a workers' restaurant, this was extended to include 86 external workers who were served for just 25 pfennigs. The employees were also able to enjoy use of the garden and the park that were practically part of Brandts' house and had access to a hospice with relaxation rooms (Löhr 1979, pp. 93–94). In Brandts' factory the working day was just $10^1/_4$ hours long (Löhr 1974, p. 7) compared with 11 to 14 hours at his competitors' places of work. Brandts was also recognized for paying the highest wages in the city (Löhr 1979, p. 93).

The gratuitous practice of this textile entrepreneur was an integral part of his business model. It included product innovations discussed above and important procedural innovations also prepared the way for modern forms of HR management. For example Brandts created a health insurance fund for his workers to help them in case of sickness or necessity. It was obligatory for all workers who had to pay 1 to 4 per cent of their salary, additionally Brandts paid 50 per cent of the total contributions (Löhr 1974, 1979, Puppke 1966, pp. 274–275). Moreover, the obligatory character of the health and insurance funds – and of other initiatives – triggered the need to involve the employees themselves in the management of the funds. The "Order of the Factory" (*Fabrikordnung*) was published for the first time in 1885 and fixed the creation of a "Council of Elders," which was to mediate between the owner-entrepreneur and the workers, and to care about the workers' problems. Employees held a majority vote in the fund management even in relationship to the owner-entrepreneur. This emancipative practice of codetermination was exceptional in an era, in which worker's benefits – if granted at all – were perceived as mere alms of patriarchal generosity. As an expression of entrepreneurial spirit ingrained with gratuitousness, the corporate practice of Franz Brandts became a precursor of the integration of workers into the internal decision process of the firm (Puppke 1966, pp. 271–276).[1] Thus, it is the "logic of gift" advanced in *Caritas in Veritate*, and implemented into Brandt's Gladbach based textile company, which lies at the roots of codetermination (*Mitbestimmung*), which is still integrated in German constitutional law.

The social innovations of Brandts' factory, aimed to increase the social welfare of the workers, were supported with a set of behavioral regulations and moral admonishment: "All supervisors had to be a model for their subordinates as far as morality and a religion is concerned" (*Fabrikordnung*, 1885, 1, p. 5, quoted by Löhr 1974)[2]. The mockery of religion and morality as well as repeated scraps leads to immediate dismissal: "dissolute lifestyle, reckless debts and repeated drunkenness" had the same consequences (*Fabrikordnung*, 1885, 4, p. 6, quoted by Löhr 1974).[3] Brandts was also famous for his demanding sexual morality. Male and female laborers worked separately where ever possible; moreover sexual relations outside marriage were also forbidden during leisure time and outside the factory (*Fabrikordnung*, 1885, 5, p. 6, quoted by Löhr 1974).[4] What today appears as a major infringement on laborers' private lives should be, however, interpreted in light of its economic consequences: In a social context without any welfare state institutions an unwanted pregnancy could lead to serious economic problems especially for the unwed mother and her child. Some workers certainly avoided the company because of these encroachments into employees' private lives. However, Brandts' workers revered him as a father and in a rather individualistic context he created family bonds of mutual responsibility. He lived among them, his house being located in the working-class neighborhood. At the center of the small settlement was a chapel built by Brandts[5] out of his personal money.

### B Civic engagement

As stated above, the social innovations of Franz Brandts indirectly influenced the emergent tradition of Catholic Social Thought as well as social legislature in Germany. The chaplain of Brandts' factory was Franz Hitze, later the very first titular of an academic Chair for Catholic Social Thought in Germany – maybe in the whole world – in 1893 at the University of Munster in Westphalia. Hitze also served as a member of the German Parliament (*Reichstag*) and influenced the social security legislation of the Bismarck period, which implemented the first Public Social Security System in human history. Thus, it can be stated that the development of Catholic Social Thought as an academic discipline as well as the emergence of the German social security system was more or less directly impacted by the gratuitousness of a Christian entrepreneur.

Obviously, Franz Brandts was not the first entrepreneurial person to make labor conditions more bearable for workers and their families. Tycoons like Alfred Krupp (1812–1887) served as a role model for many others in that respect. However, Brandts' social engagement was not limited to his firm or to his activity as a local politician. He was dominantly involved in the creation of two of the most important Catholic organizations in Germany: "Arbeiterwohl" (1880) and the People's League for Catholic Germany (*Volksverein für das katholische Deutschland* 1890). The latter was the more influential and important of the two associations. Brandts financed large parts of its activities and its headquarters was established near his factory at Gladbach. The objectives of this organization were: to confront the revolutionary aspirations of the social democrats, to promote the social contract between workers and employers, to offer social information and economic education through newspapers and pamphlets, to organize courses for Catholic associational functionaries, and to plan and lead mass meetings (Stegmann and Langhorst 2005).

The importance of the *Volksverein* not only for Social Catholicism but also for democratic traditions in the Western parts of Germany in the first half of the 20th century can hardly be overestimated. In 1914 this organization counted more than 800,000 members, mainly in western Germany. Activities included a grass-roots level Christian cultural activity that enriched the life of millions of workers and their families. The associational life of Social Catholicism (supported by educational and political materials produced by the *Volksverein*) enabled Catholic workers to overcome widespread alienation and to resist the calls of totalitarian siren songs from the Communist as well as Nazi movement; moreover, the *Volksverein* also served as the civil society backbone of the Social Catholic "Center party" and recruited many functionary elites of the Weimar Republic – including the long term Labor Minister Heinrich Brauns, who laid the foundations of the German labor law (1920–1928).

Ethical visions play an important role in the success of entrepreneurial innovation and activity. The innovator Franz Brandts is an outstanding example in that respect. His Christian values inspired not only his emancipative labor practices – framed by gratuitousness and a spirit of responsibility – but also his "social enterprise" *Volksverein*, which enriched the cultural and political living conditions for Catholic workers in early industrialized Germany. Later social historiography generally attributes Bismarck social security reforms during the 1890s to mere strategic political interest of weakening social democrats and appeasement of the rising labor movement. This representation, however, ignores the crucial role of the underlying "logic of gift" present in the entrepreneurial spirit of people like Brandts. Without his organizational skills and the visionary perspective of Franz Brandts the *Volksverein* would never have reached its decisive importance and could not have developed its emancipating dynamics for the workers and their families. Shortly after his death in 1914 the association lost much of its ability to adapt to the changing social environment. Membership decreased and a new clerical leadership of the *Volksverein* slipped into a romantic anti-capitalism, which the entrepreneur Brandts had always been keen to avoid (Baumgartner 1977).

## 3 Entrepreneurial spirit in religious movements and social entrepreneurs

Our historical examples show the role of gratuitousness as an integral ingredient of entrepreneurial spirit in the emergence of capitalist institutions (medieval times) as well as civilized forms of labor relations and social security (industrialization). Is there also a systemic place for gratuitousness in the practice of fully-fledged market economies? Today's global competitive framework exerts enormous pressure on individual entrepreneurs. Does a business practice characterized by gratuitousness help companies to survive in today's environment? If there are no contemporary examples then the reminiscence of the past is merely of historical interest. Indeed, *Caritas in Veritate* refers to the present and attributes an important role to "gratuitous enterprises":

> In the global era, economic activity cannot prescind from gratuitousness, which fosters and disseminates solidarity and responsibility for justice and the common good among the different economic players.... What is needed, therefore, is a market that permits the free operation, in conditions of equal opportunity, of enterprises in pursuit of different institutional ends. Alongside profit-oriented private enterprise and the various types of public enterprise, there must be room for commercial entities based on mutualistic principles and pursuing social ends to take root and express themselves. It is from their reciprocal encounter in the marketplace that one may expect hybrid forms of commercial behavior to emerge, and hence an attentiveness to ways of civilizing the economy. Charity in truth, in this case, requires that shape and structure be given to those types of economic initiative which, without rejecting profit, aim at a higher goal than the mere logic of the exchange of equivalents, of profit as an end in itself. (CV 38)

What kind of enterprises does the Pope envision here? Pope Benedict XVI makes direct reference to the enterprises belonging to the "civil economy" and to the "economy of communion" (CV 46). The term "economy of communion" nowadays refers to a group of around 700 organizations active on five continents (Commissione Centrale Economia di Comunione 2010, p. 7) inspired by the *Focolare Movement*. According to Lorna Gold these organizations are trying to "translate universal principles of fraternity, gratuitousness and reciprocity beyond the personal sphere and into the world of business" (2010, p. 103). However, the encyclical letter is not stating here that the "economy of communion" as such might be an alternative to the market economy or that it could substitute merely for-profit business on a large scale. Rather there are a lot of examples of "gratuitous" behavior in the for-profit sector. Topics like Corporate Volunteering and Corporate Donations are important aspects here, but even Corporate Citizenship and Corporate Social Responsibility cannot respond only to mere economic expectations without losing their own legitimacy. Those forms have grown in the context of a globalized economy, which re-defines the balance of business, government, and civil society and calls for more responsibility of business in fighting social problems. One very convincing example of such a contemporary activity is the Austrian company BauMax, a medium-sized family-owned chain of home-improvement stores with expanding activities in Eastern Europe. The "Human Dignity Program" is the expression of the companies' social commitment to disabled people inside and outside the company. This program was started in 1986: One of the employees had an accident which resulted in disablement. The family-based management did not want to lay him off in that difficult situation, rather it decided to allow the continued employment of disabled people and set up a program to make this possible. Today, all the BauMax stores in Austria and a majority in other Eastern European countries have established an ongoing cooperation with a local welfare organization (Diakonia; Caritas Youth at work, etc.) as a competent partner: more than 8,500 disabled persons in 190 organizations are supported in Austria alone. In this collaborative framework every week people with disabilities from the partner institution come into the store to help. The partner institutions receive paid service contracts to tend garden areas in the vicinity of the store, to keep parking lots clean, to fill shelves, and so on. Further, some stores engage more fully with their partner organizations and develop cooperative workshops where disabled persons produce goods which are then sold in the store. This is a conscious decision of the company to employ the disabled people thus allowing them to earn their money in dignity from their own work even when these products can be sourced more cheaply elsewhere.

Moreover, BauMax is eager to increase the proportion of disabled people in their employment. The necessary infrastructure is procured and work schedules are flexible enough to support that goal. Disabled persons are perceived as valuable employees and paid the same wages as their able-bodied colleagues. The employee magazine "XXinside" regularly reports about the progress of the company's "Human Dignity Program."

Within the BauMax chain the regional store manager has the freedom to pick a qualified local partner institution. The headquarters at Klosterneuburg, close to Vienna is supporting local activities in a subsidiary way. A dedicated manager for the "Human Dignity Program" is employed. Internally, (s)he is the contact person for all issues which arise in connection with the program. The manager helps the local markets with the integration of disabled persons and provides information about, among other things, legal obligations.

As a medium-sized family-owned company, BauMax is deeply influenced by the Essl family who own it. The Chairman of the Board, K.R. Martin Essl, has produced a strong mission statement and perceives the "Human Dignity Program" as an expression of his Christian faith.[6] Having followed this road for decades, the company is also aware of the positive side-effects of the engagement, which have grown over the years: a positive corporate identity framed by mutual respect of the employees and an increased corporate reputation among clients and in the local community.

Understanding the relationship between gratuitous activities and resulting competitive advantages is very important for a correct perception of gratuitousness as an element of entrepreneurial spirit. As Bruni (2009) makes clear, gratuitousness does not necessarily mean that nothing is received in return – giving does not necessarily mean that there is no reward or benefit. Rather companies putting gratuitousness into practice may profit from this activity legitimately in a multifold ways, because stakeholders may be more eager to work with them (see Habisch 2011).

## 4 Conclusive remarks

With entrepreneurship being perceived as serving only the economic success and profit of the owner-entrepreneur (Cornwall and Naughton 2003, p. 63), it seems impossible to understand gratuitousness as an integral element of it.

However, as Buchholz and Rosenthal (2005, p. 307) state: "at the heart of entrepreneurship are imagination, creativity, novelty, and sensitivity." We may also add gratuitousness to this list. Gratuitousness, shaping the vocation of entrepreneurs in their unknown journey towards multiple business possibilities, is a fundamental element for human development and sustainable economic progress. Only an ambitious concept of "entrepreneurial spirit" is able to cover that aspect.

In this chapter we have presented different types of entrepreneurial experiences in three historical frameworks in order to demonstrate gratuitousress as an integral component of entrepreneurial spirit. In the medieval monastic movement it was the neo-Platonist-Augustinian transcendental orientation towards the *Civitas Dei*, which enacted the approach towards rational planning and innovation (creating new organizational architectures, governance structures, etc.). The link between imagination and gratuitousness on the one hand and the entrepreneurial action on the other, is even more obvious in the Franciscan movement, which, due to its transcendental character, triggered the emergence of progressive concepts of interest and promoted the evolution of financial institutions.

During industrialization Christian entrepreneurs perceived their responsibility not only in terms of financial profit. Rather their entrepreneurial creativity was sustained by a different concept of man and reality, which deeply impacted their organizational decisions and human resources policies.

Finally, for some contemporary entrepreneurs, their Christian convictions or values shape not only their private life but also the identity and mission of their ventures. In our example gratuitousness, in the sense of engagement for disabled people, determines the corporate horizon in which entrepreneurial spirit is sustained.

Working toward a more human and conscious capitalism, which is able to overcome a mere instrumental stakeholder orientation, involves the capacity to see beyond the limits of mainstream practices (see Sisodia et al. 2007 for a similar argument). The entrepreneurs presented here show us that gratuitousness is an integral part of what we call entrepreneurial spirit: it includes aiming at purposes higher than economic success.

In order to confirm the observations of the globalized business practice of the 21st century provided in *Caritas in Veritate* more research on interdependencies and more case studies demonstrating responsible, conscious human management are necessary.

## Executive summary

During recent decades entrepreneurship has gained much importance as a mainstream research topic in economic and managerial sciences. However, so far, only limited attention has been paid to the spiritual and ethical aspects of entrepreneurial activity. The recent social encyclical letter *Caritas in Veritate* by Benedict XVI offers some innovative perspectives from a Catholic Social Thought point of view. It criticizes a superficial economic perspective on entrepreneurship and highlights aspects of gratuitousness of entrepreneurial activity – not only in a non-profit but also in a for-profit context. This chapter develops this train of thought and condenses it into the concept of "entrepreneurial spirit." This is done in an historical as well as contemporary perspective. We analyze three historical examples for that endeavor inspired by the

Christian tradition and introduced managerial, economic, and institutional innovations: (1) in pre-modern times, we focus on St. Benedict of Norcia and St. Francis of Assisi; (2) during industrialization we present the German textile entrepreneur Franz Brandts; and (3) in contemporary times of globalization we analyze some experiences of modern social entrepreneurs. We show that, in these cases, gratuitousness is an important driver of entrepreneurial spirit.

The proposals of *Caritas in Veritate* open up research perspectives on entrepreneurship, which overcome a reduction towards technical aspects and work towards a more detailed and, at the same time, more integrated understanding of entrepreneurial spirit.

## Notes

1. Business structures of codetermination deeply influenced the German economic order of "*Soziale Marktwirtschaft.*" Crafted as national law by the Catholic priest and Minister of Labor affairs Heinrich Brauns, who had previously served as a director in the *Volksverein*, codetermination was crafted again after World War II. In 1949 the *Katholikentag*, stated that codetermination (*Mitbestimmung*) in business was anchored in natural law (Spieker 2001). This unchained a very interesting controversy that finished one year later when Pius XII criticized this position considering it as too extreme and contrary to the idea of the private social contract (Pius XII 1950). Nevertheless, *Mitbestimmung* is still part of German labor law and has been very important in the development of a cooperative business culture and the lasting economic success of the German economy.
2. This is our German translation from the original. We reproduce the German text (here and in notes 3 and 4) for accurate analysis: "Alle Vorgesetzten in der Fabrik, Meister und Angestellte, sind gehalten, ihren Untergebenen in der Erfüllung ihrer sittlichen und religiösen Pflichten mit einem guten Beispiel voranzugehen und fördernd auf den sittlichen Geist in der Fabrik einzuwirken" (Fabrikordnung, 1885, 1, p. 5).
3. "Arbeiter die sich innerhalb der Fabrik öffentlicher Verhöhnung der Religion oder der guten Sitte, oder grober unsittlicher Handlungen schuldig machen, oder in trunkenen Zustände getroffen oder der Veruntreuung überprüft werden, oder Schlägerei veranlassen oder daran teilnehmen, werden sofort entlassen" (Fabrikordnung, 1885, 4, p. 6).
4. "Die weiblichen Arbeiter sollen während der Arbeit, soweit tunlich, von den Arbeitern männlichen Geschlechts getrennt sein. Ebenso ist denselben während der freien Zeit jeder gegenseitige Verkehr untersagt. Zuwiderhandlungen, sowie jeder leichtsinnige der christlichen Sitte widerstrebende Verkehr der jungen Leute beiderlei Geschlecht, auch außerhalb der Fabrik, ziehen Verwarnung seitens des Arbeitervorstandes und, falls diese fruchtlos, Kündigung nach sich" (Fabrikordnung, 1885, 5, p. 6).
5. The construction of the building was motivated by the death of Brandts' son Rudolf, who died of tuberculosis in 1889 at the age of 21 years. In 1874

three daughters died from the "white plague." In total F. Brandts had eight children.

6. See Baumax website: www.baumax.com/en/about-baumax/mission-statement/christian-ethics (accessed January 31, 2012).

## References


Acs, Z.J. and D.B. Audretsch, eds. *Handbook of Entrepreneurship Research: An Interdisciplinary Survey and Introduction.* New York: Springer, 2010.

Alford, H.J. and M. Naughton *Managing as if Faith Mattered: Christian Social Principles in the Modern Organization.* Notre Dame: Notre Dame University Press, 2001.

Arens, H., "'...das du für dich selbst fest entschlossen bist, so zu handeln.' Menschenführung franziskanisch." In U. Meier and B. Sill, eds. *Führung. Macht. Sinn: Ethos und Ethik für Entscheider in Wirtschaft, Gesellschaft und Kirche.* Regensburg: Friedrich Pustet, 2010.

Audretsch, D.B. and M. Keilbach. "Entrepreneurship capital and economic performance." *Regional Studies,* Vol. 38, 8, 2004: 949–959.

Audretsch, D.B., M.C. Keilbach, and E. Lehmann. *Entrepreneurship and Economic Growth.* Oxford: Oxford University Press, 2006.

Baumgartner, A. *Sehnsucht nach Gemeinschaft. Ideen und Strömungen in der Sozialkatholizismus der Weimarer Republik.* München: Schoningh, 1977.

Baumol, W.J. "Entrepreneurship and a century of growth." *Journal of Business Venturing,* Vol. 1, 2, 1986: 141–145.

Bazzichi, O. *Alle radici del capitalismo: Medioevo e scienza economica.* Cantalupa: Effatà, 2003.

Bazzichi, O. *Dall'usura al giusto profitto. L'etica economica della scuola francescana.* Cantalupa: Effatà, 2008.

Benedict XVI. "Saint Benedict of Norcia." Homily given to the general audience a St. Peter's Square, Vatican City, April 2008. Available at: www.vatican.va/holy_father/benedict_xvi/audiences/2008/documents/hf_ben-xvi_aud_20080409_en.html (accessed July 24, 2011).

Bruni, L. "Gratuità." In L. Bruni and S. Zamagni, eds. *Dizionario di Economia Civile.* Roma: Città Nuova, 2009.

Bruni, L. and A. Smerilli. *Benedetta Economia. Benedetto di Norcia e Francesco d'Assisi nella Storia Economica Europea.* Roma: Città Nuova, 2008.

Bruni, L. and S. Zamagni. *Civil Economy: Efficiency, Equity, Public Happiness.* Oxford: Peter Lang, 2007.

Buchholz, R.A. and S.B. Rosenthal. "The spirit of entrepreneurship and the qualities of moral decision making: Toward a unifying framework." *Journal of Business Ethics,* Vol. 60, 3, 2005: 307–315.

Cantillon, R. *Essay on the Nature of Commerce in General.* Piscataway, NJ: Transaction Publishers, 2009[1734].

Chan, C.C.A., K. McBey, and B. Scott-Ladd "Ethical leadership in modern employment relationships: Lessons from St. Benedict." *Journal of Business Ethics,* Vol. 100, 2, 2011: 221–228.

Commissione Centrale Economia di Comunione. *Rapporto 2009/2010.* Roma: Città Nuova, 2010.

Cornwall, J.S. and M.J. Naughton. "Who is the good entrepreneur? An exploration within the Catholic Social Tradition." *Journal of Business Ethics*, Vol. 44, 1, 2003, 61–75.

Dean, T.J. and J.S. McMullen. "Toward a theory of sustainable entrepreneurship: Reducing environmental degradation through entrepreneurial action." *Journal of Business Venturing*, Vol. 22, 1, 2007: 50–76.

Felice, F. *Capitalismo e Cristianesimo*. Soveria Mannelli: Rubbettino, 2002.

Fisscher, O., D. Frenkel, Y. Lurie and A. Nijhof. "Stretching the frontiers: Exploring the relationships between entrepreneurship and ethics." *Journal of Business Ethics*, Vol. 60, 3, 2005: 207–209.

Freeman, E.R. and S. Venkataraman, eds. *The Ruffin Series No. 3: Ethics and Entrepreneurship*. Charlottesville: Philosophy Documentation Center, 2002.

Galbraith, C.S. and O.I. Galbraith. *The Benedictine Rule of Leadership: Classic Management Secrets You Can Use Today*. New York: Adams Media Corporation, 2004.

Gasparski, W., L.V. Ryan and S. Kwiatkowski, eds. *Entrepreneurship: Values and Responsibility*. Piscataway, NJ: Transaction Publishers, 2010.

Gold, L. *New Financial Horizons: The Emergence of an Economy of Communion*. New York: New City Press, 2010.

Grassl, W. and A. Habisch. "Economics and ethics: Towards a new humanistic synthesis." *Journal of Business Ethics*, Vol. 99, 1, 2011: 37–49.

Habisch, A. "Corporate citizenship and private regulatory regimes: Understanding new governance roles and functions." In I. Pies and P. Koslowski, eds., *Corporate Citizenship and New Governance*. Berlin: Springer, 2011.

Habisch, A. and C. Loza Adaui. "Seasoning business knowledge: Challenging recent Catholic social thought." *Journal of Management Development*, Vol. 29, 7/8, 2010: 660–668.

Hannafey, F.T. "Entrepreneurship and ethics: A literature review." *Journal of Business Ethics*, Vol. 46, 2, 2003: 99–110.

Hannafey, F.T. "Entrepreneurship in Papal thought: Creation of wealth and the distribution of justice." In H.J. Alford, C.M.A. Clark, S.A. Cortright and M.J. Naughton, eds. *Rediscovering Abundance. Interdisciplinary Essays on Wealth, Income, and their Distribution in the Catholic Social Tradition*. Notre Dame: Notre Dame University Press, 2006.

Harmeling, S.S., S.D. Sarasvathy, and R.E. Freeman. "Related debates in ethics and entrepreneurship: Values, opportunities, and contingency." *Journal of Business Ethics*, Vol. 84, 3, 2009: 341–365.

Harris, J.D., H.J. Sapienza, and N.E. Bowie. "Ethics and entrepreneurship." *Journal of Business Venturing*, Vol. 24, 5, 2009: 407–418.

Holcombe, R.G. *Entrepreneurship and Economic Progress*. London: Routledge, 2007.

Inauen, E., K. Rost, B.S. Frey, F. Homberg, and M. Osterloh "Monastic governance: Forgotten prospects for public institutions." *The American Review of Public Administration*, Vol. 40, 6, 2010: 631–653.

Inauen, E., K. Rost, M. Osterloh, and B. S. Frey. "Back to the future: A monastic perspective on corporate governance." *Management Revue*, Vol. 21, 1, 2010: 38–59.

Löhr, W., ed. *Die Fabrikordnung der Firma F. Brandts zu Mönchengladbach. Unveränderte Nachdruck der Ausgabe von 1885*. Mönchengaldbach: Stadtarchiv Mönchengaldbach, 1974.

Löhr, W. "Franz Brandts (1834–1914)." In J. Aretz, R. Morsey and A. Rauscher, eds. *Zeitgeschichte in Lebensbildern. Aus dem deutschen Katholizismus des 19. und 20. Jahrhunderts.* Mainz: Matthias-Grünewald, 1979: 91–105.

Mair, J., J. Robinson and K. Hockerts, eds. *Social Entrepreneurship.* Houndmills: Palgrave Macmillan, 2006.

Melé, D. "Entrepreneurship and wealth creation: An omission in the social teaching of the Church?" *The IV International Symposium on Catholic Social Thought and Management Education,* Puebla, July 2000. Available at: www.stthomas.edu/cathstudies/cst/conferences/puebla/papers/mele2.pdf (accessed January 31, 2012).

Melé, D. "Integrating personalism into virtue-based business ethics: The personalist and the common good principles." *Journal of Business Ethics,* Vol. 88, 1, 2009: 227–244.

Novak, M. *Free Persons and the Common Good.* Lanham: Madison Books, 1989.

Pacheco, D.F., J.G. York, T.J. Dean, and S.D. Sarasvathy. "The coevolution of institutional entrepreneurship: A tale of two theories." *Journal of Management,* Vol. 36, 4, 2010: 974–1010.

Percy, A. "Entrepreneurship and Catholic Social Teaching." In W. Gasparski, L.V. Ryan, and S. Kwiatkowski, eds. *Entrepreneurship: Values and Responsibility (Praxiology).* Piscataway, NJ: Transaction, 2010: 195–210.

Peters, T.J. and Waterman, R.H. *In Search of Excellence: Lessons from America's Best-Run Companies.* New York: Harper & Row, 1982.

Pius XII. *Address* . Catholic International Congresses for Social Study (Fribourg Union) and Social Action (Saint Gall Union), Rome June 1950. In R.G. Kennedy and S. Rumpza, eds. *Pius XII on Work and Commerce.* Minnesota: University of St. Thomas. Available at: www.stthomas.edu/cathstudies/cst/publications/piusxii.html (accessed January 31, 2012).

Puppke, L. *Sozialpolitik und Soziale Anschauungen Frühindustrieller Unternehmer in Rheinland-Westfalen.* Köln: Rheinisch-Westfälischen Wirtschaftsarchiv zu Köln, 1966.

Rost, K., E. Inauen, M. Osterloh, and B.S. Frey. "The corporate governance of Benedictine abbeys: What can stock corporations learn from monasteries?" *Journal of Management History,* Vol. 16, 1, 2010: 90–115.

Schein, E.H., *Organizational Culture and Leadership.* San Francisco: Jossey-Bass, 2005.

Schumpeter, J.A. "Essays: On entrepreneurs, innovations, business cycles, and the evolution of capitalism." In R. Clemence, ed. *Essays: On Entrepreneurs, Innovations, Business Cycles, and the Evolution of Capitalism, Joseph A. Schumpeter.* Piscataway, NJ: Transaction Publishers, 2009.

Schumpeter, J.A. "Theorie der wirtschaftlichen Entwicklung." In J. Röpke and O. Stiller, eds. *Joseph Schumpeter, Theorie der wirtschaftlichen Entwicklung. Nachdruck der 1. Auflage von 1912.* Berlin: Duncker & Humblot, 2006[1912].

Senges, M. "Knowledge entrepreneurship in universities. Practice and strategy in the case of Internet based innovation appropriation." Unpublished dissertation, Barcelona, 2007.

Shane, S. and S. Venkataraman "The promise of entrepreneurship as a field of research." *Academy of Management Review,* Vol. 25, 1, 2000: 217–226.

Sisodia, R., J. Sheth and D.B. Wolfe, *Firms of Endearment. How World-Class Companies Profit from Passion and Purpose.* Upper Saddle River, NJ: Wharton School Publishing, 2007.

Sommerrock, K. 2010. *Social Entrepreneurship Business Models: Incentive Strategies to Catalyze Public Goods Provision*. Houndmills: Palgrave Macmillan, 2010.

Spieker, M. "Labor, property and co-determination: Guidelines of the Christian social teaching and experiences in Germany." *Conference Work as Key to the Social Question. The Great Social and Economic Transformations and the Subjective Dimension of Work*, Vatican City and Rome, September 2001, Available at: www.stthomas.edu/cathstudies/cst/conferences/LE/papers/spieker.pdf (accessed January 31, 2012).

Stegmann, F. and P. Langhorst. "Geschichte der Sozialen Ideen im deutschen Katholizismus." In W. Euchner, H. Grebing, F. Stegmann, P. Langhorst, T. Jähnichen, and F. Norbert, eds. *Geschichte der sozialen Ideen in Deutschland: Sozialismus – katholische Soziallehre – protestantische Sozialethik; ein Handbuch*. Wiesbaden: VS Verlag für Sozialwissenschaften, 2005.

Tredget, D.A. "Benedictines in business and business a vocation: the evolution of an ethical framework for the new economy." In D.A. Tredget, ed. *I benedittini negli affati e gli affari come vocazione: l'evoluzione di un quadro etico per la nuova economia*. Milano: Università Cattolica del Sacro Cuore & Associazione per lo Sviluppo di Banca e Borsa, 2006: 27–45. Available at: www.assbb.it/CMI/quaderno_etica_14.pd (accessed November 11, 2010).

von Nell-Breuning, O. "The image of the entrepreneur in Catholic Social Teaching." *Management International Review*, Vol. 9, 2/3, 1969: 35–47.

Weber, M. *The Protestant Ethic and the Spirit of Capitalism*. London: Routledge, 2001.

Wolf, N. "Alter Wein in neuen Schläuche. Moderne Führungsverantwortung auf der Basis der Regel Benedickts von Nursia. Moralische Werte un der globalen www-Welt." In U. Meier and B. Sill, eds. *Führung. Macht. Sinn: Ethos und Ethik für Entscheider in Wirtschaft, Gesellschaft und Kirche*. Regensburg: Friedrich Pustet, 2010: 379–393.

# 12

# Human Development: Work and Working Mothers

*Jennifer E. Miller*

> [Decent work] means work that expresses the essential dignity of every man and woman in the context of their particular society: work that is freely chosen, effectively associating workers, both men and women, with the development of their community; work that enables the worker to be respected and free from any form of discrimination; work that makes it possible for families to meet their needs and provide schooling for their children, without the children themselves being forced into labour; work that permits the workers to organize themselves freely, and to make their voices heard; work that leaves enough room for rediscovering one's roots at a personal, familial and spiritual level; work that guarantees those who have retired a decent standard of living. (CV 63)

Recent business ethics has begun to turn its focus from a norm-centered approach to one which calls for human excellence. This new approach calls for a greater understanding of the human person, the relations which are created and sustained, and the multiple aspects of continuous personal growth which, interdependent and interrelated, can be termed "integral human development." Such an ethical approach is more "personal," that is, taking into consideration all the aforementioned aspects of the human person, and is capable of encouraging and promoting human excellence at all levels of business.

This chapter seeks to investigate, with the aid of Pope Benedict XVI's 2009 encyclical letter *Caritas in Veritate* (CV), how job design can foster integral human development in an increasingly prominent group of employees: working mothers. Expanding on the definition of integral human development, which this chapter provides, both in the realm of work and the family, then the different motivations of working mothers that prompt them to enter the paid labor force will be considered: necessity, intellectual stimulation, and a quest for dignity. Beyond understanding their motivations, this chapter will then indicate the specific contributions working mothers make in their fields: greater education and the "feminine genius" or emotional intelligence, thus illuminating why their participation is so vital to both their own integral human development and that of their colleagues. Finally, the conflict of time which arises due to the obligations of working mothers to both work and family will be addressed. Different possible solutions in the realm of job design or work organization will be proposed and examined in the light of integral human development and the human excellence it promotes.

## 1 Integral human development: work and family

Does work, as understood and performed in the majority of businesses, contribute to human excellence? Does it allow the multiple aspects of the human person to flourish in such a way that the person may perform his work better and more creatively as well as participate more fully in the life of society and of his family? Such a question recalls one of the drawbacks that Adam Smith noted to the division of labor in his *Lectures on Justice, Police, Revenue and Arms*. A person who spends the entire day thinking about the seventeenth or an eighteenth part of the pin making process, although he might produce a fantastic number of pins, is not apt to be a person who develops himself through work (Smith 1896, p. 255). It is only the poorest definition of work which understands a person's job as an exchange of fatigue and labor for economic retribution (Melé 2010, p. 4) and not an opportunity for excellence, "effectively associating workers, both men and women, with the development of their community" (CV 63). Such excellence cannot be obtained or fostered by merely respecting basic human rights or avoiding outright abuse of its employees. Although such norms are important as a basis for businesses and working relationships, true business ethics, concerned with excellence, demands an environment conducive to integral human development.

### A Work in integral human development

This notion of business and personal excellence, termed integral human development, can be more fully understood by examining Pope Benedict XVI's social encyclical, *Caritas in Veritate*, and the tradition upon which it draws. The social encyclicals, from *Rerum Novarum* in 1891 (RN 40) to *Caritas in Veritate* in 2009 (CV 45), proclaim that the human person, created in the image and likeness of God, is called to action: "The Lord God then took the man and settled him in the Garden of Eden, to cultivate and care for it" (Genesis 2:15). The newly-created person is not portrayed as a passive recipient of paradise; rather, this person is called to participate in God's work of creation by further developing the world around him. Work is not a punishment for sin but a means for personal growth in excellence.

Unfortunately, many employees perform a type of work which makes them passive recipients of executive orders, analogous to being part of the process that makes one of Adam Smith's pins; such work design denies them the opportunity for personal growth and collaboration with others for excellence. However, the characterization of work found in the social encyclicals, as an opportunity for self-growth and not merely a necessary evil, can contribute to a better understanding of the manner in which work should be approached and designed. It cannot be considered a simple means to an economic end. Although certainly necessary for the survival of both the person and his family, work is also personal, because through it the person develops and leaves upon his work the impression of his personality (RN 44). As Pope John Paul II noted in his 1981 encyclical, *Laborem exercens*, the person "is therefore the subject of work... he performs various actions belonging to the work process; independently of their objective content, these actions must all serve to realize his humanity, to fulfil the calling to be a person that is his by reason of his very humanity" (LE 6).

Integral human development hence promotes a continuous "progress 'from less human conditions to those which are more human'" (CV 8). As a fundamental dimension of human life, (Manzone 2003, p. 10) that is, as a means to becoming "more human," the process of work and the way and manner in which it is performed becomes more important than the final product (Manzone 2003, p. 34). This does not mean that production and earnings are to be disregarded or neglected since businesses and the economic system would then cease to exist. Rather, the necessary and personal aspects of work, if correctly understood and developed by society and business, become mutually beneficial to the integral human development of the working person and the environment in which he lives and works. This development is the true end and excellence of business.

Integral human development also includes all aspects of the human person (CV 18). These aspects of the human person are comprehended within, but are not limited to, the economic, social, and political areas of life. In other words, integral human development is concerned not only with equal participation in the market, education, and free and peaceful democracies (CV 21), concepts which come quickly to mind when development is mentioned, but also those personal elements which are usually considered to belong to the "private" sphere: sexuality and marriage (CV 51). Hence, although part of man's integral human development is dependent upon his working, it cannot be forgotten that the modern "economy is such that it requires the integration of many other human dimensions than just the purely economic" (Martin 2004, p. 47).

## B The family in integral human development

Within this understanding, integral human development substantially embraces the family, a community of life and love founded on matrimony and the privileged place of "responsible procreation," which "represents a rich social and economic resource" (CV 44). As the Holy Father mentions in his encyclical and economists can easily demonstrate, demographic growth is an asset in developing countries (CV 44, see also, Murphy 1997, p. 193). Children provide not only a type of security for the family of which the state is incapable, but they are also the laborers who construct the structure necessary for economic growth. It is for this reason that great emphasis is now being placed upon "human capital" (Becker 1993, pp. 392–395). Along the same line, the decrease in births in more economically developed countries has become a social and economic liability. Social security and welfare systems are becoming more difficult to maintain as the pool of contributing workers is shrinking (CV 44). These systems thus become a battleground between the generations, as disadvantaged members of society seek to insure the well-being of their particular group. Consequentially, the growth, or lack thereof, of the family is not only a private affair but also has important societal and economic repercussions.

The importance of the family is not only due to the biological fact that the person is the result of a union between a father and a mother: families, in their essential function, play an indispensable role in the integral human development of the person. It is they who are responsible for forming this "human capital" or, as Amartya Sen has noted in his expansion of the concept (see Sen 1999, pp. 295–296), the person by whom and for whom the economic order exists. It is in the family that the human person first learns how to be in relation. This socialization of the person is indispensable not only for his personal identity but also for the good of society. In his interaction with the other members of the family, the person is initiated into "the relations between the sexes and the generations...education leading to an active solidarity...the fact that the rights we have as persons are exercised in relation to the rights of others" (Belardinelli 1996, p. 112). This socialization contributes evidently to the political good of society. Sergio Belardinelli (1996, p. 114) contends that when the family is not able to fulfill its function the results are a breakdown of society: addiction, suicide, the abandonment of the elderly, numerous homeless in large cities, and a substitution of communication with hours spent in front of the television. However, it is just as important in the economic sphere, where transactions without trust are impossible. It is in the family that the person is also educated with a trade or to professional work while contemporaneously being educated as to the meaning of work. "In fact, the family is simultaneously a *community made possible by work* and the first *school of work*" (LE 10) Hence, the family is necessary for work, in that it be done and that it be done well (*Compendium* 249) just as work is necessary for the family. This emphasis upon the importance of the family is even more pronounced when we consider that "projects for integral human development cannot ignore coming generations, but need to be *marked by solidarity and inter-generational justice*" (CV 48; italics in original).

Unfortunately, in a time when unemployment is growing and positions of stability can be scarce, uncertainty about work forces many to delay the infinitely precious life-projects of marriage and family. This results in a psychological and spiritual suffering which can only negatively impact their work (CV 25, Manzone 2003, p. 11). According to the Italian sociologist, Pierpaolo Donati, it could be demonstrated "that the majority of modern pathologies derive from...the lack of recognition of the political, economic, social, and cultural services that the family performs for the person and for society" (Donati 2008, p. 100). Pope Benedict XVI cites these reasons as the impetus for his predecessor, Pope John Paul II's, support of the International Labor Organization in his appeal for "decent work" (2000). In the light of integral human development, the definition of "decent work" must be amplified to include pay which allows families to meet their needs, a stipend which helps them to send their children to school, and time to "rediscover...[their] roots at a personal, familial and spiritual level" (CV 63).

## 2 Working mothers

Having laid a basis for understanding the problem at hand, we will now turn our attention to the working mother. Here, although we use the phrase "working mothers" to indicate women who work in the world of paid work, there is not any implicit devaluation of work done in the home by women who do, or do not, possess a paid job. In fact, this author believes that the contributions of women who devote themselves to the family and to the human and personal formation of their children, especially those who do so exclusively, deserve a greater recognition by the State. Proposed measures, such as the recognition of domestic work in the GNP of their respective countries as well as subsidies given to mothers to enable them to choose whether or not they prefer to enter the paid labor force, should be more intensely investigated and proposed by political organizations and bodies (Holy See 1983, article 10).

Unfortunately, the subject of the working mother is often the elephant in the room where hiring is concerned. The demand for recognition of the mother's contributions and a desire for her integral human development in the business and economic sphere, as well as her role in the integral human development of her children, can best be understood if we first examine mothers in the public domain that they now occupy.

## A The presence of the working mother in today's labor force

Let us take the United States as an example of the trend in some of the more developed countries. In 1890, during the industrial phase of the economy, women made up only 15 per cent of the labor force in the United States (Becker 1996, p. 131). In 1950, the number of women engaged in work other than the domestic work of their own homes was still little more than 25 per cent. It was not until 1980 that notable progress was made. At that time, over 40 per cent of women had begun to work outside the home; that number has just recently come on par with the percentage of working men (A.A.V.V. 2009, p. 7). Comparing the percentage of working women to the overall number of women shows an even more dramatic picture. The female population working in countries of similar economic development, such as Denmark, Sweden, Great Britain, Germany, the United States, France, and Japan, varies from 60 to almost 75 per cent (A.A.V.V. 2009, p. 49). This presence is by no means negligible. Even more interesting are the reasons given for the increased participation of women. Some authors insist that women work more now as compared to the recent past due to market forces which make it more profitable (Becker 1996, p. 131) while others characterize this movement as a means to independence (A.A.V.V. 2009a, p. 7). Generally, however, women's motivation for dedicating time outside the home to paid employment can be grouped into three areas, very often interrelated: necessity, a desire for intellectual stimulation, and a means to assert one's dignity.

## B Reasons women work

First, while the picture of the woman content to stay at home and occupy herself with the domestic sphere may seem to be taken straight from a sitcom in the 1950s, 70 per cent of American couples stated that if finances were not a problem, one parent would be present at home to raise their children (Vollmer and Vollmer 1997, p. 58). These numbers speak even more loudly if we compare them to the statistics on working women just examined. Assuming that the presence of the mother would be that required at least during the first few months of the child's life (Matlary 2003, p. 239) it can be presumed that many mothers work because they feel it is an economic necessity (A.A.V.V. 2009b, p. 50). This point is quite poignantly illustrated in a recent study examining working mothers in the national labor market of Hungary. "Research made by Balint-Kollo (2007) clearly shows that subsidies paid for child-rearing available to women irrespective of whether they stay at home or work (like GYES and GYED, the Hungarian maternity leave subsidies) increase the value of staying at home and help others to stay away from work for a longer period of time" (Bencsik and Juhasz 2010, p. 82). It is interesting to note that an increase in economic resources, allowing mothers to choose whether or not to return to work, resulted in a significant number deciding to invest exclusively in their children. As one reader of *The Economist* remarked in a letter to the editor, "You cite a study that finds mothers, on average, spent the same time on child-care in 2003 as in 1965. It is naive to suggest that equal time means equal quality. A stay-at-home mother is able to give care as and when it appears to be needed; a working mother can give care only when it fits into her schedule, which may not be when it is most beneficial to the child" (Froomes 2006, p. 17). Necessity, we can then conclude, is one of the great motivators which has moved women into the world of work.

A second motivation is a desire to put theory into practice. Women living in countries with greater female participation in the market actually tend to be more educated than men. In the United States, they earn 57 per cent of Bachelor degrees, 59 per cent of Master's degrees, and 50 per cent of doctorates (A.A.V.V. 2008, p. 40). Being more educated, they are also more likely to work (A.A.V.V. 2009b, p. 50). "My drive to go into teaching theology was primarily to put into use this precious credential I had achieved after so many years," one professor, a mother with children, wrote. "At every cost, I wanted to preserve the intellectual, social, and personal contacts that the workplace provided for me" (Washbourn 1984, p. 160). As the trend towards higher education for women continues to prevail, with 2.6 million more female than male college students projected for 2011 in America (A.A.V.V. 2009a, p. 7), the workforce must be prepared to accommodate the growing numbers of educated mothers ready to enter the professional world.

A third motivation for women's presence in the business world is its role in the affirmation of personal dignity. Martha Nussbaum, bringing our attention to those women in less-privileged societies, notes that access to work and other economic possibilities allows women bargaining power in the face of domestic abuse or sexual brutality (2000, p. 293). Moreover, the self-affirmation that work in the economic sphere bestows upon a woman is strengthened not only by the fact that she is able to provide for her family but also by the realization that her capacities for growth and development are being brought to life (O'Connell 1994, p. 60). Thus, the question of the integral human development of the working mother is one which traverses not only the social classes of the rich and the poor but also the globe.

## C Contributions women make

The specific contributions women make to their fields can be viewed under two aspects. The first one, as indicated above, is through higher education. If Bacon was correct, and "knowledge is power," working women have definitely cornered the market. Furthermore, they usually "come to the workplace with know-how and skills (that is, with a human capital stock) that far exceed those of their male counterparts" (Caselli 2002, p. 76). This propensity came to the forefront in the Graemeen Bank, where women predominate as customers and have shown themselves to be shrewder in the handling of money (Salvini 1999, p. 158).

The second aspect of female contribution, important for business, is the specific difference found in women. Although one must always be cautious about attributing a specific characteristic to an entire group, it is indisputable that certain characteristics, rightly or wrongly, have traditionally been attributed to women, especially in their roles as mothers, and are now being elaborated in feminist theories of work. Women are also widely credited with what Pope John Paul II called "the feminine genius":

> the fact that God "entrusts the human being to her," always and in every way, even in the situations of social discrimination in which

> she may find herself...These women are owed much by their families, and sometimes by whole nations. (MD 30)

This attribute is, in the field of social sciences, sometimes called "emotional intelligence" (Condren et al. 2006). Delineated by the strong bond created between employers and employees, it occurs when the employer is considered to be able to relate effectively to her employee. Leadership is argued to be more efficacious when these "human qualities," which tests reveal to be more often present in working women, are involved (Condren et al. 2006). Another characteristic related to a proficiency in human relations, also generally applied to women, is an innate ability to multitask. It cannot be denied that in a business world, continuously more marked by networking, persons better at creating social relations and handling several tasks at once will have an advantage (Caselli 2002, pp. 80–81).

## D Working women: understanding the conflict

We have now examined both the reasons women work and the contributions they make to their respective fields of work. The economic, intellectual, and personal development they receive from the public realm, coupled with the personal elements they are able to provide, create a relationship which is mutually beneficial for both parties: business and women. However, working women face a conflict whose resolution, although necessary for true excellence in work, is not easily delineated.

The time when most women enter into the business world is also when they begin having children. Janne Matlary (2003, p. 237) quite aptly calls this period the "life-phase squeeze." Foundations must be contemporaneously laid, then, for two important life-projects: for the professional life and also for family life. Although these life-projects are to be complementary and mutually enriching, as an integral human development would require, the combination quite often leads to exhaustion. Neither one can reasonably be delayed if a woman hopes to achieve both. A delayed entry into the work force often means the loss of opportunities for professional development, promotion, and economic restitution (Matlary 2003, pp. 238–239) while the delay of maternity leaves a woman in a fight against time. Tens of thousands of dollars have been spent in the fertility industry by women who have waited to have children. This has become such a habit among women in the business world that now campaigns are being planned to inform them of the consequences of delayed motherhood. "The facts are stark: According to a January 2002 report on aging and infertility in women, published by the American Society for Reproductive Medicine, a woman's fertility begins to decline in her late twenties and drops precipitously around the age of 35" (Rosen 2003, p. 70). This means that a woman in her forties, even with the aid of technology, has less than a 10 per cent chance of bearing a child (Rosen 2003, p. 70).

These work–family conflicts do not become any easier once the child is born. Women who do enter the business world and decide to have more than one child may feel that they have let their employer down, that they are "always pregnant" (Matlary 2003, pp. 238–239). Simultaneously, they may feel that they are neglecting their family and children. The conflict mothers experience between their commitment to work and to family is well-documented in psychological and sociological studies. Women lament that they are unable to perform their roles in the home and at work to the best of their capacity, much less effectively. They blame problems their children may be having in their absence (Guendouzi 2006, pp. 901–909). The difficulty in resolving this conflict is perceived culturally as well. Sarah Palin, during her candidacy for vice-president of the United States, was depreciated by a media which insisted that a woman with a large family could not be both a good mother and a valid candidate (A.A.V.V. 2008, p. 40). One may well argue that "there will be no equality between men and women in the workplace until the specificity of women as child-bearers and child-carers is recognized and is brought into the equation" (Martin 2004, p. 44).

As previously stated, "decent work," according to *Caritas in Veritate,* must provide time for the family. In the light of *Laborem exercens,* the social encyclical promulgated by Pope John Paul II in 1981, this insistence upon businesses granting time for the family can be re-read and understood in a way that pertains particularly to the mother engaged in the professional and economic sphere. Pope John Paul II expresses this need in the following passage:

> Experience confirms that there must be a *social re-evaluation of the mother's role,* of the toil connected with it, and of the need that children have for care, love and affection in order that they may develop into responsible, morally and religiously mature and psychologically stable persons. (LE 19; italics in original)

Mary Ann Glendon, Learned Hand Professor of Law at Harvard and mother of three, makes the point that women who choose to devote themselves more fully to their families are often criticized by society. The move for women's rights seems to have forgotten that they were originally fighting for a recognition of a woman's value *as a woman*, and not merely as a worker; the result is a contemporary societal attitude that often denigrates the role of the mother by reaffirming that only paid labor has any value (Glendon 2003, p. 35). An authentic promotion of woman's integral human development, however, should allow her the opportunity for excellence both within and outwith her home. "The *true advancement of women* requires that labour should be structured in such a way that women do not have to pay for their advancement by abandoning what is specific to them" (LE 19; italics in original).

How then, can work be adapted or organized so as to allow for a woman's full participation in both the business sphere and in the family? What kind of resolution would make it possible to foster the integral human development of the working mother, in such a manner that both her paid labor and her work in the family are truly appreciated?

## 3 Proposed resolutions

The proposed resolutions to these questions must be carefully investigated in the light of integral human development including the economic as well as the familial spheres, benefiting both and neglecting neither. One of the answers most often given to this question is subsidized maternity leave and childcare, subsidized either by the business at which the woman works or by the government. Maternity leave and childcare provided by the business are immediately apparent as a risky proposition. Once this is legislated by the State, businesses will seek to minimize damage to productivity. In other words, such a law would lead to lower-paying jobs for, and to lower employment of, young women and women with children; employers, of economic necessity, must seek a balance between work done and restitution paid (Becker 1996, p. 47).

The alternative, state-subsidized childcare, seems to present a more probable solution. Sweden is constantly mentioned as the exemplar in this regard. With subsidized childcare, mandatory paid leave for parents, and the encouragement of part-time work by mothers, it boasts a record number of more than 80 per cent of working mothers with young children. This is quite a contrast to the 40 per cent in West Germany and 60 per cent in the United States (Becker 1996, p. 103). However, the statistics must be examined more closely. Although this employment rate for working mothers is quite high, three-quarters of women work in the public sector as private companies are still reluctant to hire them. Furthermore, promotion also becomes more difficult. Whereas in the United States, 11 per cent of senior managers are women, this position is only reached by 1.5 per cent of Swedish women (A.A.V.V. 2009b, p. 51).

The question of childcare becomes even more complicated if we couple it with other considerations. For instance, childcare does not seem to allay the working mother's feelings of guilt concerning her absence (Guendouzi 2006, pp. 901–909). This could be due, as Becker points out, to the fact that "[m]any psychologists and other professionals in the field of child care argue that young children often need their mothers' care, and a fierce debate is raging on whether many are hurt by their mothers' absence" (1996, p. 103). In summary, the subsidization of childcare does not provide a decent work environment that respects either the economic or the familial spheres of integral human development.

A more feasible solution and one which calls for true excellence by taking into account the integral human development of all concerned would be initiatives created by businesses themselves, the organizations which are most aware of this conflict and the concrete circumstances of each particular situation. Cultivating the integral human development of working mothers should not merely be a benefit offered by companies who are willing to take the "losses." It should be remembered that the "economy needs ethics in order to function correctly – not any ethics whatsoever, but an ethics which is people-centered" (CV 45), that is, concerned with integral human development.

Promising ethical and economic solutions could center on flexible working time. Including more than the "part-time" position, so often sought by, or offered to, working mothers, flexible working time is becoming more desirable both for future employers and employees. It encourages creative initiatives on the part of both businesses and working mothers, responding to the demands of "*integral human development [which] presupposes the responsible freedom* of the individual and of peoples" (CV 17; italics in original). In an attempt to foster personal excellence and responsibility, businesses are beginning to judge their employees by annual, instead of weekly, working schedules. In Germany and Sweden, more than 90 per cent of companies offer flexible working time. This usually means that hours for work can be selected or compressed. Job-sharing or working from home are additional options. Another exciting possibility is that in which the structure of the job is regarded in the light of a long-term commitment. Since the age of retirement is being extended, some companies are offering the possibility of structuring one's career in order to allow for five years of leave

(A.A.V.V. 2009b, p. 51). Such options are attractive not only to the working mother but to any worker who decides to pursue a new academic degree, to travel, or to realize other important life goals.

Such is the demand for decent work for working mothers that various models and aids have been created to allow businesses to become family-friendly (Sorrenti et al. 2010, pp. 4–5). Businesses seeking to alter job structures or implement family-friendly policies can contact organizations whose aim is to facilitate this process. In Spain, Nuria Chinchilla and Partners promote and aid implementation of a model called "Empresa Flesible & Familiarmente Responsable" (EFR©), which defines family-friendly practices, identifies those already present in a specific business, highlights the relevant cultural factors in aiding the development of these policies, and later measures the impact of their implementation (Sorrenti et al. 2010, p. 4). They sport international partners in Argentina, Colombia, Guatemala, Italy, Panama, Canada, and Venezuela (online information is available at www.nchpartners.com/). Another notable process, the Family and Work Audit, has been developed by *Beruf-und-Familie* in Germany and is also present in Austria and the northern provinces of Italy (online information is available at www.beruf-und-familie.de/).

With the aid of such policies, work–family conflict becomes work-family enrichment, a reciprocal beneficial influence between these two important aspects of a "more human" life. Evidence to support this claim can be found in a 2010 study published in *The Journal of Psychology*. In this study, of 220 working adults, participants were questioned as to the possibilities of flexible working time offered by their businesses, their job satisfaction, and turnover intentions (McNall et al. 2010, pp. 67–68). The hypothesis was that "the resources…an employee gains in his or her work role (e.g. flexibility) may directly improve his or her parenting role or may indirectly produce positive affect (e.g. enthusiasm, alertness, high energy), which, in turn, benefits the employee's interactions with his or her family" (McNall et al. 2010, p. 64). As work-family enrichment seems to be comparable to integral human development, albeit in a very circumscribed mode which touches upon the elements in which we are interested: work and family, the fact that this study positively confirmed its hypothesis becomes key. A mutual enrichment, or human development, can follow from a balanced relationship between these two aspects of the person's life. The study further mentioned that 90,000 employees in a recent survey indicated work–life balance as one of the most important elements considered in accepting and continuing in a job (Galinsky et al. 2008, 2010,

p. 77). It is therefore not surprising that businesses that have attempted work-family reconciliation through flexible job design find that they have lower turnover, greater productivity, and possess an advantage in attracting talented workers (Sorrenti et al. 2010, p. 4–5; see also McNall et al. 2010, pp. 61). In this perspective, it becomes very easy to see that integral human development must be respected and sustained: it is not only important for the person who works and desires a decent situation but also becomes important for businesses who want to attract good employees.

## 4 Conclusion

This chapter has allowed us to investigate more profoundly the meaning of integral human development as elaborated in *Caritas in Veritate*, attempting to understand how it can contribute to greater excellence in business ethics. Since work is not to be understood as merely a necessity for survival but also an opportunity for self-realization, "progress 'from less human conditions to those which are more human'" (CV 8) must allow the person, and more specifically the working mother, to realize herself in and through the process of work. Integral human development also indicates that work must be harmoniously integrated with other aspects of human life, especially the family, in which the person is formed and learns to live in relation to others. The creation of such a work environment, conducive to creativity and personal growth, is the mutual responsibility of an ethical business and the worker concerned. Thus, instead of leaving the integral human development of the working mother to government legislated and regulated subsidized maternity leave and childcare, responsible organizations should investigate and implement alternative job designs. These "flexible" designs can be chosen and formulated by businesses in such a manner so as to allow working mothers to be both "working" and "mother" while also responding to the economic needs of the business. Only in this manner, by truly respecting the integral human development of working mothers and their families, can decent work be ensured and excellence in business obtained.

## Executive summary

The encyclical *Caritas in Veritate* calls for a greater understanding of the human person, the relationships which are created and sustained, and the multiple aspects of continuous personal growth which, interdependent and interrelated, can be termed "integral human development." This chapter seeks to investigate, following this encyclical, how the organization of work can foster integral human development in an ever more prominent group of employees: working mothers.

It is argued that a woman must be able to develop as both a "worker" and "mother," for the benefit of herself and society. The motivations behind her entrance into the business world, financial necessity, a desire for intellectual stimulation, and a quest for dignity, create a broad picture of the contribution that the business world makes to the growth of a woman as a person. The examination of the specific characteristics she brings into the work environment (greater education and the "feminine genius" or emotional intelligence) demonstrates how she reciprocally contributes to the integral human development of the people with whom she collaborates. Finally, an investigation of the conflicts that arise between work and family, allow for a consideration of some of the more prevalent options that would allow a working mother to both "work" and be a "mother." Although subsidized childcare may seem like a feasible option, its benefits are dubious. Flexible working time, which permits the working mother to create a schedule better suited to her needs and that of her family, allows her to develop essential elements of her person that can contribute to more than one sphere in life. In addition to the standardized part-time approach, several different options, as well as programs which help to identity and implement these options, are now available. The best solution is that which takes into account the concrete needs and desires of particular businesses and their employees. It is in this way, through the mediation of flexible working time, that it appears business design can best respond to the call for excellence within the sphere of the integral human development of the working mother.

## References


A.A.V.V. "Lexington: The triumph of feminism." *The Economist*, Vol. 388, 8597, September 13, 2008: 40.

A.A.V.V. "Women and work: We did it!" *The Economist*, Vol. 394, 8663, December 30, 2009a: 7.

A.A.V.V. "Women in the workforce: Female power." *The Economist*, Vol. 394, 8663, December 30, 2009b: 49–51.

Becker, Gary. "The economic way of looking at behavior: Nobel lecture." *The Journal of Political Economy*, Vol. 101, 3, June 1993: 385–409.

Becker, Gary. *The Economics of Life*. New York: McGraw-Hill, 1996.

Belardinelli, Sergio. *Identità e funzioni nella famiglia in una società complessa.* Roma: An. Veritas Editrice, 1996.

Bencsik, Andrea, and Timea Juhasz. "Empirical study concerning women's post-birth re-establishment to the Hungarian labour market." *Perspectives of Innovations, Economics & Business,* Vol. 4, 1, 2010: 82–85.

Caselli, Lorenzo. "The difficulty of reconciling family and work." In *Fondazione Centesimus Annus – Pro Pontifice.* Città del Vaticano: Famiglia e Lavoro, 2002: 65–87.

Condren, Tommy, Barbara N. Martin, and Sandy Hutchinson. "What does emotional intelligence and gender have to do with leadership effectiveness…or does it?" *Advancing Women in Leadership Online Journal,* Vol. 21, 2006. Available at: www.advancingwomen.com/awl/summer2006/Condren_Martin_Hutchinson.html (accessed February 1, 2012).

Donati, Pierpaolo. *Perché "la" famiglia? Le risposte della sociologia relazionale.* Siena: Cantagalli, 2008.

Froomes, L.H. "The work-life balance." *The Economist,* Vol. 379, 8476, 6 May 2006: 17.

Galinsky, Ellen *et al. 2008 National Study of Employers.* Available at: http://familiesandwork.org/site/newsroom/releases/2008nse.html (accessed February 1, 2012).

Glendon, Mary Ann. "The women of *Roe* v. *Wade.*" *The Human Life Review,* Vol. 29, 3, Summer 2003: 31–38.

Guendouzi, Jackie. "The guilt thing: Balancing domestic and professional roles." *Journal of Marriage and Family,* Vol. 68, 2006: 901–909.

Holy See. "Carta dei diritti della famiglia." In *Pontificio Consiglio Per La Famiglia, Enchiridion della Famiglia,* Bologna: Grafiche Dehoniane, 1983: 507–520.

John Paul II. Jubilee of Workers *Greeting after Mass.* 2000. Available at: www.vatican.va/holy_father/john_paul_ii/speeches/2000/apr-jun/documents/hf_jp-ii_spe_20000501_jub-workers_en.html (accessed February 1, 2012).

Manzone, Gianni. *Il lavoro dal volto umano.* Roma: Pontificia Università Lateranense, 2003.

Martin, Diarmuid. "What happens when people become capital." In E. Malinvaud, ed. *Forum on the Meaning of the Priority of Labour.* Vatican City: Pontificia Academia scientarum socialium, 2004.

Matlary, Janne. "Women and work: The radical Papal teaching." In *The Pontifical Academy of Social Sciences, Work and Human Fulfillment,* Ypsilanti, MI: Sapientia Press, 2003: 237–240.

McNall, Laurel A., Aline D. Masuda, and Jessica M. Nicklin. "Flexible work arrangements, job satisfaction, and turnover intentions: The mediating role of work-to-family enrichment." *The Journal of Psychology,* Vol. 144, 1, 2010: 61–81.

Melé, Domènec. "Etica en la organizacion del trabajo: trabajo decente y trabajo con sentido." *IESE Business School Occasional Paper,* OP-172, Febrero 2010.

Murphy, William. "Famiglia ed economia nella Dottrina sociale della Chiesa." In *Pontificio Consiglio Per La Famiglia, Atti in italiano del simposio internazionale su 'La famiglia e l'economia nel futuro della società,* in *La Società* Vol. 7, 1/97, 1997: 183–200.

Nussbaum, Martha. *Women and Human Development: The Capabilities Approach.* New York: Cambridge University Press, 2000.

O'Connell, Helen. *Women and the Family*. Women and World Development Series, London & New Jersey: Zed Books Ltd., 1994.
Pontifical Council of Justice and Peace. *Compendium of the Social Doctrine of the Church*. Città del Vaticano: Libreria Editrice Vaticana, 2004.
Rosen, Christine. "Overcoming motherhood." *The Human Life Review*, Vol. 29, 1, 2003: 68–78.
Salvini, Giampaolo. "L'esperienza della "Grameen Bank": Il minicredito come strumento di lotto contro la povertà." *La Civiltà Cattolica*, Vol. 3590, January 15, 2000: 157–161.
Sen, Amartya. *Development as Freedom*. New York: Anchor Books, 1999.
Smith, Adam. *Lectures on Justice, Police, Revenue and Arms*. University of Glasgow, reported by a student in 1763, and edited with an Introduction and Notes by Edwin Cannan, Oxford: Clarendon Press, 1896.
Sorrenti, Roberto *et al*. "*Flexible organization*: un driver di successo nella gestione delle persone." *Direzione del personale*, Giugno, 2010.
Vollmer, Christine, and Alberto Vollmer. "Il punto di vista di genitori: un bisogno urgente per questo simposio." In *Pontificio Consiglio Per La Famiglia, Atti in italiano del simposio internazionale su 'La famiglia e l'economia nel futuro della società* in *La Società*, Vol. 7, 1/97, 1997: 57–60.
Washbourn, Penelope. "Women in the workplace." *Word & World*, Vol. 4, 2, 1984: 159–164.

# Index

# Index for *Caritas in Veritate* citations

## Encyclical Sections